FISHERMAN'S APPRENTICE

The Making of a Fisher of Men

DAN FLOEN

For permission requests and ordering information, email the author at floen.d@pm2online.com or the publisher at info@twopennypublishing.com

This is a work of creative nonfiction. While all the information in this book is true, some names and identifying details have been changed to protect the privacy of the people involved.

Library of Congress Control Number: 2021907359

Paperback: 978-1-950995-28-8
Hardback: 978-1-950995-29-5
eBook also available

FIRST EDITION

For information about this author, to book an event appearance or media interview, please contact the author representative at floen.d@pm2online.com or https://www.danfloen.com

Dan Floen's Fisherman's Apprentice is a book every believer will benefit by reading. His transparency, his faith, and his commitment to live for Christ through his many challenges will inspire you to overcome any obstacle in your life. Well done, Dan!

Os Hillman
Author, TGIF Today God Is First

I have known Dan and Julie Floen for twenty years or so. Early on, we were friends from a distance as members of C12 but in different groups. We were always asked to pray for Dan, and I had some awareness of what they were going through. About five years ago, our C12 groups merged, and I came to know them much more intimately. How grateful I am for our relationship. We have had many ministry and fishing adventures together. When Dan asked me to read his book, I wasn't sure what to expect. Once I cleared the deck to read it, I found myself drawn into a very real and personal experience including supernatural God stories and a faith journey that will encourage even the most desperate. I found my own faith challenged and encouraged. Thank you for sharing your story, Dan and Julie. Love you guys.

Dave Dunkel
Chairman and CEO, Kforce Inc.

I've fished with Dan for years and caught lots of fish thanks to him. Knowing his health journey, I expected Fisherman's Apprentice to be about his struggle with cancer, but it is so much more. Dan tells a captivating story of how God used a torrent of tragedies and challenges to forever change a stubborn fisherman, one who is just like me. Dan drew me in, and I found my faith strengthened by the supernatural God stories. This book prepared me for when life throws the next curveball, and it will do the same for you. Fisherman's Apprentice is a touchdown in my scorebook!

Jason Maniecki
Broker/Owner | All Pro Realty | Former NFL Player

To my wife, Julie,
who helped me hear God's voice and
encouraged me to follow through with what He said.

Contents

*And he said to them, "Follow me, and
I will make you fishers of men."*
Matthew 4:19

Foreword

Is this all there is? I thought life would be . . . more. There's no hope. Christianity feels hollow. What in the world is God doing, and why am I going through this? What is life about?

Do you ever wrestle with those questions?

If you do, Dan and Julie have a story that not only will inspire and move you; their adventure will invite you to "let down your nets one more time." As Dan is quick to share, anything less than total surrender is a toxic imitation for the abundant life Jesus has made available to you. Whether you like fishing, catching, boating, or business, Dan and Julie's honest story of trials, despair, temporary deliverance, and tragic sequels will draw you into a place of sensing that perhaps Jesus is inviting you to "drop your nets" and come be an apprentice as well.

Dan and Julie are entrepreneurs, business owners, parents, people who have scars, dreams, and went through the "valley of the shadow of death" multiple times. If you meet Dan or Julie today, they radiate love, peace, and joy and will share truth boldly. They have a contentment and peace you'll envy, yet a zeal for life that doesn't seem empty like so many. There's something different and confident about them. They have something you want. They have faced the questions I listed and more. They have faced the depths of despair, cried into the storms of crisis, and have a story to tell.

Life is not a game, but it might be a school. Too many live a life of watered-down, pseudo-Christianity, dabbling in some Jesus-flavored religiosity while operating in the delusion of self-sufficiency and quiet rebellion against the living God. That way of living is a losing proposition!

Jesus greeted some commercial fishermen after a woefully unproductive venture that left them broke, despite their best efforts and applied skill. Seeing their fatigue and frustration, Jesus suggested perhaps they should attempt one last net cast in a slightly different place. This was incredulous—borderline insulting! What did some no-name rabbi from the middle of nowhere know about fishing? Luke 5:5 records Simon's implied exasperation when he says, "Master, we have toiled all night and took nothing! But, at your word I will let down the nets." Their boat almost capsized by the haul of fish that net cast yielded.

Jesus then famously recruited those roughneck people to become lifelong apprentices to Him that they might become "fishers of men" (Matthew 4:19). It was not an easy apprenticeship. The temptation and inclination was repeatedly to seize control, to try and achieve supernatural outcomes with natural methods. Supernatural blessing is not natural!

As you enter into Dan and Julie's story, you might find yourself in their story and, perhaps, you'll hear the voice of the living God speaking to you through it. Jesus doesn't want fans, members, acknowledgement, or assent—He wants you to be an apprentice.

MIKE SHARROW
CEO, The C12 Group

Preface

I'm a fisherman, and we can be a superstitious lot. But here's one thing I know: I don't believe in coincidences anymore.

I believe in God, and since my late forties, I have put my full faith in Him and His Son, Jesus Christ. I know that may sound crazy, but trust me, I didn't come to this place easily, and I didn't decide to trust in God after He rescued me. On the contrary, I learned I had to trust Him in the middle of the long, hard struggle, day by day, minute by minute. Through the blinding storms, as waves crashed over the rail, God continuously calmed my heart and assured me that I would see one more day.

So how does one decide whether something invisible is real? Isn't it usually when a person experiences that thing for themselves? I mean, I can't see gravity, but I know it's real because I have done things that have broken several bones to prove its existence. In a similar way, I know God is real because I experience Him personally every day. I see consistent, undeniable evidence of His work in my life. When He does something special for me, I record it in my spiritual journal, which I think of as my miracle tracker. I know from continuous experience that God loves me deeply. In fact, I am in the perfect Father-son relationship with God.

Sounds nutty, right? But let me ask you: How can you tell when a father loves his son? He sends his son letters, right? The father does things for his son that the son could not have done for himself. He surprises him with special gifts. He disciplines him. He protects him. He encourages him to grow and mature. He sends his friends to advise and support him. He talks with him often. He teaches him courage and faith. He tells him the truth. I am so blessed to have two fathers like that.

Fisherman's Apprentice is the true story of how God used devastating circumstances and incredible miracles to shape me, a stubborn fisherman, into acting more like a fisher of men.

Dan

1

I pray that I may live to fish
Until my dying day.
And when it comes to my last cast,
Then I most humbly pray:
When in the Lord's great landing net
And peacefully asleep
That in His mercy I'll be judged
Big enough to keep.
—Author Unknown

Trolling for Success

The *Floen Bayou* pitches and rolls as she works her way through three-foot seas in the Gulf of Mexico. It's the summer of 2001, just past dawn, and my two work buddies and I are headed out to our favorite fishing hole, about ten miles offshore from Clearwater Pass. We named our spot "Cudaho," which is short for barracuda hole. My GPS only gives six spaces to name a waypoint, so Cudaho was the best we could come up with. Tom is at the helm, tracking our headway on GPS. Every so often he shouts out progress updates to Eric and me.

"Five miles to Cudaho! . . . Three miles to Cudaho! . . . One mile to Cudaho!"

Tom is also in charge of the music, which is critical, especially when we're over "the spot." Fishermen are very superstitious. I mean, every serious fishing boat captain around the world knows that having bananas onboard will jinx the fishing trip just as sure as your wife will kill you for putting frozen bait in her kitchen freezer. So if you've packed bananas in your lunch bag and your captain finds them, they're going overboard faster than you can say "fish on!" As for our idiosyncrasies, we've determined that we catch more fish when we have Van Halen blasting on the stereo. "You Really Got Me" is their favorite song.

As Tom drives, Eric and I prepare the rigs for action. We made our own barracuda lures last night. These are thirty-inch tube lures made of fluorescent-colored poly tubing encasing a heavy-gauge, twisted stainless steel wire. Each lure has five treble hooks evenly spaced along the length of it. We put a gradual twist in each lure, so it slowly spins like a fluorescent corkscrew as we pull it through the water. My guess is it looks like a big swimming eel or a Technicolor sea snake to a barracuda. Whatever they think it is, when the bite is on, they can't leave it alone. Their favorite color is blood red. Go figure.

"Cudaho, dead ahead!" Tom yells.

As Tom eases the boat into position at about five knots, Eric and I rig fishing lines on downrigger release clips, one on each side of the boat. We set the lures on the downriggers to about six feet deep and pull them roughly seventy-five feet behind the boat. We rig a third lure on a long line to be pulled at the surface, roughly a hundred and fifty feet back. Then we crank up the Van Halen and prepare for action.

Tom maneuvers the boat in a large, figure-eight pattern over Cudaho. We're on the second pass over our mark, and we're all singing "Dance the Night Away" along with Van Halen as line goes screaming off one of the downrigger reels.

"Fish on!" Eric yells, and like a well-oiled machine, each man springs into action at his preassigned post as angler, gaffer, or driver. We rotate assignments for each fish. For this fish, Eric is on the rod and I'm the gaffer, which means I'm the guy who snags the fish at the side of the boat with a long-handled hook and lifts the fish over the gunnel.

Eric's just getting settled into a good fighting position when the second downrigger line snaps into action as the release clip gives way to another ferocious strike.

"Got two!" Eric and I shout out in unison.

I scramble to grab the rod with the second fish on it, and Eric and I start doing a kind of fisherman's dance in the back of the boat. We're handing rods over lines, switching our positions to keep the lines tight and clear, and hollering out driving instructions to Tom.

"Hard left! Straighten out! Now, go-go-go!"

Just then the long-line reel starts screaming. "Got three!" The bite is on, and we have steady action well into the afternoon.

After a full day of fishing, it's time to reel in the lines and secure our gear for the three-hour ride back to our dock. The chatter between us is really flying at this point, and the fish stories are growing bigger by the minute. We're high-fiving each other as we replay the most memorable events of the day.

Eric shouts to Tom over the drone of the twin outboards, "Dude! When you dove for that rod with the third fish on, I thought you were going overboard! Man, I would have grabbed you by your belt if I could have reached you, but then, I figured we could always come back for you once we got our fish in the boat!"

Eric grins devilishly at Tom, trying to convince him we'd have left him in the water while we landed our fish. Tom just smirks and shakes his head, keeping his eyes on the horizon as he mans the helm.

"Who needs one?" Eric hollers out.

I trumpet right back, "I'm parched!" which means, "Yes, kind sir, I'd like a beer please."

"Me too!" yells Tom from the helm.

Eric goes rummaging through the cooler, which by now is doubling as a trash can, and digs out three AmberBocks, puts each one in a zip-up bottle koozie, and hands them out. We all clack our bottle necks together to make a toast. "Here's to good brothers and big barracuda!" Eric says. We all take a swig and settle in for the long ride home.

Our course takes us southeast from Cudaho for fifteen miles toward Egmont Key at the mouth of Tampa Bay. Today the wind and seas are higher than usual as we head into the weather off our starboard bow (the right front corner of the boat). It's getting pretty bumpy and we're starting to get wet with all the sea spray the boat is kicking up, so we swing out the clear plastic side curtains and snap them in place between the gunnels and the T-top to keep as much water and wind off us as possible. At this point I ask for the helm back from Tom because I know what my boat can handle and what it cannot. I slow the motors to 2,800 rpm, just enough to keep the boat on plane and avoid beating the hull to death in the choppy seas.

As we turn east into Egmont Channel, we pick up a following sea and the ride smooths out a lot. Now we're making good time. Just ahead is a Carnival cruise ship headed back into the Port of Tampa. We gain steadily on her, and in a few minutes we're running alongside this huge floating building. Suddenly we're feeling very, very small. We respectfully ease by her and push on toward the Skyway Bridge.

The sun is getting lower in the sky behind us as we approach the Skyway Bridge. The scene looks just like one of those postcards you see at the Clearwater Beach surf shop. We pass under the bridge, and the golden spires tower over us as they seem to reach endlessly to the sky.

As I turn the *Floen Bayou* north toward home, the seas are off her port quarter (the left rear corner of the boat). As her deep-V hull plunges into the backside of each new wave, she throws up a wall of water, shutting out the sun for just a moment.

It's on days like these, out in the vast expanse of God's creation, when the sheer bigness and beauty of it all reminds me that there is a God. He has blessed me and my wife, Julie, so richly. I say a short prayer of thanks under my breath and keep on driving.

After twenty more miles, we turn east under the Courtney Campbell Bridge and take a heading for the channel leading to my neighborhood. The sky behind us is a spectacular bright orange as we make our way along the causeway. At the wheel, it's hard for me to resist the temptation to stare at the beautiful sunset taking place behind me, but I've run her aground more than once when my eyes strayed for too long. So I keep my eyes forward and drive on.

The sun slips beyond the horizon just as I slow the motors to 1,000 rpm and tuck into our canal. It's no wake boating from here.

Cruising along just over idle speed, it's much easier to talk now over the motors.

Eric starts out. "Okay, guys, here's the deal. I say if we hadn't all been laid off, we never could have taken this week to go fishing. Think about it. You know I'm right." Tom and I nod. The three of us worked at Grainger, an industrial product distributor, for roughly fifteen years, and they recently shut down our entire department. Eric continues, "I mean, everything happens for a reason, and I think we got laid off so we can go into business together." He pauses for a moment to give us time to think about it. "So, are you guys in or what?"

Eric's question is not new. Launching a business has been a frequent topic of our casual musings all week long, but it's the first time Eric has been so adamant. Eric is the optimist of the group. Tom's the detail-oriented, control guy. I guess I'm somewhere in between, so we make a good team.

I must admit, the idea of launching a business with these guys has been growing on me. The company gave us all very generous severance packages, so if we are ever going to do this, now would be the time.

As we make the last turn near the end of the winding canal, our dock lights come into view. The boat lift is already lowered into the water and white PVC pipes mark the four corners of the lift carriage. The pipes serve as landing lights for me to line up on as I ease the *Floen Bayou*, stern first, into the boat slip.

"Nicely done, Captain Dan!" Tom says. Tom and Eric have always been impressed by how I can handle a boat. Truthfully, I like it when people call me Captain Dan. That's how I see myself, and I'm glad when other people see it too.

Eric jumps onto the dock and turns on the two gray barrel switches to start the boat lift motors and raise the *Floen Bayou* out of the water. Tom and I hand our gear to Eric on the dock and then hop out to wash the boat. "This is an awesome boat," Eric says as I'm flushing the motors. I agree with him. This boat is a dream come true for me.

The *Floen Bayou* is a twenty-five-foot Trophy center console fishing machine with twin 150 hp Mercury outboards mounted on a transom bracket. I spared no expense outfitting her for serious fishing: GPS, fishfinder, ship-to-shore radio, AM/FM CD player, live well, downriggers, saltwater wash down, and tons of rod holders. I even added a custom T-top with a half tower for spotting fish and a full canvas enclosure around the console. Out in the Gulf, I can set those twin Mercury's to 3,200 rpm and she walks right through just about anything. When those motors are dialed in right, they sound like two beautiful ladies singing to me. What can I tell you? It's a guy thing.

She only had 150 hours on her when I bought her from my neighbor Vic. He had picked her up nearly brand-new after the 1996 Atlanta Olympic Games, where she had served as an official race management vessel for the rowing events. She still sports the bronze plaque on her console to commemorate her special commissioning. Vic is not a fisherman and he almost never took her out, so she wasn't well-equipped for fishing, but Vic was meticulous about maintaining her in tip-top condition.

Most importantly, the boat has a head. A bathroom was a critical feature if I ever wanted Julie and our daughter, Laurel, to go out with me.

Our house sits near the end of a saltwater canal, a kind of marine cul-de-sac. The low traffic and deep water here make this an attractive sanctuary for all kinds of aquatic life. We regularly see manatees and dolphins, and we catch many species of fish right from our dock. Every summer we have tarpon rolling in the canal, and I've reeled in some very large fish over the years. The biggest tarpon weighed seventy-five pounds.

Julie calls our canal "nature's classroom." It truly is. What a wondrous place for a little girl to grow up. Laurel was just one year old when we moved here from Atlanta in 1999, so this blessed lifestyle is all she's ever known.

We found this house after only two days of looking with our real estate agent, Harry, who was a buddy of Julie's father, Larry. Harry looked and sounded just like Fred Flintstone, but he seemed to know what he was doing, and we figured Larry would keep him on the straight and narrow for us.

Owning a home on the water had never seemed a remote possibility to me, but the more we looked around Tampa, the more it occurred to me that this could actually happen. We had hit the Tampa housing market at just the right time. And when the reality sunk in that I could have a boat hanging on a lift in my backyard, I lost my ability to concentrate on anything else.

Picking out a house was mainly Julie's department. Oh sure, I had a vote, but let's face it, guys; we all live in our wife's house. We had looked at a handful of waterfront homes, but nothing was really hitting Julie's sweet spot. She's the kind of house shopper that knows within the first five seconds whether it's a winner or not. I've always loved that about her. She calls it "shopping like a man." Works for me!

When we pulled up to 4210 Saltwater Boulevard, the curb appeal was really nothing special compared to other houses we'd seen that day, but we decided to go in and take a quick peek anyway.

Harry opened the lockbox hanging from the front door handle and swung open the door. Julie and I peered into the house, and within five seconds we looked at each other and said, in unison, "This is the one."

Standing in the foyer we could see glass all along the back of the house, which brought in lots of light. Julie had always said she wanted lots of windows. What got my attention was on the other side of the glass. The back of this house was like a resort, with beautiful multilevel decking, tropical plantings, and tons of outdoor seating surrounding a pristine pool. An in-ground hot tub was situated about three feet above the pool and a soothing waterfall flowed from the hot tub to the pool. Best of all, just past the pool was the canal that led to the open waters of Tampa Bay. No matter what direction you looked while standing in that backyard, you saw water. I wanted to stay there forever.

What sealed the deal for me was the twenty-five-foot Fountain on the lift in the backyard, presumably left there by the owner so I could envision what my boat might look like hanging there one day. Good strategy. It worked.

Half-jokingly, but secretly wishing for a miracle, I asked Harry if the boat was included in the price of the house. Harry chuckled. "Not hardly." No surprise there. I had done a lot of research on BoatTrader.com and figured this one was worth about $85,000.

We bought our dream home on Saltwater Boulevard and moved in on Fourth of July weekend, 1999.

Having an address on Saltwater Boulevard is a lot of fun. I travel a fair amount for work, and I especially love it when the person behind the rental car counter (usually in Chicago or someplace cold) notices the address on my driver's license and says something like, "Saltwater Boulevard, huh? Must be nice!" It surely is.

Eric, Tom, and I finish washing down the boat and our gear and fire up the grill to prepare for a fresh barracuda dinner. In the kitchen Julie is preparing some fresh vegetables and a salad to go with our fish. Most people don't eat barracuda for fear of ciguatera poisoning, which can cause nausea, vomiting, and abdominal pain. We only eat the smaller fish, which have a lower probability of carrying the toxin, and we've never gotten sick. A grilled barracuda fillet with some nice mango salsa on the side is pretty hard to beat.

"Fish is ready!" Eric calls to Julie. Eric is our grill master. He likes to do it, and he's really good at it.

We usually eat outside on our lanai overlooking the pool and canal, and tonight is an especially beautiful evening. Julie brings out the veggies, potatoes, and salad, and Eric puts the fish on a platter. We all sit down and join hands to pray.

"Laurel, would you like to pray for us tonight?" I ask. Laurel is two and a half years old and is very shy about praying out loud, but after a bit of encouragement (prodding), she gathers her courage and starts out.

"God is great. God is good, and we thank Him for our food. Amen." Relieved that it's over, Laurel says, "Can I have some mac and cheese now, Mommy?"

"Sure honey. So guys, tell me all about it," Julie says. Julie and Laurel love going out on the boat with me, but not for the fourteen-hour marathon excursions we've been doing all week. Eric, Tom, and I are beat, but a man is never too tired to tell a good fish story. The lively chatter goes well into the night until way past Laurel's bedtime.

Laurel gives Eric and Tom the customary good night hug and kiss, and then Julie, Laurel, and I head off to Laurel's room to tuck her in and say prayers together.

I always get on my knees beside Laurel's bed for prayers and Julie snuggles up next to her on her bed. I usually start off our bedtime prayer and then Julie chimes in and adds whatever requests or praises I've missed. Laurel is always good for the "amen."

Julie and I get one last hug for the night and head back out to the lanai where Eric and Tom are still going strong. As I settle into my chair, I notice that Julie is looking very intently at me.

"What?" I say.

"What's that dark spot on your right jaw? Have you taken a shower today?" she asks, not joking.

"Yes," I retort with a bit of attitude in my voice. "I took a shower before dinner."

"Come here," she says. "Let me see that."

I slide my chair over so Julie can take a closer look. "How long has that been there?" she asks.

"How long has what been there?" I reply, getting annoyed.

"This dark spot looks suspicious to me. I don't like it. We should get that checked out. Why don't you let me schedule a dermatologist appointment for you?"

"Julie, relax. This is nothing," I assure her. I've never been to a dermatologist, and I see no reason to start now.

Julie concedes for the moment.

The next day Julie and Laurel join us as we fish the grass flats around Rocky Point on the far north side of Tampa Bay. We typically troll with spoons or plugs on hot summer afternoons because it keeps the air moving around the boat so you stay a lot cooler. The music of choice for flats

11

fishing (or just cruising) is Jimmy Buffett. The bite stays on pretty much all afternoon, and everybody on the boat gets several opportunities to reel in a fish.

It's getting late in the afternoon and we're getting hungry, so Julie pipes up, "How about we go to dinner?"

"Sounds like a plan!" I reply. "Let's bring in the lines and we'll head that way."

Once the lines are in and everything is secured, I point the *Floen Bayou* toward the center span of the Courtney Campbell Causeway Bridge.

It's a twenty-minute boat ride to Bahama Breeze from here, and Bahama Breeze is one of our favorite spots because we can boat up to it. This Caribbean-style restaurant sits on a saltwater lagoon at the end of our canal, and they recently built a large dock that accommodates eight boats. Julie, Laurel, and I boat over there every Sunday after church. They have a great outdoor seating area with a small bandstand, where every weekend a one-man steel drum band gives you that sense of being on an island.

On the way home from dinner, the guys are debating incessantly about what to name this company we're talking about launching. By the time we reach the dock, Julie and Laurel have heard enough, so they hop off onto the dock as Eric runs into the house after some fresh beers and a few select cigars. Eric, Tom, and I need more time on the water to get some clarity and fresh air. A man needs a place where he can think. Mine is our boat. After many beers and a few fine cigars, we come up with the perfect company name, and I can't wait to get home and try it out on Julie.

It's well past midnight when I ease the boat into the slip. We raise her up on the lift and start the water running to flush the motors. If you don't flush the saltwater out of your motors, they won't last long, so I am always religious about flushing the motors, no matter what condition I'm in. This night is no different. I take special care not to fall into the canal as I lean my head against the engine cowling over the edge of the dock to connect the wash-down hoses to the back of the motors.

Once the motors are flushed and the boat is secured, we head to the house to see if Julie is still awake. She's awake, all right. (We're just a bit loud and obnoxious, but Julie is very forgiving, as always. I do love that girl!)

"Hey, Julie," I bellow. "What do you think of this new company name? We even have the acronym figured out already! Are you ready for this?"

"I can't wait!" Julie says, humoring me.

"Julie, after intense analysis and drawing upon our forty-five years of combined experience in this business, we present to you our new company name, Professional Materials Services."

Julie lets out a huge exhale. "PMS. Seriously? Think about it, guys."

That night, with Julie coaching us, we name the company Professional Materials Management, or PM2 for short. We'll provide spare parts inventory management services to the industrial, institutional, and healthcare business sectors.

A few weeks later, in June of 2001, we take the plunge and launch PM2.

You know, few things are as powerful as starting your own business to get your prayer life into full swing. I mean, I had heard from several sources over the years that you should always expect to lose money for the first three years when starting a new business, but if every entrepreneur honestly believed that, there would be a lot fewer entrepreneurs in the world. We didn't buy that old wives' tale.

Weeds on the Line

Months later we are visiting my sister, Kathy, and her family in Minnesota for our summer vacation. Kathy's an RN and therefore is generally considered the family authority on health and medicine. As we're standing in her kitchen talking, she notices the dark spot on my right jaw and starts right in on me.

"Dan, you have to get that checked out," she says.

"It's nothing," I assure her, as if I knew.

With that, Kathy lays into me harder. "Think about it, you stubborn toad head! You're a fair-skinned Scandinavian who has scorched himself in the sun more times than I care to think about."

She has a point. When I lived in Dallas back in the late '80s, I sailed my catamaran every weekend in the Gulf of Mexico off Galveston Beach. I hated using sunscreen, and since my boat was a very wet ride, I didn't feel myself getting scorched until I came in at the end of the day. By then I would have some serious color going on. Usually by day two of the weekend, my sunburn made it too painful to wear my trapeze harness, so I would be forced to slather on some waterproof Aloe Gator to keep on sailing. That Aloe Gator stuff was horrible, like being encapsulated in tar. You practically needed a trowel to put it on, and washing it off was even worse. I used it as sparingly as I could. With all the great sun I was getting, I soon earned a nickname in Dallas that stuck with me for years: "Lobster."

"You have got to get this checked out," Kathy says even more firmly. "I need to know when this will happen and then I expect a report back."

"Geez, you can be pretty persuasive when you want to be," I say with a chuckle, trying to make light of the whole thing. "That assertiveness training in nursing school served you well. Okay, I'll get it checked out when we get back home."

Just then Julie walks over to the phone and makes an appointment for me with her dermatologist on the spot.

One week later I am sitting in the dermatologist's office with Julie. I'm not sure she trusts me to give the doctor all the details, so she came along.

Dr. Cheryl Miller walks into the room and introduces herself. Julie is the talker in these situations, in fact, in most situations. I'm an introvert, so I prefer it that way. Julie always makes a point of getting on the right side of any doctor early on because she knows this will influence the level of care I receive. She and her sister, Diane, learned this years ago when they were taking care of their grandmother. The more well liked and visible they were, the better care Granny received.

Within the first two minutes with Dr. Miller, we know where she's from, what her interests are, how many kids she has, and what they're doing. Then it's down to business. She takes one look at the spot on my right jaw and collects a punch biopsy of it, which leaves a hole that looks like I've been attacked by a paper punch.

"We'll send this off to the lab and get back with you in a few days. From now on, you need to wear long-sleeve fishing shirts, a wide-brimmed hat, and lots of sunscreen," she says with the authority of someone who's seen a lot of ugly stuff in her day. Julie assures her that I'll comply fully with her instructions.

Several days go by and I've all but forgotten about that biopsy, except for the hole in my jaw that is still healing. The phone rings. It's Dr. Miller. "Hi, Dan, we have some results from your biopsy that I'd like to share with you in my office. When can you come in to see me?"

By now Julie has jumped on the line. "We'll be there as soon as you can see us."

"I have an opening at three this afternoon if you can make it here on short notice," Dr. Miller says.

"We'll be there. See you then!" Julie assures her.

It's never good when a doctor won't give you test results over the phone.

Back in Dr. Miller's exam room, we wait in silence. When Dr. Miller enters the room, we exchange a few brief pleasantries. "Let me cut to the chase," she says with a voice of one who's not kidding around. "The spot on your jaw is a melanoma in situ. *In situ* means the melanoma cells are only in the outer layer of the skin, and it is treatable by excision. Because of the location on your face, I suggest that a plastic surgeon performs the excision. We'll contact Dr. Sanchez right away. He's the best in town and he'll take very good care of you."

She then examines every inch of skin I own, which raises more questions. "I think we need to get a biopsy of this spot on your right lower flank also," she says. So out comes the "paper punch," and I go home with a little less skin, again.

A few days later the second biopsy results are in. The spot on my back is a level two melanoma. (Level two is a measure of depth, which means the melanoma has invaded the papillary level of the skin.) I schedule an appointment to have it removed. Honestly, I think nothing of these spots, and Julie isn't sounding any alarms either, so I'm not worried.

A few days later, during my appointment at the Lakeside Cancer Center clinic, it strikes me for the first time that I am now officially a cancer patient.

I mean, the first thing Dr. Sanchez starts talking about when he comes into the room is what the five-year survival rates are for the various levels of melanoma. According to Dr. Sanchez, the five-year survival rate for melanoma in situ is 99 percent. Level two invasive melanoma, like the one on my back, has an 85 to 99 percent five-year survival rate.

Really? I think. *I'm here to get a weird-looking mole removed and you're talking about survival?*

That's a little unsettling.

Turning Point

There's something about the C word (cancer) that gets a guy thinking about the things of God. I've been a Christian all my life, but until well into my thirties, that simply meant I checked the *Christian* box on the census form. Other than that, you would have been hard-pressed to identify me as a Christian.

I grew up in a devout Lutheran family. Like a lot of guys, though, I lost my way in college, and I stayed out in the wild wilderness well into my young professional career.

A turning point came several years ago one Monday morning in Atlanta. I had recently transferred there from Dallas with a promotion, and I was driving my fellow branch manager, Paul, to a meeting at the Roswell branch. At that time Paul and I didn't know each other very well. He was married and I was single, which is to say Paul wasn't one of my drinking buddies. He asked me how my weekend went and, like most of my weekends back then, it had been a pretty wild one. I was laughing and carrying on about all the crazy stuff I had gotten into, trying to build on my "Dan the Man" reputation, I suppose.

Paul was listening quietly. Something wasn't right. I had only known Paul for a few weeks, but one thing I learned about him early on was that he was not a quiet guy.

I finished my story and waited for the response most people give, usually something like, "That sounds awesome! You're a wild man! You've got to call me next time!"

But not this morning.

After a moment or two, Paul let out a long sigh as he stared down at the floorboard of my Nissan 300ZX. Then he raised his head and told me in a purposeful and clear voice, "Brother, you have got to get back to church."

Wow. I didn't see that one coming. Suddenly I was feeling embarrassed and ashamed. I knew he was right. Even though my life in no way resembled that of a Christian, I guess the foundation my parents laid for me as a kid found its way to the surface long enough for me to sense that something was missing.

Breaking the silence once more, I said to Paul, "Maybe you're right," and I left it there. I was way too embarrassed to get into a deeper conversation with him about my faith. Besides, we had just arrived at the Roswell branch. Thank God! I very much needed to separate myself from the discomfort of that encounter. We got out of the car and went to the meeting.

Julie wasn't exposed to church much growing up. She would go with her neighbors and her grandmother whenever she got the chance, but that was about it. She seemed to me like someone who knew something was missing, but she didn't know what.

The weekend after my encounter with Paul, I asked Julie to go to church with me and she accepted. We found a church home at Mt. Pisgah United Methodist Church, and we attended regularly together. Soon we joined a

Sunday school class and even began singing in the choir. On rare occasions we would miss a Sunday, and whenever that happened, Julie would always say, "I feel like I haven't been watered today." She and I looked forward to being watered every Sunday, and we could feel a difference when we hadn't been there. We were married at Mt. Pisgah UMC on August 19, 1995.

Julie and I were both deeply entrenched and very successful in the material world, but as we grew in this church, we began to see gradual changes in each other. I noticed that Julie was becoming a warmer and more contented person overall. She was no longer just the polished businesswoman I had met on our first date. She seemed to be getting more grounded and at ease with herself. More real. I could see it in her eyes.

As for me, I had been living a double life ever since Julie and I met. During the day I played the role of nice guy and after we were married, the loving husband. But most weekends (and lots of weeknights) my buddies and I would head out to "places unbecoming a Christian" until all hours of the morning, leaving Julie at home to wonder what we were getting into. I never felt obligated to call and let her know where I was or when I'd be home. I couldn't be tied down like that. Besides, I figured she didn't need to have our whereabouts rubbed in her face. So rather than lie to her, I just didn't call. But it didn't matter either way because I had myself convinced that Julie was okay with what we were doing. After all, Julie had said she realized men had needs and she'd rather I get it out of my system at the clubs than have an affair. That sounded fair to me.

The trouble with this "boys' night out" understanding I had with Julie was that it didn't line up with what we were being taught every Sunday in church. The more I heard on Sundays, the more obvious the gap became between what I was doing and what God wanted for me. I was very conflicted. I mean, how could I sit in those pews every Sunday and keep doing what I was doing? Thankfully, that conflicted feeling would usually fade as soon as we left church. Little by little, though, I began to see a change in the balance of time I spent with Julie versus with my buddies in those "places unbecoming."

At Mt. Pisgah, Julie and I heard testimony after testimony from people who had gone through seemingly impossible situations, and we heard about how their faith in God had grown so much during that time. Life was going pretty smoothly for Julie and me, and we didn't have life-changing experiences to talk about like these people did, but they were still a great encouragement for us to hear. Subconsciously, I think I was packing each of those stories away in my head to pull out on some dark, rainy day. Over time, as stresses arose in our life, Julie and I began to think differently about them; we came to believe God was in control and we didn't need to worry.

Even as involved as we were at Mt. Pisgah, it was always hard for me not to feel like an imposter. I would come to church every Sunday and try to act all pure and innocent like everybody else there, but I knew I was not like these people. Oh, I wasn't so naive as to think I was the only guy in those pews who had an occasional lustful thought (okay, maybe more than occasional), or cussed at work, or drank too much. But knowing I was among many men who were in the same place didn't make me feel any less an imposter.

One day, about one year into our marriage, I was invited to join a Mt. Pisgah men's group that met every Tuesday night at 6 p.m. I was mortified! *My cover has been blown!* I thought. *They've seen through my facade, or worse, they've seen me coming out of someplace sketchy, and I'll be walking into some kind of tribunal. Oh, that's just perfect!*

I figured refusing the invitation would be as good as entering a guilty plea, so I resolved to go in and attempt to save face as best I could.

That first Tuesday evening I was more than a bit tense, not quite knowing what to expect. But as guys were sharing and encouraging one another, I realized I wasn't there to be put on trial but to be a part of a team. Each week we would share our individual struggles and successes and hold each other accountable to our personal goals. What got said in that room stayed in that room. It was the only way to instill trust. That's how brothers are made.

In this group I quickly learned I was no different from any of these men I went to church with every Sunday morning. And that was saying a lot. I saw these guys as pillars of the community, men I looked up to. But every guy had his own personal struggle he was working through. These guys were just like me.

Oh, I still felt like an imposter, but I figured misery loves company.

Now, at forty-five, I feel reasonably secure in my faith, but it has never really been tested.

Clearing the Line

It's plastic surgery day at Lakeside, and Julie and I are casually sitting in the waiting room. The thought occurs to me that we could pray, but I decide not to bring it up. I figure this thing is no big deal and God has a lot of bigger fish to fry. After a few minutes, a nurse calls me from the waiting room to walk me back to the procedure room. I kiss Julie and she smiles at me with eyes that say I'm going to be just fine.

"See you in a few. I love you!" Julie says.

"I love you too!" I tell her.

The nurse looks like she's fresh out of nursing school. "Hi, I'm Kelly and I'll be the nurse assisting Dr. Sanchez with your procedure today."

"Nice to meet you, Kelly. You done this before?" I say in a jesting tone, but seriously wondering.

Kelly laughs and comes right back with, "Once or twice."

"I feel better already," I reply, not quite sure what to make of her comment.

We arrive at the procedure room, and it is drastically colder in this room than anywhere else we've been in the clinic. "We keep the temperature at sixty-eight degrees in here to keep the germs down," Kelly informs me. I figure that's a good thing.

I lie down on the table and Kelly is getting me situated when Dr. Sanchez comes in. He's got on his full surgery attire: scrubs, disposable hair cover, shoe covers, mask, protective eyeglasses, and surgical gloves.

"Wow, you look like you're loaded for bear, Doc," I say.

Dr. Sanchez laughs and says, "We want to make sure we give you your money's worth today."

Dr. Sanchez starts explaining the incisions he's going to make, and he's talking about some flap of skin he's going to make to cover the area where the cancer will be removed. He's using a lot of big words and I can't visualize this flap of skin he's describing, so I only follow about half of his explanation, which is why Julie usually comes with me. But she's not here.

"Are you ready to get started?" asks Dr. Sanchez.

"Let's do this," I reply.

After numbing me with lidocaine, the procedure goes on for what seems like thirty minutes. As he's finishing up, Dr. Sanchez says, "We'll send this tissue off to the lab and check for clear margins and I'll call you in a few days, okay?"

"Okay," I reply.

This is the first time I've heard the term *margins* outside of my high school typing class. Clear margins means there is no trace of cancer along the edges of the tissue that was removed. If the margins are not clear, we do this all over again, but Dr. Sanchez cuts deeper and wider next time.

I walk out to the waiting room to find Julie reading a book. She looks up and gives me a huge smile as if she doesn't even notice how bandaged up I am.

A few days pass, and the right side of my face is starting to heal nicely when the phone rings. It's Dr. Sanchez.

"Hi, Dan," he says. "How are you feeling?"

"I'm doing just fine," I say.

"Well, Dan, unfortunately, the tissue sample did not come back with clear margins, so we need to schedule you to come back in so we can take some more tissue. I know this isn't the news you want to hear, but I know you want clear margins, just like I do," says Dr. Sanchez.

I let out a long sigh and tell him, "Yes, I do."

The second time around goes pretty much like the first. A few days later Dr. Sanchez calls me again and this time the margins are clear. *That's behind me now,* I think.

A few weeks pass and the scheduled appointment date arrives to go in and have the spot on my right lower flank removed. Dr. Miller does this procedure. This lesion is deeper than the one on my jaw, and man, it feels like she's digging to China. I don't mind telling you that really hurt! I walk out of the clinic that day a few ounces of flesh lighter.

A few days later the call comes from Dr. Miller. The margins are clear. *All right, I am now cancer-free and I can get on with my life.* It's been a hectic few weeks and I need to go somewhere I won't be thinking about cancer, where I can be free and breathe. I walk down to the dock, fire up the boat, and head out to go fishing.

2

Taking on Water

We launched PM2 in June of 2001, and Julie's been bankrolling the company by working some dreadful jobs. We've been heavily drawing upon several lines of credit and have already burned through the money we got from a large sale of stock. It's now January 2004, and that old wives' tale about losing money for the first three years of being in business is proving to be true and is starting to wear on me. I spend a lot of time every day wondering if we're going to make it or not.

At this point the cash from the stock sale is long gone and the balances on our lines of credit are nearly all maxed out.

About once a week Julie and I have "the talk." It starts out like this: "Julie, our credit lines are nearly maxed out, and looking at our current rate of spending, I figure we've got about thirty days of available funds left before I've got to start looking for a real job."

Thirty days comes and goes, but in that time we've landed a small deal, so there's hope but still not enough cash to float the boat. So we dip into the line of credit a little deeper and we pray for a better month.

Hope can cloud your judgment when you're in business for yourself. I liken it to my golf game. I mean, I was a pretty good golfer when we lived in Atlanta and I have the potential to make some amazing shots, and once or twice in an entire round of golf, I do make an amazing shot. Many of my other shots are bitter disappointments, but my great shots are the ones I remember most. That gives me just enough hope to entice me to come back for another round.

Since we moved to Tampa in 1999, Julie has been laid off three times. At this point she's resorting to taking jobs she never would have considered before just to slow the bleeding. Unfortunately, we need more than a tourniquet. We need a miracle.

These days Julie often comes home crying, tortured by unscrupulous employers. She'll often call me on her way home and ask me to put the boat in the water. The boat is our refuge.

It's now March, and Julie and I are having "the talk" again.

"Julie, we keep praying for more business, and God is bringing us a little at a time, but it simply is not enough to sustain us. What is He trying to tell us here?"

After a long pause, she says, "Maybe He's telling us it's time for you to send out your resume."

"I think you're right," I tell her. "What have we got to lose? Besides, if God doesn't want me to go out and get a real job, He'll make sure I don't get any offers."

"That's exactly right," Julie says.

In the next few weeks I find a lot of really good job openings that I'm a perfect fit for, and I'm beginning to think this is what God wants for me. I go on several interviews and I get to the final round on most of them. Every one of these jobs is right in my wheelhouse, and I think I'm going to have some tough choices to make between the offers I'll be getting.

Not one offer comes.

Licking my wounds after an abysmal job-seeking outing, I go in prayer to consult with God. "Lord, I take it You want me to stay put, but for the life of me, I can't see where the funds will come from to continue on. Father, please speak loudly and clearly to me so I won't miss what You want me to do. I'm at the end of my rope here. Please send help."

After three years of struggling to survive, I'm starting to lose sight of the value PM2 brings to the marketplace. Tom lost sight of it several months ago and sold his shares to me and Eric so he could go and work full-time with his dad. I think we should probably fold up our tent, but we have nowhere else to go. So now it's just Eric and me manning this sinking ship. And Julie is bailing water.

Larry Goes Home

It's June 2004 and Julie's dad, Larry, has been battling cancer for nearly a year.

Larry was very successful in business before he retired a few years ago. He's always been a big, strong man with a booming voice that surely sent fear into the heart of any boy who had an eye on dating one of his two daughters.

The trouble was Larry had a weakness for scotch, and it had finally caught up with him. The cancer started in his prostate, but quickly moved to his stomach. Larry's entire stomach was removed a few months ago, so now he can only eat very small amounts at a time. It's the world's worst weight-loss program. He's lost at least seventy-five pounds.

I ride along with Larry and his wife, Bettye, to what will prove to be his final doctor's appointment. Even after losing seventy-five pounds, Larry is still a big man, but he can barely move under his own power. I came along mostly for my ability to maneuver him in and out of the car and in and out of his wheelchair.

Larry sits in the doctor's office looking like a yellow zombie. He's severely jaundiced from cirrhosis of the liver. His liver has been weeping for weeks. Every so often the doctor has Larry come in to drain the fluid off to make him more comfortable.

Sitting there with us in the exam room, Larry's eyes are staring into nothingness, and the expression on his face is that of a man who knows he has played his last card. He stopped speaking a few days ago, except for an occasional one or two words to help us understand his needs.

The doctor comes in, takes one look at Larry, and slowly shakes his head.

I don't think Bettye realizes how bad things really are until the doctor speaks up.

Addressing Larry directly, the doctor asks him how he's feeling. Larry just looks at him, without uttering a word. "Larry, I thought you stood a decent chance of beating this thing, but darn it all, your liver has gotten you."

The doctor looks at Bettye with sad eyes and says, "I'm sorry."

We take Larry home and Bettye calls hospice.

The next day Julie, Bettye, and I are sitting in Bettye and Larry's house and we have a dilemma. Hospice can't provide twenty-four-hour care for Larry, but Bettye can't physically maneuver him on her own.

It's clear somebody needs to move in and live with Bettye and Larry until he passes. I'm looking around the room, really hoping it's not me, but knowing in my gut that I'm it. PM2 is dead in the water and Julie, Diane, and Diane's husband, Randy, all have full-time jobs. I am clearly in the best position to help, but I've never watched anyone die. I weaseled my way out of going to my own grandfather's funeral, and now I'm staring down the prospect of being with Larry through his dying process. This was not on the top of my list of things to do.

Suddenly this incredible feeling comes over me, like God just sent a depth charge straight to my heart. And then everything becomes perfectly clear. God has PM2 at a standstill for this very reason. He's making me available for Larry, and I have a very important mission to fulfill, a mission much bigger than helping a man die without pain. This mission is about showing a man the way to heaven. But it's just as much about developing me. I have to do this. Besides, I'm afraid to think about what God will do, or not do, if I don't accept this assignment.

"I'm your man," I tell Bettye. "I'll go home, pack a bag, and be back here later this afternoon, okay?"

"Are you sure, Dan?" Bettye asks.

"This is the most sure of anything I've ever been," I tell her.

Julie and Diane's mother, Martha, died when they were four and six years old respectively. She was a deeply religious woman. I don't think Larry ever forgave God for taking Martha from him so soon. In fact, I think the first time he set foot in a church after Martha's death was thirty years later for our wedding in Atlanta.

Now that Larry's death is imminent, my conversations with Julie move to where Larry will spend eternity. For Julie and me, that is the only question that matters at this point. It's funny how people rarely think of heaven or hell until someone is dying. So we begin devising our plan to share our faith with Larry and attempt to lead him to Jesus.

"There's no way I can talk to Daddy about this," Julie says with a look on her face somewhere between fear and deep sadness.

Julie and her older sister, Diane, respect their daddy deeply. He's provided very well for them, and he's always been there with wise advice for daily living. The girls have a healthy fear of their father. When Larry told Julie that he'd call the cops on her himself if he ever caught her with drugs, Julie believed him. Julie and Diane trusted him fully to carry out whatever discipline he promised them. That's healthy fear. Telling their father what to do, or worse, giving him spiritual advice, was unthinkable.

Julie continues, "I'm his little girl. He's not going to take spiritual advice from me. I think he needs to hear this from you, Dan. If you get the chance, will you do this for me?" she asks.

Her eyes are so hopeful. I realize she's right. I'm the one. "Yeah," I tell her. "If I get the opportunity, I'll talk with him."

Sharing Jesus with Larry is going to be an extremely tough assignment. He's been angry with God most of his adult life, and he's a very stubborn and determined man. Part of me thinks we've already waited too long to have this conversation. He's so physically uncomfortable now that he's not talking much at all. Any conversation we do have is going to be a one-way street. On the other hand, maybe that's not a bad thing. Either way, I am uneasy but determined to take the opportunity when it presents itself.

Two days have passed, and Larry has steadily slipped deeper into the abyss. He's very jaundiced, and his belly is badly distended from all the fluid that has built up from his weeping liver. The doctor won't drain anymore fluid off him because he says it would just be delaying the inevitable. Larry hasn't eaten anything for several days. He's so weak I am starting to have trouble getting him out of bed to the bedside toilet. I call my dad, who is visiting from Minnesota with my mom, and ask him to come over and help me with him during the day. Dad comes immediately.

Larry stopped talking several days ago. The only sounds he is uttering now are deep moans and short grunts as he tries to get comfortable. Alas, for Larry, getting comfortable has become an elusive goal. Larry's eyelids are at half-mast and the sparkle is gone from his eyes. He just stares across the room into nothingness all day long, rarely blinking.

Earlier today a Hospice nurse named Laura came out to the house and sat down with us to explain what we could expect from here. This was when I learned what the "death rattle" is. Laura explained this is the sound a dying person makes after they've lost their cough reflex and the ability to swallow. This causes an excess build-up of saliva in the throat and lungs and causes a deep rattling sound as the person breathes. Laura told us, "When you begin to hear the death rattle, you will know Larry's time is very close."

After Laura had answered all our questions, she reached into her bag and pulled out a white four-by-six-inch box. "This is your emergency kit," she said. "Some people call it a comfort kit. Your Hospice nurse will be here with you during the day, but at night you're on your own. This box contains several prescribed medications that will allow you to help Larry if he appears in distress or great discomfort. Keep this box refrigerated at all times."

Laura pulled out the first vile. "This is morphine," she said. "Give this to Larry for pain or shortness of breath." She put the vile back in the box and pulled out the next one. "This one is Ativan, for anxiety, nausea, or insomnia." She put that vile back in the box and pulled out the last item in the comfort kit. "And last but not least," she said, "this little white bottle is Atropine drops. This will help to minimize the death rattle."

After our meeting with Laura, Julie and I realized Larry's time on earth is shorter than we thought. So we decided I should talk with Larry at the first sign of him being alert enough to listen. We figured the best time to catch Larry alert and awake is around the time when Dad and I are moving him to and from the bedside toilet. Larry clearly feels like he needs to use the bathroom quite often, probably because of all the pressure the liver fluid is putting on his bladder. He tries to get up by himself, but he can't. So we watch him continuously through the open door of his room from the family room.

Dad and I hear Larry grunting and groaning, which we've learned by now means he's trying to get out of bed to go to the bathroom. Dad and I run into the room to help him up. We get Larry to the bedside toilet and then get him situated back in the bed.

Larry is awake and alert now. I figure this is my chance. So as Dad heads back out to the family room, I stay behind and pull up a chair alongside Larry's bed.

There, beside Larry's bed, I do my feeble best to talk to him about my faith, how God is the one I put my trust in, and how I want to go to heaven when I die. But my words don't seem to be sinking in. My words sound empty to me even as they leave my lips, and Larry's not responding to me in any way. Something's not right. I start to get very uncomfortable as I hear myself rambling aimlessly. So I wrap up my little sermon as quickly as I can and stand up to say a short prayer aloud beside his bed.

"God is right here with you, Larry," I tell him. Larry is just staring into space. I give his hand a squeeze, then turn to leave the room.

Wow, what a bitter failure that was. I mean, I know I'm not supposed to be the one who does the saving. That's God's job. But I did hope to tell a compelling enough story to get Larry to take a step back toward God. I didn't do that.

Then it hits me: I am not God's chosen messenger to Larry. It's Julie.

I walk into the living room where Julie is waiting.

"Julie, I attempted to talk with your daddy just now, but I don't think it went very well. I don't know how to explain it, but I just didn't sense that God was speaking through me to Larry, which leads me to think I am not God's chosen messenger here. Julie, I think it's you."

Julie instantly gets wide-eyed, and a look of deep fear comes upon her.

I don't say anything. I can see she needs to chew on this for a bit.

After a few moments, Julie's eyes come down and the look of deep fear gives way to one of acceptance with great trepidation. "As hard as it is to even think about, I believe you're right, Dan. It's got to be me."

I am certainly relieved it's not me, but mostly I'm happy for Julie that God has given her this opportunity to talk with her daddy, scary as it is.

Julie takes a few minutes to gather herself, and after a while, she musters the courage to stand and point herself toward her daddy's room.

"You can do it, Julie. God will be with you, and He'll give you the words."

"I sure hope so because I have no idea what to say."

With great determination and resolve, Julie enters her daddy's room, trembling in fear. Larry is staring expressionless as she moves over to his side. "Hi, Daddy," she says.

Larry gives no response; he just keeps staring into space.

"Daddy, I love you very much. I know you are in pain and that you are staying here for us. I want you to know that it's okay for you to go when you are ready. You have raised me to be a very self-reliant and capable woman. You have always protected me and given me great advice to live by."

No response.

Sensing that her daddy is not hearing her, Julie pauses to pray silently. "Dear Jesus, He's not hearing me. Please give me the words that he will hear."

Julie breathes deeply and takes his hand. "Daddy, I don't know what happens next. I believe there is a heaven and I pray that I will see you there. I think it's a pretty good place to be. I just hope that you believe this too. I really want you to be healed... and whole... and happy. And I want to see you again. But I guess it's up to you."

Just then Larry turns his head and looks Julie square in the eyes, tears running down his face. His countenance is like that of a man who has seen the face of Jesus for the first time.

"I love you, Daddy," she says. Julie gives him a long hug, then leaves the room.

Julie's daddy goes home to heaven that night, June 17, 2004.

It's All Yours, God

It's now July 2004, and PM2 is still going nowhere. I fulfilled my duty for Julie's dad and, to be honest, I really expected God to bless our business right after I did. Nonetheless, here we sit, dead in the water without the slightest puff of wind in our company's sail.

I must say, though, that walk through the desert with Larry changed my life forever. A deep sense of purpose and peace comes over you when you are walking with a man through the valley of the shadow of death. I felt honored to have been chosen to be there with Larry. Most of all, I was happy to know that he made it home. Still, the reality is that we are sinking here.

"What is God trying to do?" I ask Julie out of utter frustration. "He won't let me find a job elsewhere, but He's not helping us survive in this business either. So what's the deal? I'm at a total loss. What am I not doing that He wants me to do?"

Julie pauses for a moment. Then, in a calm voice, she says, "Maybe you should ask Him."

I've mostly learned to keep my mouth shut when Julie says something that really annoys me. I mean, does she think I haven't been praying about this constantly? I've been talking to God incessantly on this topic and He's not answering me. She wants me to go right back to the same well again, like that's done any good up to this point. Geez!

Julie's looking at me like she's expecting a response from me, but I'm not ready to give her one because she won't like it.

Sensing that I need to work through some things, Julie quietly leaves the room so I can be alone with my thoughts. She knows I need time to process things, especially when they involve my business and livelihood.

I need a change of scenery, so I walk out our sliding glass door to the back patio. I grab a fishing rod on my way out to the dock. Every man needs a place to escape with his thoughts. I do some of my best thinking when I'm fishing.

It's a sunny afternoon in Florida as I fan cast with my favorite plug along the seawall and around the pilings of our neighbors' dock. I've caught tons of fish casting from our dock, but not usually in the middle of the afternoon. Mornings right after sunrise are best, so I'm not surprised that nothing is biting. But I don't care. As they say, "A bad day on the water beats a good day in the office every time."

I saw a video on YouTube recently called "Tale of Two Brains" by a guy named Mark Gungor. He talks about the differences between a man's and a woman's brain. He says a woman's brain is like a bowl of spaghetti and everything is connected to everything. I think this is how Julie can carry on two or three conversations at the same time. On the other hand, he says, a man's brain is made up of a bunch of boxes. We only use one box at a time, and when we're done with that box, we put it back neatly on the shelf. A man also has what he calls a "nothing box." This is where a man goes when he needs to detach his brain from the rest of the world for a while.

When I'm fishing, I'm often in my nothing box. When I'm in my nothing box, I'm not distracted by the troubles of the world. I'm at peace and available. In fact, the best time to strike up a conversation with me is when I'm in my nothing box because you are likely to get my unfettered attention.

I reel in my plug and I'm taking aim at a fishy looking spot along the seawall when I hear a faint whisper in my head.

"The business is Mine, Dan. It always has been. Turn it back over to Me and I will take care of you. Trust in Me."

Whoa! What was that? I'm all keyed up as the thought occurs to me that God might have just spoken to me. Was that really Him? How would I know if it was? One thing I know for sure: if that really was God talking to me, we've just entered uncharted territory here.

I keep on casting as I try to sort out what just happened.

There was something about this voice that was like nothing I've ever heard before. The voice was calm and sure. I didn't feel threatened by it. In fact, I was drawn to it.

Have you ever had that sixth sense when you're sure about something but you can't explain how or why? You just know. I think this happens for Julie a lot more often than it does for me, but at this moment I have no doubt in my mind that it was God speaking to me.

So now that I know that was God talking, I'm left to wrestle with the words He said to me.

Giving my company to God seems pretty drastic at first, but then it quickly occurs to me that I haven't done any good with PM2 up to this point, so I figure God can't possibly do worse with it than I have.

You know, it seems like we never give the steering wheel to God until we have nowhere else to turn. It doesn't take much faith to trust God when there's nothing to lose. I'm disappointed in myself for waiting until I got to this point. Geez, I am such a sorry excuse for a Christian!

After I'm done beating up on myself, I dust off and start thinking about what it would look like to give the business to God. I conclude I have to treat this like a literal change of ownership. If I'm no longer the owner, that means I'll be working for God. Working for God does have a nice ring to it. I mean, everything I've ever learned about Him tells me He'd be a great guy to work for. This is starting to feel more and more like the right thing to do.

I make a few more casts with no bites, but I'm not paying attention to the water anymore. Then I take a deep breath and ask God once again, just to be sure I heard Him right the first time, "Is this really what You want me to do, Lord?"

The reply comes instantaneously. "Yes, Dan. Trust in Me."

I stop casting and lay my fishing rod down on the dock. I stand up and stare out over the water, not focusing on any single object. It's decision time, and I'm struggling to gather my courage to take the plunge.

Now, I've never been skydiving, but I think this is what it must feel like just before you jump out of a perfectly good airplane for the first time. Your head tells you that your parachute will open, but your instincts are screaming at you not to leave the safety of the airplane. I expect it takes most people a few moments to gather their courage before they take a flying leap.

As I'm standing on the dock, I get this mental image of God being my skydiving buddy. You know, this is the person who straps you to his chest and you take the plunge together. With your instructor secured to your back, you get a front-row seat as you hurtle toward the earth together, but your buddy's done this many times. He's right there with you, and he'll make sure you land safely. So even though this means I'm still jumping out of an airplane, figuratively speaking, I feel strangely at ease with the whole idea.

I take a deep breath and begin to pray. "Okay, Lord, effective immediately, PM2 is Yours to do with what You will. Please forgive me for being so stubborn. You are now the owner, Lord. Tell me what You want me to do and I will do it. If You want PM2 to be successful, so be it. If You want it to fail, so be it. But if PM2 is to fail, I just ask that You provide other work for me so I can take care of my family. Do whatever You want with PM2 and lead me in the direction You would have me go. I ask this in Jesus' name. Amen."

Excited, I head back into the house to tell Julie what just happened. I find her reading a book in the family room, and I tell her the whole thing. I finish my story and I don't have to wait long for her response. "Dan, I'm so happy you heard from God on this! I can't wait to see what He does now! It's gonna be awesome! Just you wait and see, love!" It's as if she'd been patiently waiting for me to finally discover this simple truth. Julie's thinking has a way of getting places well before mine does. A bunch of boxes just can't compete with a bowl of spaghetti.

I, too, am excited about this step I just took, but I'm not as optimistic about the future as Julie is. But I gave PM2 to God, so now I need to trust Him to lead us and provide for us.

This Changes Everything

I didn't sleep much last night. I couldn't shut off my brain. I mean, I gave my business to God yesterday and then I laid awake all night thinking about all the implications of doing that. For starters, what will our employees think of the idea? Do we tell our customers and new prospects about this? Should we change our mission statement? Does this change our key business objectives? Should we openly market PM2 as a Christian company owned by God? My list of questions goes on and on.

But before I can answer any of these questions, I need to figure out how to present this to my partner, Eric. I only own half of the company. Excuse me, God only owns half the company . . . so far.

In PM2's three years of existence, there's no one I talk to more often than Eric. Julie kids me and Eric about her having two husbands because we appear joined at the ear by a telephone wire. Eric and I have grown very close manning this sinking ship together. Adversity either pulls people together or breaks them apart. It drew Eric and me together.

Eric and I talk about everything, almost, but not God. I think it's fair to say Eric isn't as far down the path spiritually as I am, but then again, I really don't know where he is on the path. How would I? We never talk about it. I figure this is my opportunity to bring God into the conversation with Eric. So I dial the phone.

Eric answers the phone with the usual, "Hey, man, what's up?"

"Oh, not much," I tell him. "I've just been doing some thinking . . ."

"Uh-oh, is it time for another circular conversation?" Eric says half-jokingly. I'm famous for what he calls circular conversations. This is where I bring up some hypothetical business situation and tell him how I think we would respond to it. Then I take Eric through a drawn-out debate on the alternatives we could choose, which invariably leads right back to the conclusion I made at the beginning of the conversation. Eric just comes along for the ride, knowing exactly where it will wind up.

"Sorry, man. No circular conversation this time," I tell him. "This time I'm skipping right to the conclusion. Are you ready for this?"

"Dude, you're scaring me, but go ahead," Eric says.

I take a deep breath and come right out with it. "God told me He wants us to give the business back to Him. I've already told Him that my half of PM2 is His for Him to do with what He pleases. So I want to know if you'll join me in this with your half of PM2."

Dead silence. One thing I've learned about the sales process is that once you've asked for the sale, the next person to speak loses. So I'm not saying a word. After a moment I hear a long sigh on the line. Then more silence.

A few more moments pass and then Eric finally speaks. "Man, you know me. We've worked together a long time, and we trust each other. Dan, if you truly believe this is what God told you to do, you know I will follow suit. You know that, right? That's what we do. Brother, we are in this thing together. I just wish I knew what it looks like for God to own the company."

I cover the phone receiver and let out a huge sigh of relief. "Yeah, me too. I think He'll show us in time. We just have to take this first step and trust that He'll take care of the rest."

"Yep, that's right," Eric says. "I'm in. It's all going to be good, Dan. You'll see."

Wow! So now Eric's encouraging me on the benefits of giving the business to God. In a matter of just a few minutes, he's embraced this idea and is selling it right back to me. He got there a lot faster than I did. I guess Eric is further along the spiritual path than I gave him credit for. Or he's got serious thrill issues. Either way, Eric's the eternal optimist, a true and loyal friend. This is the stuff brotherhoods are made of. I'm excited about working with Eric under our new ownership!

Up on Plane!

Most mornings I wake up with a knot in my stomach. The constant pressure of mounting debt and no business coming in has a way of getting you all twisted up inside. Somehow, though, this morning is different. I feel very much at peace. Waking up without a knot in my stomach is something I haven't experienced since we launched PM2 three years ago.

Yesterday we gave the business to God. So this morning I guess that makes us a wholly owned subsidiary of the Kingdom of God. I find there's a sense of relief and security that comes with knowing PM2 is owned and directed by "the Lord of Heaven's Armies." After all, if God is for us, who can be against us, right? I mean, if I were God, I wouldn't want my business to fail, so that makes me feel pretty confident.

Eric and I operate PM2 from our homes, so we never have to drive to work. It's a sweet deal. In fact, if you look beyond the reality that we're losing tons of money, this is the best job I've ever had.

I grab some breakfast-to-go from the kitchen on my way down the hall to my office. As I'm sitting down at my desk with my first cup of coffee for the day, the business phone rings. This is a significant event. Business has been nonexistent lately, and I've begun to wonder if the phone company has cut our lines.

"Professional Materials Management, this is Dan. How may I help you?"

"Hey, Dan. It's Karen Jackson. Long time, no see!" Karen is the last boss I had before our entire department got laid off back in 2000. We always got along really well.

"Hey, Karen! What the heck are you up to these days?"

"I've been with CSI for a few months now and I'm their VP of Operations," she says.

"Wow! That's sounds great. Are you having fun yet?" I always try to keep it light with Karen.

"Well, let's just say it's interesting," she says. "We've just landed a huge deal in New York City, and I'm calling to see if PM2 is in a position to help us out with it. So, are you guys still kicking?"

"Yep, we're still hanging in there, and we'd love to help. What kind of support are you looking for?"

We talk for the next thirty minutes or so as she lays out the scope of work she needs PM2 to fulfill. As she's explaining it all, I'm punching away on my calculator figuring out what our rates should be and how much business this would amount to for PM2. It's the biggest deal in company history.

As far as I can tell, God just took His first official action as PM2's new owner.

3

Band of Brothers

Julie, Laurel, and I started attending Heritage United Methodist Church in Clearwater in 2000, a few months after we moved to Tampa. We were having a tough time finding a church that could hold a candle to what we experienced at Mt. Pisgah in Atlanta, and Julie stumbled upon Heritage one day as she was out running errands. Did God lead her there? Julie called me and said, "I found where we're going to church this Sunday." We fell in love with the church right away and have been regulars ever since.

About two years ago, in the fall of 2004, I started attending the Heritage men's prayer group at church. They meet at 6:00 a.m. on the first and third Fridays of each month. Most mornings I'm the youngest guy there, which is to say that the majority of the guys are retired or near retirement age. Our pastor, Dave, generally leads the group, but he often passes the baton to one of the guys to lead it. I've never been asked to lead, which is understandable, given the spiritual giants in the room.

I first heard about the Heritage men's prayer group in casual conversation with one of the group's regulars one Sunday morning. He told me what a great bunch of guys it was and how valuable it was to him, but I distinctly recall not being invited to join them. I got the impression this was a very close-knit group, a band of brothers, and they were very careful about letting anyone in who might threaten the chemistry of the brotherhood.

Finally, very early one Friday morning, my curiosity and desire to be a part of this group outweighed my fear of rejection, so I got in my car and headed to the church. I didn't know which room the guys met in, but as I drove into the parking lot, I saw a few guys streaming into the church, so I parked quickly and jumped out to follow the crowd. Once inside the front door, I could hear voices coming from the workroom, so I headed down the hall. I arrived at the workroom to find a few of the guys gathered around a coffee machine waiting to fill their cups.

J.R. was the first to greet me. "Hey, Dan, how are you doing, man? More importantly, what are you doing up so early?" he said with a grin. J.R. was our first Sunday school teacher at this church. He's got a great sense of humor and is a likeable guy. He made me feel welcome right away.

I filled my coffee cup and followed the crowd down the hall toward the parlor, where about twenty chairs were arranged in a circle. It reminded me of the men's group at our church in Atlanta. There didn't appear to be any assigned seats, so I picked out a spot and sat down. As guys were streaming in, one by one, they were doing what brothers do.

"Hey, Rick, your Seminoles really stunk up the place last week!" said Chuck, a diehard Gator fan.

Rick fired right back, "Yeah, I warned them not to put your mom in the game, but they never listen to me!"

A man in a double-breasted blue suit with a matching orange Gator tie and handkerchief walked in a few steps behind Rick. "Hey, everybody, Richard's here, so I guess that means we can start now," Rick jabbed. "I didn't hear any sirens this morning, Richard. Is that why you're earlier than usual?" I quickly gathered that Richard was an attorney and that he had a reputation for always being the last man there.

Richard just grinned and told a lawyer joke. "What's the difference between a dead skunk in the road and a dead lawyer in the road?"

"What, Richard?" the group responded.

Richard smiled wide and said, "There are skid marks in front of the skunk!"

The group erupted.

Pastor Dave allowed the pokes and jabs to continue for several minutes. In fact, he was right in the thick of it. After a few minutes, Dave quieted the group and read a short passage from a book; then he posed a few questions to the group.

After some spirited conversation about the questions, Dave brought it back together and asked for praises and prayer concerns. He went around the circle of chairs, one man at a time. Every man had something he needed the group to pray about or something he was thankful for. Some of the guys were obviously in great pain as they expressed their concerns over a loved one, or a job situation, or a health issue.

When Dave came to me, I asked for prayers for the business.

After Dave had gotten all the way around the circle, he invited us all to stand up and join hands. Instead, the guys put their arms across each other's shoulders, which meant these guys were close.

"You men have all heard the prayer concerns and praises this morning," Dave said. "So I'm going to start us off in prayer and then I invite any of you who want to pray for these concerns to speak out as you are led. Bill, will you close our prayer time for us?"

Bill nodded.

As I stood in a tight circle with these men praying for one another, a deep sense of duty and honor came over me that I was now part of this band of brothers, and I was responsible to pray for them and support them in any way I could.

Contrary to the preconceptions I had coming in, I was welcomed into the group with open arms. There were no prerequisites, no selection criteria, no rites of passage, as I had thought. These were just men of faith who trusted God and trusted each other.

Bill closed the prayer with the eloquence of a man who had done it many times before. His words were so inspiring and encouraging. It felt more like a pep talk before the big game than a prayer, and I was energized to go out and be a better man and a better Christian.

Bill closed with, "And all God's people said . . ."

"Amen!" the guys said in unison.

Cruising Along

It's Thursday, January 5, 2006, about a year and a half after we gave the company back to God. PM2 has been cruising along steadily since the first big deal God brought us. Still, I spend a lot of time worrying about the business. I figure just because God's taken care of PM2 this far doesn't guarantee He'll continue that indefinitely. Plus, the economy has been in decline all year, and there are plenty of indicators out there that say tough times are coming.

I ran a report from QuickBooks to look at how PM2 sales had done each quarter since the day we opened our doors. Then I plotted it on a graph and added a red line on the timeline to show when we gave the company back to God. Here's what I found.

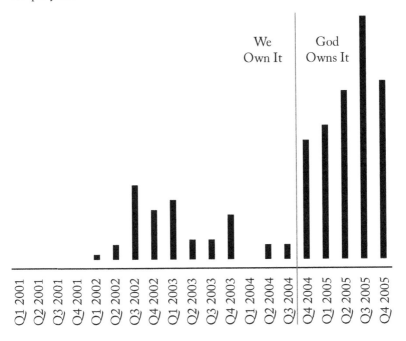

Wow! Back in '04, God said He would take care of us if we gave PM2 back to Him, and I knew things were going pretty well, but I never realized how dramatic the change was until I plotted it on a graph. It was like a light bulb came on after we gave PM2 back to God and it's been burning bright ever since. Looking at the business from this perspective, I feel a whole lot better about our chances in this declining economy.

Since 2004, we've maintained a team of at least ten people, and we did almost $1,000,000 in sales in 2005. Not bad for a company we weren't sure would still be around by this point.

But lest I start believing I'm the reason for this success, God gives me frequent reminders about who's really in charge. I mean, most of the brilliant ideas I come up with wind up being dismal failures. The truth is, nearly all the great opportunities we've been presented with have come from places I wasn't even looking. Oh sure, I've made business connections over the years that are bearing fruit now, but I rarely even know about some huge new business opportunity until it's dropped into our lap. They just seem to come from nowhere. I think this is God's way of keeping me humble and dependent on Him.

Twelve Christian Fishermen

Today is the first Friday of the month, and I'm sitting around the circle with the guys in the Heritage men's prayer group.

Since my first day in this group over two years ago, I've been constantly asking for prayers for the business. I think by now I'm getting very predictable.

I took the seat right next to Pastor Dave this morning. I've noticed the seats next to Dave always fill up last, like he has leprosy or something. I don't know why that is, but I think that being a pastor has got to be one of the loneliest jobs on earth. I mean, you always have to be there for others, and you wind up carrying all that stuff around because you can't share it with anybody. So even though I am among the first few guys to arrive, I took the seat on Dave's immediate left. I don't know; I guess I wanted him to know he wasn't alone.

After the normal small talk and a few well-placed jabs around the circle, Dave calls the group to order. Then he turns in his chair to face me and says, "Dan, how can we pray for you this morning?"

Wow, that's a new twist. Dave usually starts with a short lesson or a question for the group to ponder before jumping into prayer requests. Not this morning. I am seated to his left, so I'm up first. Now I understand why no one sits next to him in the circle.

The guys are waiting for me to say something. I lean forward in my chair, elbows resting on my knees, staring down at the floor. I feel so lame asking for more business every single time I come here. I mean, God has been providing for us just like He said He would, and I'm starting to feel guilty about constantly asking God for more business.

After a bit of a pause, I let out a deep sigh. Then I start. "Dave, I've been sitting here every Friday morning for over two years and it seems like all I ever ask for is for more business, as if that's all life is about. The fact is, God's been providing for us in amazing and miraculous ways. You see, two years ago my partner and I were ready to throw in the towel. But then one day God told us to give the business back to Him, and He's been blessing His business ever since. So this morning I don't have any prayer requests, just a whole lot of thanks to God."

Dave smiles at me like he's been waiting for this day for a long time. "Amen to that, Dan!"

As Dave continues around the circle, I look up and notice Jim staring intently at me from across the room. He looks like he has something on his mind.

Jim is a cornerstone member of the church, and if the congregation ever appointed lifetime elders, he'd be one. Jim did very well in business and sold his meat distribution company a few years ago.

I got to know Jim when he and his wife, Carol, volunteered with several other "seed couples" to help start a small satellite church called The

Compass. Julie and I led the music there every Sunday morning, and once in a while we could even sweet-talk Laurel into singing a solo for them. It was a very small, intimate group of twenty-five or so, and we all became close friends. So when the church decided to sell the building to another local congregation, the group started its own Sunday school class back at Heritage, aptly named "The Compass Class," which Jim and Carol led.

As our morning session is coming to a close, guys are standing up, shaking hands, and poking fun at each other as good buddies do. From across the circle, Jim appears to have something to say to me and he very intently makes his way across the room.

"Hey, Dan, I've got something for you to think about," Jim says. He's always very direct with me; it's one of the many qualities I love about him.

"What is it?"

Jim has a very serious look on his face. I figure this must be important. "I understand your company has been doing well for a while now. What is your annual revenue and how many employees do you have?"

I have no idea where Jim is going with this, and I normally wouldn't tell just anyone what our numbers are. But I trust him, so I answer. "We're doing around $1 million a year and we employ anywhere from ten to fifteen people." I feel like saying, "Why do you ask?" but I know he'll tell me anyway and I don't want him to know I feel threatened by his question.

Jim continues, "Before I sold my business, I was a member of a Christian CEO group called C12. It made a big difference for me on how I ran my company. I've been waiting for your company to grow before I shared this with you because you need to be at least a one-million-dollar business and have five employees to join C12. It costs money to be a part of, but now that your company is a little bigger, you may want to check it out."

Now, Jim's been a salesman for many years, but I'm definitely not getting the hard sell right now. In fact, he appears almost reluctant to share C12 with me. I sense that he values this group so deeply that he wants to choose wisely whom he brings into it. It's like he's protecting it, and he's been waiting and watching me to decide whether I would be a safe addition to the group.

It feels like I've just been invited into a very elite club, and I'm really flattered that Jim thinks I pass muster. Clearly Jim has an unrealistically high opinion of me. I mean, I'm just a kid in a forty-year-old body and I have no idea what I'm doing running a business. The thought of joining this elite group is extremely intimidating, but having the chance to be a part of C12 compels me to push beyond my fear. "I'd love to learn more about this, Jim. Who do I need to talk with to see about joining?"

Jim asks me for my phone number and email address and tells me he'll put me in touch with the group chairman, Scott Hitchcock.

"I look forward to meeting him," I tell Jim. "Thanks for sharing this with me."

A few days later Scott calls me at the office. He spends the next few minutes explaining how each member of C12 sees himself as a steward of God's business and that they view their businesses as more than a money-making machine; they're a ministry. The real value of C12, he explains, is in the relationships of the group and the godly wisdom and life experiences that each member brings to the table. I'm beginning to see why Jim thinks C12 is so special and worth protecting. Then Scott invites me to come as a guest to one of the next meetings.

I accept.

A week and a half later I'm headed to my first C12 meeting. The group meets at the Centre Club, a very nice executive club at the top of the Urban Towers in South Tampa, the ritzy part of town. I'm not intimidated in the least, nope, not me. (Yeah, right!)

When I get to the conference room, a tall, white-haired man is at the doorway and he's bantering with the guys inside the room. He looks very distinguished and seems to have a joyful countenance about him.

"I hope your wife knows, Tom!" he says playfully.

"Yeah, she keeps me on the straight and narrow!" Tom replies.

"Well, that's certainly a relief!" retorts the white-haired man.

As I approach the doorway, the man turns toward me, and in an instant his eyes widen and his smile brightens, like he's just been reunited with a long-lost friend.

"Well, hi there! You must be Dan," he says. "I'm Scott Hitchcock. Welcome, my man. Come on in. We are so glad you're here!"

I can feel the love in the room right away as the guys are throwing barbs back and forth and carrying on like old friends. Scott calls the group of twelve or so to order, and the guys all take a seat around a long conference table with a nice view of the Tampa skyline. Scott introduces me and then asks me to say a few words about myself and the business I run. Okay, now I'm intimidated. I mean, I'm sure PM2 is small potatoes compared to the businesses these guys all run. I hope they don't ask me how big PM2 is. Thankfully, they don't.

For my benefit, Scott explains the agenda for the day. The group meets once a month from 9 a.m. to 4 p.m. with two main segments. Each month the morning segment is entitled "Working on My Business" (as opposed to working in my business). Scott says there's a big difference between the two. The afternoon segment is entitled "Working on My Ministry in God's

Business," which looks at ways we can enhance our ministry both in and through the business. Other agenda items throughout the day will also include a morning devotion, prayer time, something called "to-dos," lunch, and a core business presentation by one of the group members.

Scott wraps up the morning devotion and to-dos and then moves into the prayer request and prayer time. Each of the men shares their praises and concerns, and we write them down on a sheet that says "Prayer Concerns." Something about writing down the prayer concerns makes this process very meaningful and important.

After everyone in the room has spoken, Scott says, "Remember, guys, to pray for these concerns at least once a week until our meeting next month. At that time we'll share all the ways God has been answering our prayers. So let's move into our prayer time this morning."

We all bow our heads.

The first man leads out. Then another man chimes in after him. Then another and another. As I listen to their prayers, I am struck by the passion and conviction of these men as they cheer each other on in prayer and cry out to God for their brothers in need. It's deeply inspiring, and I'm surprised when tears start coming from seemingly nowhere. I guess I never saw how desperately I needed this kind of support. When I realize I have found it, the tears of relief and joy come from a place I have kept sealed away for a very long time.

The prayer winds down, and Scott makes a few closing remarks and asks for God's blessing on our lunch today.

Toward the end of the afternoon session, Scott launches into the open forum time in the agenda. This is where guys can ask about any issue they are facing and get advice and counsel from the group. A guy named John jumps in right away.

"All right, I've got a question for the group," John says.

I recognize the company name on John's name tag. He runs a huge business and I'm sure his question is going to be way over my head, but I'm curious to hear what kind of challenges "real" companies deal with.

"I have an employee who's decided it's a good idea to start dating one of our key customers. Any of you guys ever dealt with that?" John asks.

Unbelievable! I just dealt with this issue a few months ago. Several of the guys leap to John's aid as they share their experience and counsel on how they handled the issue when it came up in their company.

I'm flabbergasted (and relieved) to realize these men all face the same issues I do, regardless of how big their company is. These men are starting to resemble me, I think—just a bunch of guys trying to do their best with what God has given them.

After this inspiring day, I'm sold on C12. The next day I fill out the membership application and send it to Scott along with a check for the first month's dues.

First Things First

Today is C12 day, December 21, 2006. I've been a C12 member for eight months, and I'm amazed how fast the time has gone. I've learned so much, and for me, the biggest value of this group is in the way they hold me accountable and teach me to be more faithful and disciplined in all aspects of my life.

C12 is where I learned the phrase "speaking the truth in love." Sounds harmless enough, right? Boy, what a wake-up call I got. I know these guys love me as their Christian brother, but when they speak the truth in love to you, it can be brutal. I guess they love me too much to let me stay where I am.

Our chairman, Scott, is fond of using another phrase, "like iron sharpens iron," to describe how a C12 group counsels its members. (This phrase is in the Bible somewhere. You can look it up.) Honestly, I don't think this phrase accurately illustrates what our group does. I think our group acts more like a blacksmith. First they turn up the heat on you until you become malleable. Then they pound you into shape over an anvil. Of course, this is all done while speaking the truth in love, but these guys carry big sticks and they're not afraid to use them.

I've been told I can be a little hardheaded at times, so having a blacksmith pound me back into shape is probably a good thing. My group started pounding on me from the first day after I became a member. This may sound like harsh treatment, but I'm certainly not going to waste $500 a month on C12 dues to have the guys blow smoke up my skirt. I'm paying for these guys to be brutally honest, and let me tell you, I'm getting my money's worth.

To be fair, this group is not about beating its members into submission. We pray for each other and encourage one another. It's a fun and positive group to be a part of. Just don't come into it thinking you're not going to be pushed.

I have picked up so many valuable things since joining C12 that it's hard to keep track of them all. It's a good thing we get C12 binders to put the monthly material in because I often refer to a prior segment.

The very first thing my group started pressing me on was my company's mission statement. The guys asked, "How can you call yourself a company owned by God and not even mention Him anywhere in your mission statement?" I didn't have a good answer. I knew they were right. Was I just going to give this "Christian company" thing lip service, or was I actually going to step up and live it? It was a matter of integrity.

Here was my company mission statement before my C12 group got ahold of me:

> *Professional Materials Management (PM2) will provide customized business solutions that ensure our clients a fast path to return on investment. We will improve our clients' business effectiveness through the delivery of:*
> * *Customized Content Services*
> * *Materials Management Services*
> * *Consulting Services*

Sounded very professional, I thought, but the guys said it was too long and there was no mention of God anywhere in it.

Here's the new mission statement I came up with:

> *To honor God as we position our clients for success in inventory management.*

Better, huh?

Once the group straightened out my mission statement, Scott moved to the next priority he saw for my Christian development: journaling. Really? A journal sounded like a diary to me. Only teenage girls write in diaries, not grown men. I'm a man's man, and I could not see myself writing in a journal.

But Scott wouldn't let up on this journaling thing. Month after month he would ask me, "Dan, have you started journaling yet?"

"Not yet, Scott."

"Why not, Dan?"

I'd sheepishly grin and say, "I guess it hasn't made it to the top of my to-do list yet, Scott."

This month is no different, and Scott starts in on me right away. "Dan, have you finally decided to start journaling yet?"

"I'll start soon."

"What's wrong with today?"

Beaten down and realizing Scott is not going to let up until I do this, I finally concede. "All right, I am putting it on my to-do sheet to start journaling by our next meeting in January."

"Oh, next meeting, huh? I guess this isn't important enough to start today?" Scott is grinning, but I know he's serious.

"I'll do my best, Scott."

Journal Your Day on the Water

After months of incessant pressure from Scott and the C12 guys, I've decided to give journaling a whirl. I made it one of my C12 to-dos, so if I don't at least start journaling by our next meeting, I will be "allowed" to pay ten bucks for not doing it. (Our C12 group treasurer keeps an envelope full of all the ten-dollar fines the guys have paid throughout the year. By the end of the year, the group usually has several hundred dollars in the envelope to do something good with around the Christmas season.)

Okay, so here goes nothing. I'll just start writing about the first thing that comes to mind.

January 9, 2007

I seem to spend my waking hours worrying and wondering whether God will take care of His business. Thank God I have Julie to help me with my faith, and Eric too. I just don't see it, Lord. I mean, I see all of the opportunities You've laid out before us, but none are turning into revenue yet. I know I can't know the future, Lord. And I know You will make things happen at the snap of Your fingers, and I will know exactly what Your plan was after the fact. Please forgive me for worrying so much all the time.

Would anyone be surprised at what I chose to write about in my very first journal entry? Of course not.

I write in my journal five days a week, usually on weekday mornings. Quite often I'll add more comments later in the day because something significant happened I want to capture. Strangely, I am noticing a certain cause and effect going on here that I never expected to see.

More and more often, I see that events and circumstances are often directly linked to the choices I make. One might say, "Well, of course, genius! When you put your hand on a hot stove, you get burned!" No, what I'm talking about goes much deeper than that. I'm talking about those times when I'm doing something harmless like checking out who won the latest Hooters bikini contest (or something even more spicy) on the internet, and then very soon after, something bad happens in my life. I am seeing this correlation with increasing frequency. It's like God is allowing me to experience pain and loss to teach me personal discipline.

Now, I don't know about you, but for me it's a little spooky to think that God might really be watching me everywhere I go and knowing every thought I have. That's just scary. But I must say, having this perspective that God is watching makes me think twice about what I'm about to do and where my mind goes.

Thankfully, I can easily convince myself that God isn't really watching, so I don't have to feel guilty. Sadly, this blissful feeling never lasts very long. It's always interrupted by some calamity. And when I look back at my journal, I'm able to connect the dots, and I'm reminded once again of who's watching me.

Don't get me wrong. It's not all doom and gloom to have God watching me. In fact, the positives outweigh the negatives. Yes, God disciplines and redirects me, but He also rewards me when He sees me doing what He wants me to do. Usually, when God rewards me, it's something to do with the business, like some big new lead or a landed contract. I think God knows how important the business is to me, and He uses it as leverage to keep me inside the channel markers. For example, I've noticed that whenever I take time out in the morning to pray with Julie and rededicate the business to God, something good usually happens for the business that day. Knowing this, you would think I would pray with Julie and rededicate the business to God every single morning, without fail. Nope.

We often learn in church and Sunday school about how many times the Israelites screwed up and how quickly they forgot about the many miracles God performed for them, and I think, *Holy cow, those people were idiots!*

Then it hits me. I'm just like them.

Stay over the Fish

I have been journaling for about two weeks now and I must say, this isn't nearly as painful as I expected it to be. I'm a man of few words. I expected to run out of things to say in my journal pretty quickly. But that hasn't happened yet. What I've discovered is that my journal is acting as a tool to help me pay closer attention to what God is doing each day. And since I'm paying closer attention, I find I have plenty to write about. Of course, compared to Julie's abundance of words, my journal entries are pretty short, but I figure God knows what I mean and I'm trying my best not to bore Him with long, drawn-out epistles.

January 10, 2007

I'm still not sleeping well, Lord. I know You have a plan. I just hope it doesn't include PM2 losing our people or us losing the home You have blessed us with. Please, Lord, show me what's next on the horizon for Your company and Your people. We all need some peace right now. Please, Lord, if it's Your will. We will glorify Your name, whatever comes.

January 18, 2007

First call this morning was from a big distributor. Thank You, Father! And thanks for the wonderful conversation with Karen yesterday. I never would have guessed she would want to represent us. You are so amazing, Father! Thank You. Thank You!!

CHAPTER 3

January 19, 2007

You kept right on giving yesterday. Thank You, Father! I met Cory and Tracy of Covenant House and they need us to set up a large food pantry for them. And then, as soon as I got home from our C12 meeting, John in Houston called with a big new opportunity.

I went to our Friday morning men's group today, and for the first time in a long time, I am not freaked out about the business. I trust You, Lord. Thanks for Your leading, Father. Thanks for the many things You are laying before us!

January 20, 2007

I fell into a tailspin today, out of control. (Got sucked in by the internet again.) Father, I am ashamed that I can't control my thoughts any better than this. Please forgive me. How short my memory is, Lord. Do I not think You are watching? Please forgive me!

January 21, 2007

Father, I am bracing for something bad to happen in response to my tailspin yesterday. Lord, please forgive me and let Your business and Your people prosper today and this week. And we'll praise Your name, Lord! Thank You for Your daily nudges and reminders.

January 23, 2007

In these few days of initial journal entries, I went back to read them and was disappointed at how terribly fickle I am. Up one day, down the next. Not the sign of a well-disciplined, trusting soul, Father. Please forgive me for my doubts.

January 25, 2007

Father, You are so amazing! Only a week ago, I was saying how much we needed some consulting work, and out of the blue, we have five consulting opportunities we are bidding on. Thank You, Lord!

And so on and so on . . .

As I think about my journal entries thus far, I'm realizing how little control I have over any outcome. God is in control. I am hanging minute by minute on the hope that God will provide for us, and I see a direct connection between my faithful obedience and God's provision.

I can't see even one second into the future. Oh, I plan for the future, and I definitely worry about the future, but I sure can't predict it. This is not to say that I have no idea what I can expect to happen, though. It's kind of like fishing. If I drop my line in a stagnant, polluted swamp, I can expect to catch scrub fish, or a turtle, or nothing at all. But if I fish in pristine water over the right structure, the possibilities of what I may reel in are endless. There's a sense of great anticipation for that next big fish when you know you're in the right spot.

"Never leave fish to find fish."
Moses, 1200 BC (according to folklore)

There's a rule in fishing that says, "Never leave fish to find fish." In other words, as long as you're catching fish, stay right where you are. I think this rule seems obvious enough, and I follow it religiously when I'm out on the water. But I'm discovering this rule also applies to life. When you're in a good spot with God and He is blessing you in a big way, why would you ever leave that spot and strike out on your own to search for better fishing grounds? I know this is going to sound ridiculous, but I do it all the time, just like the Israelites in the Bible.

Will I ever learn?

4

An Ominous Discovery

It's September 20, 2007, and for a few weeks now, I've been noticing a lump on my back, just inside my right shoulder blade. Every time I get in the car, my car seat hits me right on that spot, and it's starting to hurt just enough to be an annoyance. It feels like a big cyst or something, about the size of a grape. Anyway, I showed it to Julie this morning and we called our dermatologist, Dr. Miller, for an appointment to get it checked out. Ever since that little skin cancer incident, almost six years ago now, she and Julie have watched me like hawks. But I'm past that magic five-year mark. (This is the point where doctors say you're clear of cancer if you don't have any recurrences within five years, so I'm not expecting this to be anything.)

It's September 24, Julie's birthday, and we're waiting in an exam room. A faint knock comes on the door and in walks Dr. Miller. She's very quiet and shy, an introvert like me. We catch up for a few minutes, with Julie leading the conversation, and then the good doctor gets down to business.

"Let's see what you have there," she says.

I show her the lump on my back.

"Uh-huh," she says. "That could be several things, but it's probably a cyst. Would you like me to take it out today?" She's barely finishing her sentence as Julie pipes up. "Absolutely!"

I don't get a vote. This lady has been cutting on me for more than five years now, removing anything that looks the least bit suspicious. I've been told I look like I've been in a knife fight and lost. I'm a regular at this by now, so I roll over on my stomach and wait for the lidocaine.

A nurse comes in to numb the area around the lump. The needle goes in again and again all around the lump. Clinching my teeth, I think, *Holy smokes! She's really going deep with that needle. That lump must be well below the surface this time.*

We wait a few minutes for the lidocaine to take effect and then she comes back into the room. "Are you ready?"

"I can't wait," I answer.

And so she begins. I can feel pressure, as she and Julie make small talk, but no real pain. It's about what I'm used to from the many previous procedures she's done on me. Everything else she's taken off up until now has been on the surface of my skin. But now it's starting to hurt, a lot!

I let out a deep groan. "Good gracious, are you digging to China?" My whole body is tensed up as I brace for the next jolt of pain.

"We almost have it," she says. "Just a little more to go."

Then silence.

Lying facedown on the procedure table, I turn my head to catch a glimpse of Dr. Miller in the mirror on the wall. All the color in her face is completely gone.

"This doesn't look good," she murmurs with a tone of fear in her voice.

Julie and I don't say a word. We just look at each other.

"We'll send this down to pathology right away," she says. "We'll give you a call in a few days to let you know what we find out."

A few days later Dr. Miller's office calls me in for a follow-up appointment. It's melanoma. So she books an appointment for me with Dr. Sanchez, the guy who did my right jaw several years ago. He needs to take out some more flesh around the spot on my back to get clean margins.

A few days later surgery day has arrived. Julie and I are waiting expectantly for Dr. Sanchez in one of the exam rooms. Julie and I aren't talking much. Then Julie takes my hand and she says a prayer for me. A few more minutes pass and in comes Dr. Sanchez. He's got a very serious look on his face. He doesn't waste any time getting right to the point.

"Well, guys, I know you came in for some surgery today, but after seeing what Dr. Miller removed from your back, we're going to shift gears. Dan, you have metastatic melanoma, which means this tumor has spread from somewhere else in your body. So the first thing we need to do is a CT scan to see if it has spread anywhere else. We'll get you scheduled ASAP for the scan and then we'll make plans from there. Does that make sense?"

I nod without uttering a word.

"Do you have any questions I can answer at this point?" asks Dr. Sanchez.

"I don't think so. Not right now, anyway," I tell him.

He looks me in the eye, shakes my hand, and says, "Dan, I'm worried about you. We'll get you an appointment with one of our melanoma oncologists before you leave today. We need to get on this right away," he says.

Those words got my attention. I'm pretty sure it's a bad thing when your surgeon tells you he's worried about you.

Divine Appointment

God's plan is so complex, and I am constantly amazed at how the pieces of the puzzle fit together. Sometimes it takes years before I see the full picture. Case in point: I've known my friend Rob for several years. I sing tenor with him in the church choir. He's a fisherman, so we hit it off right from the start. I like singing with Rob. Our voices blend well together, and he reads music, so I can pick up the songs a lot faster following Rob's lead. But mostly what I like about Rob is his kind heart. Rob is a genuinely nice guy and lives out his Christian faith in the loving way he treats everybody he meets.

Rob manages the radiology department at Lakeside Cancer Center. I've known this for years, but now I see how this puzzle piece fits into God's plan. We were assigned an oncologist yesterday in Dr. Sanchez's office, but we have no idea who this guy is or whether he's any good at what he does. Julie knows that all doctors are not created equal. Some are truly gifted and talented, while others simply are not. Julie wants to make sure we get the very finest oncologist Lakeside has to offer. So Julie calls Rob, and he immediately leaps into action, polling his fellow "Lakeside insiders" on who the best melanoma oncologist is.

Rob calls Julie back a bit later. "Dr. Blake is who you want, hands down," Rob tells her. "He's world renowned for the things he's doing to treat melanoma. The trouble is, he's booked three months out. Let me see what I can do to get you an appointment with him. Stay tuned, guys."

"Rob, we love you!" Julie exclaims in appreciation.

The next morning Rob calls Julie first thing. "I was able to speak with Dr. Blake's nurse and you two have an appointment with Dr. Blake this

Friday morning at 9 a.m. Can you make that time?"

"Are you kidding?" Julie screams. "Of course we can make it! Thank you, thank you, Rob! We knew God put you in our path for a reason, and now we see why! Thanks again, Rob!"

God clearly has a plan and I am beginning to not believe in luck anymore.

Start of a Journey

It's Friday, appointment day with Dr. Blake, and we're sitting in an exam room of the melanoma clinic at Lakeside Cancer Center, waiting for the results of the CT scan and whatever is next. Julie and I hold hands and say a short prayer together. After just a few minutes, two quick raps come on the door and Dr. Blake steps into the room. He's a thin but physically fit man, about my age, I figure, and I can tell he's a nerd. The bow tie gives that away immediately. But hey, a nerdy doctor is a good thing. We exchange introductions and some small talk; then Dr. Blake gets right to it.

"Mr. Floen, you have two masses that concern me, one on each of your adrenal glands. You also have a third mass in the soft tissue just above your right hip bone. So the first thing I'd like to do is a needle biopsy of one of the adrenal masses. This will tell us for certain whether they are malignant or benign."

I appreciate how this guy is so direct. He doesn't sugarcoat anything; he just tells us what the situation is so we can make informed decisions and get moving on a course of action as soon as possible. He's obviously seen a lot of this disease before, and I am getting the very clear sense that we don't have any time to lose.

"So," he says, "we'll get the biopsy scheduled right away. In the meantime, how do you feel right now?" He starts with a long list of questions like, "Have you had any headaches or loss of vision lately? How is your energy level? Have you gained or lost more than ten pounds in the last month? How is your appetite? Do you get night sweats or chills?" And so on . . .

"I feel fine," I tell him. "In fact, if it weren't for the masses, I'd never know anything was wrong."

"That's a good sign, Mr. Floen," he tells me. "If the disease had progressed very far at all, you would be feeling a lot worse than you do. So let's see what the needle biopsy tells us and we'll make plans from there. We'll schedule a follow-up appointment next Friday to go over the results with you."

"Thank you, sir," I say as I stretch out my hand, and we shake on it.

"We'll see you in a week, Mr. Floen."

Two days later I'm back at Lakeside for the needle biopsy of my adrenal gland, and the following Friday morning we're back in Dr. Blake's exam room, waiting to hear the results. Julie and I say a prayer together as we wait for Dr. Blake.

After a cordial "Good morning," and a handshake, Dr. Blake gets right to business. "Mr. Floen, the biopsy results came back showing malignant disease on your adrenal gland. I expect the other masses are malignant as well. We could take out the mass on your right side, but you can't live without your adrenal glands so we can't remove them. Taking anything out right now doesn't make sense because of the systemic nature of your disease. The only reasonable approach for treatment has to be a systematic one, which treats the disease wherever it may exist in your body."

As I listen to him, the first question on my mind is, how long do I have? Obviously he gets that question a lot because he jumps right to the answer before I can ask it.

"Mr. Floen, I can tell you that the average life expectancy for this stage of disease is about eight months. That being said, my average is better than that. My patients are surviving as long as twelve to eighteen months."

I had prepared for bad news, but that's even worse than I had anticipated. I'm not sure how to process what he just said. I glance over at Julie and she's doing her best to keep a neutral expression, but all color has drained from her face. I look down at the floor and think, *Wow, he just said twelve to eighteen months like that's a good thing. Twelve to eighteen months doesn't sound like much to be proud of. And he hasn't mentioned the word cure at all. I guess everybody dies.*

As I struggle to rationalize what's happening, my mind flashes back to all the times as a younger man when I should have died and thought about how God protected me every time. I'm convinced I am still here only because my parents were constantly praying for me. I mean, I should have died several times while driving drunk on my KZ400 motorcycle in high school. Or how about the time when I jumped the median heading into oncoming traffic with my parents' Chevy Citation? My friends Karen and Cindy were in the front seat with me, and I'm convinced God protected me because He didn't want to see the girls get hurt that night. Then there was the time when I jumped off the back of my catamaran to retrieve my favorite hat. The boat just kept on going and I was easily a mile from shore. I never wore a life jacket. I should have drowned that day, but a boat picked me up just before I ran out of strength to swim.

I figure God has kept me around longer than I deserved already, so I look at this death sentence as the end of a very generous set of life extensions from God. I pray silently, "God, if this is the end, I am prepared to accept it and be satisfied with the full and exciting life that You have given me. Everything else from this point forward is just gravy. On the other hand, wouldn't this be a great time to show everyone a miracle? My vote is for a miracle. What do You think, God?"

Dr. Blake lays out his plan of attack for us. He tells us there are several types of chemo and various trials available, if I qualify for them. He begins to explain how important it is to do the treatments in the right order, so as to leave the most options available to us in the future. I interpret that to mean, "We really don't know which of these drugs will work, if any, so we're going to try as many of them as we can."

I hadn't noticed the lump in my right side before, but now that I know it's there, I can feel it very easily. It hurts when I press on it. Dr. Blake says he wants to leave it in as a physical indicator to tell us whether the treatments are having any effect. Sounds like a good idea to me. This way I won't have to wait six weeks for the next set of scans to know whether anything good, or bad, is happening. It occurs to me that God might have put this lump there for my peace of mind.

Dr. Blake continues to explain the recommended course of treatment. He'll start with a clinical trial to see what kind of response that gives us. If that doesn't work, he'll go to another drug, which is essentially an immune system accelerator. If that doesn't work, he'll break out the "Big Guns," a mixture of high-power traditional chemo drugs. If the "Big Guns" don't work, assuming I am still alive, there may a new trial out by then that we can try. He talks about survival rates in terms of months, not years. Again, the word cure is never mentioned.

Chemo, huh? Lovely. I've seen what chemo does to people. Pretty much all I know about it is that it kills everything in its path, not just the cancer cells. Walking through the corridors of Lakeside, it's obvious to me which patients are doing chemo. They're the ones who look like Auschwitz prisoners.

That night I am talking with God in my journal.

October 17, 2007

Okay, Lord, I guess we're going to do this the hard way. Father, I was so disappointed today. I really thought a miracle today would have spoken so loudly, more loudly than some doctor getting the credit for curing me. So now I am gearing up for a battle. Father, I reject the illness in my body, and I claim the redeeming and healing power of Your Son, Jesus Christ! I expel this cancer in the name of Jesus Christ!! I will make this my mental focus, working and fighting against this thing that the enemy has done. I know it's not Your will for me to be sick, so I plan to fight because of what has already been given me through the saving grace of Jesus. AMEN!!

Since our meeting with the doctor, Julie has been researching on the internet about stage four metastatic melanoma. She says the odds are stacked way against me. I think she senses that I don't need to hear exactly how bad my odds are, so she spares me the gory details. She's right; I really don't want to know.

Over the years I've watched people as some horrific crisis enters their life, and the most frequent question they ask of God is, "Why me?" I've never asked that question. I guess I think I had it coming to me. I mean,

I've done some stupid stuff in my life, and I'm still carrying around some serious character flaws. I think God got tired of waiting for me to make the necessary changes, so He organized a little intervention for me. As I see it, this thing is not about cancer. Cancer is simply a tool God is using to get my attention. Oh, He's got my attention, all right. So now God and I have some remodeling to do.

Listening Prayer

As the days pass and Julie and I struggle to settle into our new reality, I am spending a lot more time in the Bible. I'm straining to find any shred of guidance and direction I can glean from God's Word to make sense of what's happening here. It's funny how folks only pick up the Bible after everything else they've tried has failed and their world is falling down around them. I guess I'm no different.

A few weeks after the diagnosis, I began earnestly searching through the Bible for any shred of hope I could hang on to, and I came upon Romans 8:28, which says, "And we know that for those who love God all things work together for good, for those who are called according to his purpose."

This verse has formed the basis for my understanding of what is happening right now.

A few weeks ago our C12 chairman, Scott Hitchcock, gave us all a little book called *God Guides*. It's by Mary Geegh, who was a missionary in India for thirty-eight years, from 1924 to 1962. This little book is only sixty pages long, which is perfect for me because I am not a big reader, but it's packed with story after story of how she used this thing called "listening prayer" to hear directly from God. Until I read this book, I only heard what

God had to say when He hit me across the forehead with it. This book taught me how to stop, clear my mind, listen, and wait for God to speak. Sometimes He speaks right away. Other times it takes a long stretch of waiting and listening. And sometimes I get the sense He wants me to come back later when I'm ready to rephrase my question. I always get an answer, though. There is a great sense of peace that comes with that.

God Clears the Way

Julie's been tirelessly researching cancer treatments until long after I've gone to bed every night. She's on the phone all day, gathering information from various clinics and medical resources from around the world.

Julie has coined a phrase lately for people who don't seem to understand why she's working so hard to keep me around when it's obvious to them what the endgame is. She simply tells them, "I don't want *a* husband. I want *this* husband." That's an awfully flattering thing for me to hear, and I'm trying not to let it go to my head.

She has so much faith. I really don't think she expects to lose me. I think she's working like this to make sure she doesn't miss the slightest message from God or some smidgen of information from the medical community that might offer me the feeblest chance to stay here longer.

So when Julie's mammogram came back looking ominous last week, Julie simply didn't have time for it. Her response was to go to God in faith and simply ask Him to "just make this go away."

A few days later she went in for her follow-up mammogram appointment, and after the exam, the nurse came in with a very puzzled look on her face. The lumps were simply gone. Just gone. Vamoose!

Norman Vincent Peale wrote, "Expect great things from God and you will receive great things from God. Expect a miracle." Julie expected a miracle, and she got one.

Okay, so it's back to work for Julie on keeping me around!

Taking the Point

My dad and I have always talked regularly, at least every week or two. He's a very unassuming man and he tries not to intrude into my and Julie's life, so I'm usually the one who picks up the phone first to call him. Ever since I got the diagnosis, though, he's been calling me almost every morning.

It's 6 a.m., and the phone rings. Dad knows I'm awake by now.

I give him my usual greeting, "Hey, man, how are you doing?"

"Good morning, my man. I'm fine. Are you getting any sleep these days?" he asks.

"Not so much," I reply.

"I can understand that," he says. "Dan, ever since you got this news, I've been praying and asking God what He has to say about this. And I'd like to share with you what I've heard from Him, if that's okay."

"Please, by all means."

Dad pauses for a moment. "I believe God is saying, 'I trust you to stand tall here, Dan. I'm going to be with you. You can do this. I want you to focus completely on Me and I'll take care of the rest,'" Dad says.

Dad continues. "God is going to use this to His glory. There is going to be a miracle. We don't know what the miracle is yet, but we walk in faith, knowing God is in charge. Son, you have been drafted to be in this army. You're at the point, and God is right there with you. We don't know how the battle ends, but you're going to be okay. Don't despair. Hold on to your faith. Whatever happens, it's all good. Jesus said, 'My burden is light. Take My yoke upon you in faith and I will be with you.' Jesus took point for us, Dan. Now it's your time to draw others to Him."

I sit there holding the phone in silence, letting Dad's words sink in. He isn't saying a word. He knows I'm processing what he just told me.

After a little while, I begin to embrace Dad's godly perspective. Suddenly this great sense of honor comes over me that God has entrusted me with this amazing, special assignment. And I don't ever want to let God down. Don't get me wrong; I am petrified, but it feels like an honor.

Dad's perspective is a game changer for me. That night I sit down and write in my journal about being on point.

On Point

On point, all your senses go on high alert. You hear the faintest whisper. You spot the slightest movement ahead. You can smell everything and detect the enemy's foul stench from miles away. On point, talking too much can be fatal, so you watch and you listen. On point, you constantly pray as you are walking.

And when you're under attack, with bullets whistling by your head and mortars exploding all around, you block out all else and focus on your platoon leader. Your platoon leader frequently uses signals to communicate with you, so you dare not take your eyes off him for long. He gives an order and you obey it immediately and without hesitation because you know He is the only one that will get you through this.

On point is where you learn about faith and the power of obedience.

As strange as it may sound, I feel thankful for this responsibility and very special mission. And I'm humbled that God thinks I am worthy of the task.

The next morning I'm at Friday morning men's group at church. As soon as the group is all gathered, Pastor Dave pulls a chair into the center of the circle and asks me to take a seat. He then anoints my head with oil and invites the men to gather around me and lay their hands on me. David opens the prayer and then each man prays for me in succession.

All our friends and family now know the situation and calls, cards, and emails are starting to pour in. This one came from Jim and Carol:

Dear Dan,

I woke up this morning and you were on my mind. I walked into the living room where Carol was doing her devotions and she said you were on her mind. Know in the quiet times with God you are on our minds—prayed for, rooted for, and asked for healing. We are blessed to get to know you and Julie and look forward to many years together, learning, growing, and having fun. Long ago I listened to Chuck Swindoll on the radio on the way to work. One day he said to remember the following:

"We are all faced with a series of great opportunities brilliantly disguised as impossible situations."

We don't by any means believe yours is an impossible situation, just another great opportunity. Give 'em heaven!

Love,
Jim & Carol

Every day I learn of more and more people who are praying for my healing. I'm sure it's hundreds of people by now. I sure hope God decides to heal me or there's going to be a lot of disappointed people out there. No matter what happens, I hope I will bear this burden in a way that always brings glory to God.

You Are Already Healed!

It's C12 day today, and the guys are going around the table as we always do in our morning session, sharing their praises and prayer concerns. They all know about my diagnosis, and all I can think of to say is, "Guys, please pray for me, that I would carry the burden of this special assignment with honor and in a way that glorifies God. Let me not cower before the fight. Let me stand tall in faith, accepting whatever path God would have for me. Pray that God will work through me to bring others closer to Him."

As I look around the table, the guys are spontaneously rising from their chairs and heading toward me. Scott comes over and gets down on his knees in front me and lays his hands on my hands. The rest of the guys all circle around and lay their hands on my shoulders and head. Scott leads out in prayer and the rest follow. But these prayers are like nothing I've ever heard before. These men are actually thanking God for healing me, as though it's already happened. They are praying with such certainty in their voices that I'm beginning to believe them, that I am already healed. I've never heard anyone pray like that.

Mark 11:24 says, "Therefore I tell you, whatever you ask for in prayer, believe that you have received it, and it will be yours" (NIV). That's exactly what these guys are doing: praying as though I have already been healed.

Suddenly a deep sense of peace and comfort comes upon me, and I am not worried anymore. I feel strong and courageous because God is already in the fight for me.

That prayer session forever changes my perspective on how to pray.

At the end of the day, as the guys are shaking hands and saying their goodbyes, Chris, who runs a small advertising firm, walks over and shares his testimony of being healed from a certain death spinal disease he had. Chris has a glimmer in his eyes and a certainty in his voice, as though he has been party to a miracle and there's just no question in his mind about what God has done. Then Chris looks very intently into my eyes, puts his hands on my shoulders, and says, "You are already healed. You are already healed. Dan, you are already healed!" Chris says it with such conviction that I think I may actually believe it.

Lord, help me manage my doubts!

Brother-Sister Time

My sister, Kathy, came down from Minnesota this week to visit me. She's a nurse, which is to say she knows way too much about where this thing is probably headed. It's not pretty and she knows it. I get the sense she wanted to come quickly and spend time with me because this may be the last time she'll see me healthy, or alive. So I'm taking her fishing, just the two of us. We need some brother-sister time.

It's a beautiful day on the bay, and we have a good day of fishing. Kathy takes a lot of pictures of me throwing the cast net, rigging the lines, and driving the boat. I take pictures of her with the many fish she catches. Though it's left unspoken, we are both taking pictures to capture as much of these good times as we can so we can remember them when things get really ugly.

Being on the boat helps me forget about my cares. This is just what I needed before heading into battle.

Gone, Gone, Gone

It's October 25, 2007. We started chemo treatments yesterday at Lakeside, and so far I don't feel any worse for wear. I am taking pills for the trial I'm on. It's a blind study, so I don't know if I'm taking a placebo or the real thing, but I didn't sleep well and I had weird dreams all night long. Today I'm a little tired but otherwise fine.

A few days later Eric and I are headed to Wilmington for an important sales call at GE. This deal could be huge for PM2, and it's ours for the taking, it appears.

I board the plane in Tampa and settle into my seat.

A few months ago I bought this awesome set of ear buds so I can just faintly hear the flight attendant over the speakers as she explains the safety features of the airplane. These ear buds give me a quiet and peaceful place, no matter how much chaos is happening around me.

A few minutes after take-off, the flight attendant comes back on the speaker and tells us it's okay to use our electronic devices. So I dial up "A Pirate Looks at 40" by Jimmy Buffett on my iPod, just at a low enough volume where I can think, and settle in for some quiet time with just me and God.

In the still of this place, with only low music in the background, I am praying fervently. Suddenly I feel two very sharp pains, ten seconds apart, lasting five seconds each, near the tumor in my side. *That's got to mean something,* I think. But what?

The next morning I'm up at 5 a.m. I turn on the light and roll out of bed. As I rise for the day, I glance down at my pillow. It's got quite a bit of hair on it, my hair. *Hmm, that's weird,* I think, but I don't give it a second thought. I can't let a few extra hairs on my pillow distract me. I mean, I've got places to go and people to see today.

In the shower I'm lathering up with that tiny bar of soap they give you and I drop it. As I bend down to pick it up, I see a bunch more hair around the drain. Then the reality sinks in. It's the chemo. I'm losing my hair, and fast.

I get dressed in my usual client meeting uniform: a white button-down PM2 logo shirt, tan wool trousers, and a blue double-breasted blazer. I'm meeting Eric for breakfast downstairs this morning and as I head out the door I take one last look in the mirror, just to make sure I don't have any stray toothpaste or shaving cream on me. Nope, no toothpaste or shaving cream, but tons of hair on the shoulders of my blazer. What to do?

Here's a cancer trivia fact I learned recently. When you lose your hair from chemo treatments, your hair isn't falling out from the roots; it's breaking off at the scalp. Knowing this, I figure if I can keep my hair in place somehow, it won't break off so quickly, and I might make it through today's meeting without going bald.

I squeeze out a huge glob of extra-hold styling gel and very gingerly apply it all through my hair. I figure the gel should hold my hair in place, but I've got to refrain from touching my hair all day. This might be a challenge because I tend to run my hands through my hair a lot. By the time I'm done applying the gel, my hair feels like a helmet. Perfect. That ought to do it!

At breakfast I tell Eric about my hair falling out. "I need you to watch my shoulders today in the meeting. If you see me start to shed profusely, give me a signal or something to let me know so I can brush it off or excuse myself, okay?"

"You got it, brother," Eric says with a look of deep commitment on his face. "Dan, everything is going to be just fine. Don't worry. You'll see." Eric's always good for an encouraging word. I'm not quite as sure as Eric is.

Later the same day . . .

Woohoo! The extra-hold gel strategy worked. My hair is still intact and the meeting with GE could not have gone better!

My hair stays in place for the entire plane ride home. When I arrive home, the house is empty. Julie is in North Carolina tending to her aunt Truda, who is dying, and Laurel is still at school. She's in third grade.

I've been consciously avoiding touching my hair all day long, but I'm safe at home now, so I figure now's as good a time as any to see what the damage will be if I rough up my hair a bit. I give myself a two-handed head scratch and run my fingers through my hair. As I do this, the hair is raining down on my office carpet like an autumn tree that decided to drop all its leaves at once.

I run to the bathroom to survey the damage. My hair looks significantly thinner. For some reason, as I stand there in front of the mirror, I feel motivated to grab a wad of hair and pull. As I do this, I can hear my hair breaking off. I wind up with a fist full of hair. I give a tug to another tuft of hair and the whole thing breaks off. This isn't going to end well. Everywhere I grab, the hair is coming off in chunks. For a guy who has always had great hair (just ask anyone), this is surreal.

I keep pulling chunks of hair out until I'm left with a few ratty-looking tufts and the uneven low fuzz from the thousands of broken off stems of hair. I figure I might as well finish the job, so I break out my mustache trimmer and buzz off the rest. Then I put a new set of blades in my razor and shave my head.

It's now 4:30 p.m., time to pick up Laurel from school. And I'm bald. Not wanting to shock her, I put on a baseball cap and head out the door. I arrive at school and go to the after-school care room where I find Laurel working on a beautiful drawing. As I walk up to her, Laurel looks up at me with a puzzled look in her eye and says, "Daddy, did you get a haircut?"

I take off my cap and say, "Yep, I sure did. How do you like it?"

I hope I didn't warp her for life.

The next day, Julie arrives home and takes my new hairdo in stride.

New Look

By now, our whole company knows I'm bald, but very few of them have seen me yet because our people are located all over the country. So I decide to shoot a video to show them my new look. (You can watch the video on my website: danfloen.com.)

I hope I didn't scare anyone. I probably have delusions of grandeur, but at some level I think our team members may be wondering what will

become of PM2 and their jobs if I don't make it. I'm not sure what I can say to comfort them. From their vantage point, things probably look bleak for me.

Ronnie's Revelation

Ronnie is one of our best 1099 contractors. He's been with us for several years, and I've gotten to know him very well. Ronnie is a deep Christian man who is very much in touch with God. In fact, the rest of our team members recognize this quality in him as well, so I recently asked him to be our PM2 chaplain. Never have I met a man so in tune to what God is saying to him. So when Ronnie tells me God speaks to him, I believe him.

Ronnie and I typically talk at least once a week, but strangely, I haven't heard from him for going on two months now. I'm wondering if he's okay, so I call Eric to see if he knows anything. Ronnie is a very private individual who doesn't share his problems with many people, so I'm not too surprised when Eric says he hasn't heard anything.

I decide to give Ronnie a call. Ronnie picks up and he greets me with the usual, "Hello, Mr. Floen!"

"Brother Ronnie!" I reply. "How are you doing, man?"

"Awe, man, I am blessed as always, my friend!" he answers.

"Well, Ronnie, we haven't talked in a while, so I just wanted to check in with you. What's going on with you lately?" I ask.

"Oh, just staying busy," he says and stops talking.

Usually I would get more details about exactly what Ronnie's been up to, how the family is doing, and so on, but today something is different. He doesn't seem as comfortable with me as usual.

After a few more minutes of small talk, I muster the courage to say, "Ronnie, I sense you have something weighing very heavy on your mind. Is it anything you'd like to talk about?"

Silence.

Knowing Ronnie to be a reserved and soft-spoken man, I give him all the time he needs.

"Dan, God told me something a few weeks ago and I've been really wrestling with whether I should tell you or not."

Oh dear Lord, what could Ronnie have been told that would have him struggling so much with it? Did God tell him I'm going to die soon? I'm not sure I'm ready to hear that! I take a deep breath.

"Ronnie, you shouldn't tell me if you're uncomfortable with it. But if you do choose to tell me, I promise I'll do my best to accept whatever it is at face value."

More silence.

A long time passes. Then Ronnie finally breaks the silence. "Dan, I am reluctant to tell you this because it's very risky for me to say it, but God spoke to me about your cancer."

"He did? What did He say?" I ask.

Ronnie sighs and pauses for another moment. "God told me that He's going to heal you."

I let out a deep exhale. That is so much better than all of the other things I was imagining.

"Ronnie, thanks for telling me. I can see how that would be a risky thing for you to say. I mean, what if you heard God wrong? What if I hang my every hope on what you just told me and I die anyway? I'm sure that would be a tough thing to live with. But one thing I know is that God does speak to you, so I appreciate you telling me. Don't worry, Ronnie, I won't hold you responsible if I die," I tell him jokingly, and Ronnie laughs. "But I sure do appreciate knowing that He told you this. Thanks again for telling me. This was a brave thing you did. God bless you, Brother Ronnie."

It's Going to Get Ugly

I've been awake since three this morning, thinking, worrying, praying, and straining to hear God's voice. This morning I have just one question for God: "Am I going to survive this?" I mean, I know God told Ronnie He would heal me, and that certainly made me feel better about my chances, but God hasn't told *me* directly yet what His plans are.

So as I lay there in bed, I continue to pray, wait, and listen.

The minutes pass by as I try my best to keep my mind clear from distractions and focus only on hearing God's voice. It's probably only been a few minutes, but it feels like an eternity as I wait. Then, as I'm trying to corral my thoughts and refocus yet again, God breaks the silence. I don't think His voice is audible, but nonetheless, His words to me are loud and clear.

"This is not about the cancer," He says. "I am going to do a work in you and glorify My name in the process. It's going to get ugly before it gets better, but I will be with you all the way. Trust in Me. I am going to heal you in My own way. Just do whatever I say."

Man, that was exciting, and a little scary. I mean, how ugly is it going to get? And what does God mean by healing me in His own way? More importantly, where is He going to heal me, here or in heaven? I don't have the guts to ask Him for clarification yet because I'm not sure I'm ready for the answer, so I choose to hope He means He's going to heal me here.

By 7:30 a.m., Julie is up and getting her first cup of coffee in the kitchen, so I head out there to tell her what God told me in the wee hours of the morning.

"Good morning, darlin'," Julie says as she greets me with a hug and a kiss. "How are you doing?"

"I think I heard God say something to me early this morning," I tell her.

"Oh really? What did He say?"

"He told me this is gonna get ugly before it gets better. He said He's going to heal me in His own way and that I just need to do whatever He says."

Julie's eyes begin to well up, and she pauses for a moment. She has this look of utter amazement on her face, and I'm wondering what just happened.

"Dan, my love. That is exactly what God told me."

I am beginning to understand that our God is a God of unity, not division. The same Holy Spirit who lives in me lives in Julie. As amazing as it is that Julie was told the exact same thing I was, it really shouldn't surprise me.

So there it is. From here, we simply buckle up, hang on for the ride, and be sure to do whatever God says.

The Pebble

At 6 a.m. I take a seat with my cup of coffee around the circle at our Friday morning men's group. Pastor Dave opens our session with a short story as he often does to get us thinking. This morning the topic is about what it means to be a true friend.

Dave looks up from the book he's been reading and his eyes scan the group, slowly and intently, long enough for us to start becoming uncomfortable. The group goes completely silent, so quiet I can hear air coming from the HVAC register in the ceiling above my head.

Then Dave poses a question. "Gentlemen, would you say we're all friends around this circle?"

We all start looking at each other and heads begin to nod in agreement.

"Well, everyone except Bill," says Mike, our resident comedian, and then a short flurry of jabs and wisecracks go around the circle.

Dave waits for the group to get quiet again, then poses another question. "Let me ask you to ponder something for a minute," he says. "How do you differentiate a true friend from someone who might only befriend you for their own purposes?"

As the guys chew on this question, a few share examples from their lives of what a true friend acts like.

Bill, a sales manager for a large cell phone company, tells a story of how a friend of his supported him in a particular business situation, how the value of their friendship outweighed the price they would both pay in their careers for walking away from a very large but shady deal.

Chris, a former marine, tells about the bonds he formed while in the service, how men fight battles for their friend beside them in the foxhole, not for the stated mission of the company. "Foxholes are where friends are made," Chris says.

A few other guys chime in with their examples of what a true friend looks like, and after each man has spoken who wants to, Dave asks us for our praises and prayer requests. Then we all stand, arm in arm, and Dave closes our session, praying for each man and their request by name.

As the group is breaking up, Jim walks over to me with a look that says he's got something very important to tell me. I've seen this look before, when he told me I needed to join C12.

"Hey, Dan," he says, "I just want you to know something."

"Really? What's that, Jim?"

Jim just smiles and then bends down to take off his shoe. He comes back up with his shoe in his hand and he shakes it. It sounds like there's something tumbling around in there, like a rock or a hunk of metal. Jim is just standing there, shaking his shoe, and smiling at me. He doesn't look bothered at all that there's something in his shoe. In fact, he appears quite pleased that it's there.

So now I'm really confused.

Jim tips his shoe over to empty it and a smooth pebble rolls into his palm. It's slightly smaller than a pea.

Holding the pebble in the palm of his hand, a deeply thoughtful look comes over him. "Dan, I put this pebble in my shoe to remind me to pray for you. Every time I feel the pebble, I pray for you. I just wanted you to know."

I'm speechless, fighting back tears.

Jim gives me a big bear hug and says, "No matter what happens, you're going to be all right. I love you."

"I love you too, Jim."

A true friend is willing to be uncomfortable for you.

5

Julie Joins C12

Even though my C12 group is believing in a healing miracle, they've advised me and Julie to start getting my affairs in order. I too am believing in a miracle, but if I have misinterpreted God's intentions, I want to make sure Julie and Laurel are taken care of in case I wind up leaving them. So Julie and I have hired an attorney to get my will figured out.

Then there's the question of who's going to run PM2 if I die. At the very least, who's going to keep the wheels on the bus while I go through chemo treatments and whatever else is in store for me? I think it's Julie and Eric, and they both agree. I figure I can help get Julie up to speed on the day-to-day stuff, but who's going to support her from a leadership and business strategy standpoint if I'm in a coma, or dead? I think this is where my C12 group comes in. Julie has told me several times what a positive influence C12 has had on my life, and now it's her turn to experience it for herself. So I pick up the phone and call Scott Hitchcock to sign Julie up as a new member.

A Massive Catch

Ever since the diagnosis I've been worried about how we are going to keep PM2 going. To be honest, I was worried about that since way before the diagnosis. But now we're playing for real. If we don't figure this out before I make my exit, even if it's only temporary, PM2 is in great danger of folding. So I've been praying a lot lately for God to bring us something big to tide us over until I either recover from this disease or we've had time to train Julie to run PM2 with Eric.

So today is my birthday, December 13, and God has just provided in a huge way!

We've been working on closing a very large deal at Northwestern University for several months now, and today we won it. This deal represents half of our annual revenue, enough to keep our team very busy for at least six months. So I am making a video for our team to announce this momentous occasion. I put on my motorized Christmas elf hat and proceed to tell our team the great news and how God just gave us an early Christmas present. (You can watch the video on my website: danfloen.com)

I figure this deal will float PM2's boat long enough for us to see what's at the other end of the tunnel for me. At the very least I don't have to worry about PM2 surviving for the next six months. Now I can concentrate on surviving cancer.

Taking Care of the Temple

I am still doing remarkably well with the chemo treatments, but we've been told they have a cumulative effect. So while I still can, I try to stay as physically fit as possible. I figure the better I take care of my body, the better chance I'll have of enduring the chemo treatments and, ultimately, surviving this thing. I've started lifting weights and running. I run two laps around our neighborhood, which is just over two miles, and work out five days a week, usually weekdays. I take weekends off to recover.

The news of my impending demise has traveled around our neighborhood, and when I run, our neighbors often greet me with a thumbs-up or a "Go, Dan!" It's humbling to be cheered for in this way and it motivates me to keep going, but it's also a stark reminder of my highly improbable odds of survival.

My current goal is to bench-press two hundred pounds. When I've lifted as much weight as I safely can on my own, I call Laurel to spot for me, just to see how much I can max out at. She's only nine years old, and she was scared to spot me at first, but she's learned that she really only needs to lift ten pounds or so, just enough to help me up with the weight, and only if I ask for help.

Laurel always cheers me on. "Come on, Daddy! You've got this! You can do it!"

When I lift the weight, she gives me a big "Woohoo!" and a high five. If I can't lift it without her help, she always tells me, "Good try, Daddy. You'll get it next time."

She is such a great motivator.

I guess Laurel thinks I'm some kind of bodybuilder. Funny, I know, but I don't want to spoil her image of me. According to everything we've heard about these chemo treatments, I'll be getting weaker soon enough, so I choose to let her keep this image of me as long as I can.

December 28, 2007

I have an image that I use to motivate myself during my daily run.

Julie and Laurel are on a train that is leaving the station. They're calling to me and reaching for me as I run to catch them. I'm running and running, praying and running.

My eyes well up at the very thought of missing the train and not going with them, and I find new strength and stamina to carry on and run faster. I finally reach the step of the train where Julie and Laurel are cheering me on. I grab on to their hands and jump.

I make the train. Praise God almighty! I make the train!

Dear Lord, let me stay here with Julie and Laurel!

Farewell Fishing Trip

My hair has begun to grow back, at least until we start the next round of poisoning . . . I mean chemo. Meanwhile, the tumors are still alive and well, and although not growing terribly fast, the threat of my impending doom is very real and ever present.

Eric's not saying it, but I get the sense he wants to give me one last great fishing trip before I leave the planet. It's February 2008, and Eric has sprung for a yellowfin tuna fishing trip off the coast of Venice, Louisiana, for me, Dad, Eric, and Eric's father-in-law, Larry.

It's a cool, sunny morning out in the Gulf of Mexico, and our captain, Billy, has already put us on some amberjacks at the base of an oil rig. Now we're about seventy miles offshore, anchored on top of what the local fishermen call "The Lump." Captain Billy has a pretty foul mouth, but he appears to know what he's doing, so I try to tune out his bad language and focus on the fishing.

This is prime yellowfin tuna grounds, according to Captain Billy. We're anchored in a pretty swift current, and Captain Billy is continually cutting chunks of bonito (a small species of tuna), which makes an oily, bloody chum slick that we're hoping will bring the yellowfins to our boat. The fishing method is like chumming, really. You put a chunk of cut bonito on your hook and drop it into the water. Then you gradually pay out line to let your bait move with the current as naturally as possible. For three hours we do this.

Nothing.

We're now into our fourth hour, with no bites whatsoever. It's getting quiet on the boat, and guys are starting to head to the cooler for a break and something to eat or drink.

Suddenly Captain Billy breaks the silence. "Big mako behind the boat!" We all look up to see this huge, dark shadow swimming about thirty yards behind the boat.

"Looks like about an eight-footer," says Captain Billy.

We watch for a few minutes more as the big shark cruises back and forth, but it never takes our bait. And then, as suddenly as the big mako appeared, he's gone.

A few more minutes go by, and Dad gets a strike on his line, but the fish gets off, so he reels in his rig to check his bait. Meanwhile, I'm fishing on the same side of the boat as my dad, and my bait is still out there. As the five of us are trying to guess what that was that just hit Dad's bait, my rod takes a sudden jerk toward the water and then the line starts screaming off the big Penn International reel. "Whatever this is can pull like a locomotive!" I yell.

"Everybody else, lines in!" yells Captain Billy, so the guys all pull in their lines to keep my line from getting tangled or cut off. "Now, head to the back of the boat and fight him from there! Keep your line tight. Don't give him any slack!"

Several minutes pass as I do this dance with whatever is on the other end of my line, giving line as the fish runs and taking back line as he allows me to. I am giving more line than I am taking back.

"He's coming up!" yells Captain Billy, which makes no sense to me because my line is still pointed straight down into the water. A few seconds later an enormous gray monster leaps out of the water about a hundred and fifty yards to the port side of the boat. "There's the mako we saw a little while ago," says Captain Billy. "Looks like about three hundred pounds."

As the fight continues, I can hear Captain Billy talking on his cell phone to one of his captain buddies. "We've got a three-hundred-pound mako on the line out here. You ever land one before? Any suggestions?" And I think, *You mean you've never landed a shark this big before?*

I keep on pulling and reeling, reeling and pulling. Then the line goes limp.

"He's off," I say.

"Looks like he cut your leader," says Captain Billy. (We're fishing with monofilament leaders, expecting tuna, not sharks.)

"Man, I'm glad we got to see him," I tell the guys. "That was amazing!" For me, that shark was the fish of a lifetime, and maybe the last of my lifetime.

So, in the event I must leave the planet sooner than I'm hoping, I'll leave it having one last great fishing experience under my belt, just like Eric planned.

6

Broken Arrow

I didn't sleep well last night. We're headed back to Lakeside to get the results of the last scans. Today I find out how much longer I have to live. I wonder if this is what the guys on death row feel like as they wait to see if they'll receive another stay of execution.

As Julie and I wait to be called into one of the exam rooms, I pray under my breath, "Father, help me handle the news with honor and in faith that Your plan is perfect. Keep me humble and righteous in Your eyes when You do Your great deed so that all glory and credit will go to You. I will deflect all praises and accolades aimed at me directly to You. I promise. Please, Father, I ask You once again, please let the scans show that Your healing work is already done or in process. I ask in the name of Jesus. I love You. Amen."

A nurse calls my name, and she leads us to an exam room to wait for Dr. Blake. When he comes in, he gets right down to business. "Well, Mr. Floen, unfortunately the tumors have not responded at all to this trial. In fact, they are growing and multiplying. I recommend we start the 'Big Guns' on Monday."

He explains that the "Big Guns" are a combination of several of the strongest traditional chemotherapy drugs available. Apparently the goal is to obliterate everything in sight.

As I try to process Dr. Blake's recommended course of action, a scene from the movie *We Were Soldiers* comes to mind. In it, Commander Hal Moore (played by Mel Gibson) and his battalion of 450 soldiers are surrounded by 2,000 Vietcong in the Ia Drang Valley of South Vietnam. They've been under heavy attack for three days. The enemy has broken through the battalion's lines, and they are now engaged in hand-to-hand combat and in grave danger of being overrun.

As a last-ditch resort, Commander Moore directs the code words *Broken Arrow* to be sent out over the radio, which instructs all fighter bombers in the area to "direct all fire to my position."

A few minutes later, as the bomb drop ensues, the forward air controller who called in the order watches in horror as scores of enemy soldiers and his very own comrades are blown to bits before his eyes.

The battalion suffers extremely heavy casualties, but it ultimately wins the day.

Starting the "Big Guns" on Monday feels like calling in a bomb drop on your own position. You know there will be heavy casualties on both sides, but this is your only chance for survival, so you call it in and pray you won't be among the dead after it's all over.

Boat People

We are boat people, pure and simple. I mean, this is the only life Laurel has ever known. Heck, she's been on a boat ever since we could cradle her baby carrier between the gunnel and the console of our old twenty-foot Aquasport. We've made so many great memories on our boats. We are so blessed.

With the "Big Guns" looming in my future, I get the sense that we won't be spending much time on the boat in the coming weeks (or months, or maybe ever again), so I figure we better get in what we can this weekend. So my ladies and I spend much of the weekend on the boat, and we do all our favorite things. I'm hoping this won't be the last time. We troll the grass flats for sea trout or whatever will give our line a tug. I watch the lines and listen to Jimmy Buffett while the girls relax on the bow cushions. We hook a few ladyfish, and Laurel reels them in. We feed a few of them to a pod of dolphins that have been playing and jumping in our boat wake.

After a great day out on the boat, we tie up to the dock at Bahama Breeze for a nice dinner on the patio as we're serenaded by live steel drum island music. *This is why we live in Florida*, I think. "Thank You, Lord, for this wonderful life You have given us." I'm praying this highly cherished part of our family's life isn't coming to a close forever.

One Week in Paradise

This morning Dr. Blake called to say I also have a cancer lesion in the neck of my left femur, just past the ball that goes into my hip socket. The concern is that I may break my leg, so Dr. Blake is recommending surgery to install a pin to reinforce it. This would happen right after my first week in the hospital getting the "Big Guns."

Jeez!

It's now Monday, and I'm back at Lakeside to get a PICC line installed and check into the hospital for a week of chemo treatments. A PICC line will give the nurses easy access to give me IV drugs without having to stick me every time I go in for treatment. Up until now I've been avoiding them putting in anything like this because I see it as conceding defeat in a way. The other option I was given was a port (a more permanent device), which sounds even more like admitting defeat to me, so a PICC line it is.

As long as this PICC line is in, they don't want me to work out my upper body because it could dislodge the PICC line. That really sucks because, the way I see it, staying as physically fit and strong as I can is critical to this fight. For now, I guess I'll concentrate on lower body workouts and running.

With a new PICC line in my arm, I head over to admissions to get checked in for the week.

I packed a small duffel bag this morning full of fishing shorts and T-shirts. I do not intend to wear that ridiculous hospital gown they give you (you know, the one that's open in the back). In my mind, I am a short-term visitor in this place, so I am not about to get comfortable with the standard-issue uniform.

I tell Julie about my position on the hospital gown and she politely relays it to the nurses on the floor. Julie comes back to tell me the nurses agreed not to push the gown on me unless I'm going to surgery or someplace where they'll need "easy access." That works for me.

Julie packed a bag as well. She plans to stay here with me all week, so she asks our nurse for a cot. Laurel is staying at home with my mom and dad, who have come down to help. The list of side effects from these drugs is as long as your arm, so she wants to be with me if anything goes wrong. One thing we learned early in this journey is that cancer is a team sport. Everybody needs a health care advocate, and Julie is relentless and tenacious in this role. With Julie at my side and God out ahead of me, I just might survive this thing.

Julie and I both brought our laptops and cell phones with us so we can work. The hospital has free Wi-Fi and the cell signal on this floor is pretty good, so we should be in business.

We get settled into our room and I look at the clock. Time has gotten away from me. Shoot! I have a conference call in two minutes. I rush to get situated with my client papers and join the call. A few minutes into the meeting, the facilitator gives me the floor to present PM2's capabilities and experience.

Just then one of the nurses walks in holding an IV bag in one hand and pushing a cart full of medical supplies with the other.

"Hi, Mr. Floen. I'm your nurse, Michelle, and it's time to get this show on the road," she announces loudly. Michelle sees me on the phone and covers her mouth sheepishly. "Sorry!" she whispers.

While I pitch PM2, Michelle takes my blood pressure and my temperature. As I'm describing the pieces of information we need from the client, Michelle lifts up my shirt and applies ten adhesive leads all over my chest. The probes are ice cold and I'm doing my best to not react verbally on the phone.

Last but not least, Michelle hangs the IV bag containing my special cocktail for the week. "You're all set, Dan," Michelle whispers and smiles.

I nod and smile back at Michelle.

"Thanks, John. We look forward to serving you. Have a great week! Goodbye."

I'm probably fooling myself to think the client didn't know something unusual was happening on my end of the line, but I think the call went well nonetheless.

Each of the following days in the hospital I write in my journal.

March 11, 2008

Good morning, Father. Tough night last night, mostly couldn't sleep because of the clicking IV machine. Very low blood pressure today. Please help me stay on mission.

Dave L. and Arch J. from church came by today. Bill G. came later in the day. They each prayed over me and it felt good.

March 12, 2008

Another tough night last night. Fever, pounding heart, hot and cold. Couldn't get comfortable. Feeling fine this morning, aside from lack of sleep. Father, please allow this treatment to work so that I can continue leading Your business for You and impacting others for Jesus along the way.

March 13, 2008

Father, thanks for granting Dad's request last night to give me a decent night's rest. I woke feeling the best I have felt since I got here. You are obviously shielding me from a lot of stuff, and doctors and nurses are commenting in disbelief on how good I look. Thank You, Father!

Please, Father, continue Your healing work in my body so I can shine like a beacon for You!

Laurel opened her children's Bible and read the story of how Your Son, Jesus, healed the blind man. It's the very same story Julie and I

have been studying in recent devotions. Thanks for the added reminder.
We both believe that You are healing me for the purpose of glorifying
Your name. Thank You for entrusting us with this responsibility! We
will not let You down, Father. All the credit and glory goes to You!

March 14, 2008
Father, You have made me a phenom around here! Nobody can believe
how well I have handled the treatment, thanks to You, Father. One
more day in paradise and we go home!

After surviving the first week of the "Big Guns" in style, Julie and I
head home.

Getting Pinned

It's Tuesday, March 25, 2008, hip-pinning day. After a few tough days
following the "Big Guns," I finally turned the corner enough for Dr. Blake
to schedule me to install the pin in my left femur.

We're waiting in a pre-op room for a few minutes when a doctor walks
in and introduces himself. "Hello, Mr. Floen, I'm Dr. Lee, and I'll be the
one installing a nail in your left femur today."

A nail? I figure it's just another name for a pin. Whichever it is, a pin
or a nail, it sounds small to me, and Dr. Lee doesn't give me any reason to
think otherwise. I just want to get this show on the road, so I don't belabor
things by asking a bunch of questions.

Dr. Lee then pulls a black magic marker from the breast pocket of
his scrubs and says, "All right, Mr. Floen, one last very important detail."

Then he writes, "NOT THIS ONE" in all capital letters on my right thigh. He smiles and says, "We don't want to do the wrong leg, now do we, Mr. Floen?"

Smiling back, I tell him, "And we certainly don't want to have to make a claim against your malpractice insurance, now do we?"

We both get a good laugh and Dr. Lee says, "See you when you wake up!"

The surgery goes as planned. No surprises. Except one. When I wake up, I have little to no pain. Before the surgery I prayed God would protect me, and it looks like He's doing just that. Even hours later, after the pain meds I left surgery with have worn off, I still have very little pain.

As nurses file in one after another to offer me pain meds, I smile and tell each one, "No thanks. I'm doing just fine."

Everybody is scratching their heads. I mean, who comes out of surgery not needing any pain meds whatsoever, not even an aspirin?

I'll tell you who. Someone who is being protected by God. That's who!

The nurses don't want me getting out of bed today, so they left me a bed pan on my bedside table. What they don't realize is that I've never used a bed pan, and I darn sure don't intend to start using one now. You see, I put bed pans in the same category as hospital gowns. They're only to be used in extreme emergencies. My leg feels fine. Besides, I figure it's stronger now that the pin is in there, so what's to stop me from walking to the bathroom, or anywhere else for that matter? Julie makes me promise not to leave the room. She doesn't want me to get anyone excited at the nurses' station. I agree to stay put inside the room for the night.

The next morning breakfast arrives at 8 a.m. sharp. Don't get me started on hospital food.

After breakfast, I get up to go to the restroom. As I'm washing my hands in the sink, I hear a knock at the hospital room door, and I hear Julie say, "Come in."

The door swings open and there stands a young man and a woman in blood-red scrubs, one holding a cane and the other, a walker. And they brought one of those thick, webbed belts they use to help get a patient out of bed or to hold them up as they hobble along.

Looking at Julie, who is seated next to the bed, the young man says, "Hi, I'm Mike with occupational therapy and this is my partner, Allison. We're here to see if you're ready to take a few first steps this morning on that leg. We brought you a cane and a walker, whichever you prefer."

Just then they both look to their left to see me standing as tall as I can in the restroom doorway.

Puzzled, Mike asks, "Which one of you is the patient?"

"He is," Julie says, pointing across the room at me.

"I won't need those things you have there," I tell them.

"Are you sure you don't need these, Mr. Floen?" says Mike. "You just had surgery yesterday."

Smiling, I simply say, "Allow me to take you on a stroll around the third floor."

They look at each other with that same perplexed look the nurses gave me yesterday when I refused all pain meds.

For a stroll we go, with Mike and Allison in tow. I am doing my best not to limp. It's not a fast walk (after all, I just had surgery), but I am walking deliberate and steady. I overhear Mike saying to Allison, "I've never seen anything like this before. Have you?"

"Nope," Allison replies.

"Pretty amazing," Mike says.

But considering it is God who is protecting me, I don't think it's surprising at all. Amazing? Yes. Miraculous? Yes. Surprising? Not at all.

We finish our little tour of the third floor, and Mike and Allison take the cane, walker, and belt away with them.

A week later I'm back in Dr. Lee's office for a follow-up visit. They took two X-rays, one of my left hip and upper thigh, and one of my lower thigh to my knee. I remember thinking, *Why are they taking a picture that far down my leg? The pin is in my hip.*

When Dr. Lee shows me the digital pictures on his computer monitor, it all becomes alarmingly clear to me. *Holy cow! That's not a pin or a nail. It's a full-blown rod that goes the whole length of my femur, all the way down to my knee!* I guess I should have asked a few more questions on surgery day. But then again, I don't guess it would have changed the outcome very much.

Now that I've seen how big that so called "pin" is, suddenly my leg isn't feeling so good!

I'll Still Love You When . . .

We are now deep into the heat of battle. I'm lying in bed, too weak to get up, except to shuffle to the bathroom and back.

The sun is setting, and I can see the warm amber glow coming through my window. I'm really needing some good words from God right now, so I roll to my left to turn on my nightstand lamp and grab my Bible.

As I flip the pages, scanning for something that might speak to me, my eyes land on Psalm 91. And I begin to read.

Those who live in the shelter of the Most High
will find rest in the shadow of the Almighty.
This I declare about the Lord:
He alone is my refuge, my place of safety,
he is my God, and I trust him.
For he will rescue you from every trap
and protect you from deadly disease.
He will cover you with his feathers.
He will shelter you with his wings.
His faithful promises are your armor and protection.
Do not be afraid of the terrors of the night,
nor the arrow that flies in the day.
Do not dread the disease that stalks in darkness,
nor the disaster that strikes at midday.
Though a thousand fall at your side,
though ten thousand are dying around you,
these evils will not touch you.
Just open your eyes,
and see how the wicked are punished.
If you make the Lord your refuge,
if you make the Most High your shelter,
no evil will conquer you,
no plague will come near your home.
For he will order his angels
to protect you wherever you go.

*They will hold you up with their hands
so you won't even hurt your foot on a stone.
You will trample upon lions and cobras,
you will crush fierce lions and serpents under your feet!
The Lord says, "I will rescue those who love me.
I will protect those who trust in my name.
When they call on me, I will answer,
I will be with them in trouble.
I will rescue and honor them.
I will reward them with a long life
and give them my salvation." (NLT)*

The words grab me like God Himself is speaking right to my face. It's exhilarating. I take a deep breath in and let it out slowly.

"Thank You, Father. This is what I've so been needing to hear. Thank You!"

I go back to read the whole chapter again, and then again, and then a fourth time, trying to memorize what I can and imprint these words on my brain.

As I continue to read and memorize, Laurel softly approaches my bed and enters the warm glow of my nightstand reading light.

"Hi, sweetheart," I say in the most normal sounding voice I can muster, trying not to show her how utterly spent I am.

"Hi, Daddy."

Laurel seems a little somber, but that's nothing new these days. My heart has ached for her as I've watched her deal with the fear that I may be dying soon. She doesn't seem as comfortable around me these days. I get the sense she's trying to distance herself from me now, so it won't hurt so bad when I'm gone.

She hands me a drawing she's done for me.

"Aw, thanks, sweetie. What's this?" I ask as I begin to get a closer look at her drawing.

In her sweet innocence, Laurel says, "Daddy, do you think you look like the young man or the old man in my picture?"

Tears immediately start to well up, but I gather myself and say, "Laurel, I'm afraid I look like the old man right now. But God is taking care of me, and this is only temporary. Just wait and see what God does here."

"Okay," she says.

She leans over and gives me a long hug. "I love you, Daddy."

"I love you too, sweetheart. Don't worry, honey. We're all gonna be all right. Let me pray for us, okay?"

"Okay," she says.

Laurel is hugging me tightly, and I can literally feel the fear and worry emanating from her body. I start to pray. "Dear Lord Jesus, Laurel and I just want to thank You for healing me. We know You said it would get ugly before things got better, and it looks like we're into the ugly stuff right now. But we know that You always keep Your Word, so we know that our family will come through this stronger than ever and that Laurel's daddy will be around for a long time to come. Thank You, Jesus. Amen."

"Amen," Laurel says. She kisses me on the cheek and stands up to leave my room. "I love you, Daddy," she reminds me again. "Sleep tight."

"I love you too, sweetie. Sweet dreams. I'll see you in the morning."

"Oh, dear Lord, Laurel has always seen her daddy as a strong man. Please help me live up to that, spiritually, mentally, and physically!"

Got Your Ears On?

Growing up in the '70s in Omaha, Nebraska, my buddy Rob owned a 1972 Jeep CJ5. It was green with gold-and-white stripes that ran across the middle of the hood, down the sides, and to the back. Rob spent a little extra for a nice set of knobby tires and chrome wheels. That Jeep was beautiful, and a pretty good chick magnet too. It seemed like we always had girls riding with us.

On hot summer days we'd take the top down and cruise all our usual spots and hangouts. On weekends we'd go four-wheeling on the outskirts of town. In the wintertime we'd make a little extra money pulling cars out of snowbanks.

In 1977, the movie *Smokey and the Bandit* starring Burt Reynolds hit the silver screen, and all of sudden it seemed like everybody in the world had to own a CB radio. Rob followed suit and installed one in his Jeep, complete with a big whip antenna.

We started learning the CB lingo of the trucker fraternity. It was a whole new vocabulary, and there was this list of "10 codes" you had to know. For example, 10-4 means "Okay, message received." If you wanted to know where someone was, you would say, "What's your 20?" 10-100 means you gotta go number 1; 10-200 is fairly obvious. If you had a pretty girl riding with you, you were said to have a nice "seat cover" or "hood ornament." If you wanted to know if your friend was tuned into your CB channel, you'd use his call sign (or "handle") and say something like, "Rubber Duck, Rubber Duck. Got your ears on? Come on."

I've found that communicating with God has a few things in common with talking on a CB radio.

For starters, you have to be on the right channel. I mean, if your friend is on channel 23 and you're on channel 17, you're not going to do much communicating. The same is true with God and me. He has shown me which channels He uses to communicate with me, and if I go to those channels, I will always hear from Him. The channels God uses to talk to me are devotions, prayer, the Bible, and my Christian friends.

Second, you've got to have your "ears on," as they say in CB lingo. You have to be listening. It seems like I do my best listening when I'm in the deepest trouble, after all of my personal efforts have failed. Is that ridiculous or what? I wish I had the personal discipline to be listening earlier and more often. You'd think by now I would have learned this, but alas, I forget too often what God has told me and done for me. But when I finally do decide to be still and listen, God will sometimes speak directly to me in the quiet of my soul.

March 7, 2008

Father, You have been speaking so clearly to me lately, especially in the past week. Through the morning email devotions You send me, You have prepared me, directed me, and comforted me. As we're waiting to see if the latest treatment is working or not, You have sent devotions that met me exactly where I was each day. First, it was one entitled "The Waiting Is the Hardest Part." Then one about "Strength or Weakness." Then "Nothing Is Impossible." Then "Walking Humbly" and "Fearing God." Then "The Suffering of a Saint" and "The Depth and Width of Your Calling." This morning it was simply "Peace." In the storms of life, Jesus says, "Peace! Be still."

This morning my brothers in the Friday morning men's group spent the entire hour praying for Julie, Laurel, and me. I am so thankful for these mighty men of faith.

The Biggest Loser

I've been trying to eat Burger King Whoppers, French fries, and milkshakes every day and packing away as much food as I can, but I am still losing weight. Lakeside recommends drinking Ensure meal replacement drinks, but Julie looked at the nutritional facts on the label, and the amount of sugar in Ensure could choke a horse. Julie read a study recently that said sugar feeds cancer, so we won't be drinking any Ensure in my lifetime. That suits me just fine because Ensure tastes nasty.

Doing heavy chemo and being nauseous have heightened my sense of smell. I mean, there are certain foods I can't even be in the same room with. If I get even a whiff of something disagreeable, I demand that Julie leave the room with it or I risk making a trip to the bathroom to pray to the porcelain god.

Julie's been pushing me hard to eat more and more often, but I'm usually too full to pack anymore in or too nauseous to even think about it.

This morning I weighed 141 pounds, an all-time low.

"Dan, I'm really sorry that you don't feel like eating, but you don't have a choice," Julie tells me in a loving but firm voice. "You cannot lose any more weight. It's just that simple. So you're going to have to find a way to get in more calories."

I scowl at her with a look of great displeasure, hoping she'll back off and leave me alone.

"Honey, you can be mad at me if you want to, but I am more willing to let you be mad at me than I am willing to lose you," she says. "Like I told Dr. Blake, I don't want *a* husband. I want *this* husband. So be mad at me if you want, but you have to eat. You promised me you would do your best to stay here with me, remember?"

"Yeah," I reply begrudgingly.

I pinch my nose and start eating what Julie has brought me.

For about a week now, Julie has been tracking my food intake to see how many calories it takes to maintain or gain weight. Ever since I started this chemo, my heart has been racing at a constant 110 beats per minute, even at rest. It's no wonder I can't gain weight with my motor running so fast all the time. This chemo has me more amped up than if I chugged a six pack of Red Bull in one sitting.

Julie has concluded that I have to eat at least three thousand calories a day to maintain my weight. The trouble is, I'm lucky to get 1,500 calories in a day because the nausea has killed my appetite. The thought of doubling my calorie intake when I'm nauseous all the time sounds impossible. But I made Julie a promise, so I'll try my best.

As it turns out, I'm not the only one losing lately. It's mid-June and the Northwestern University job has just wrapped up, and PM2 is losing money as fast as I'm losing weight. Even though God provided for His company with this job, my absence from the sales process is making me wonder about the health of our project pipeline.

The "Big Guns" are starting to take their toll on me. My whole system is under siege as it tries to manage bodily functions while under the most merciless pounding it has ever received. I've done some dumb stuff in my life and abused my body a lot, but none of that stuff was anything compared to this. Good cells and bad cells alike are under attack. I just hope more bad ones are dying than good ones.

In recent weeks I've spiked massive fevers and landed back in the hospital several times. Each emergency hospital visit reminds me of just how precarious my situation is right now. My body is fighting and adjusting to each new attack as best it can, but if the tide turns too quickly, my defenses will be overrun, and I'll be among the dead on the field of battle.

Today I weigh 142 pounds, but it fluctuates day to day. That's about 18 pounds under my usual 160. Julie has noticed that when I drop below 142 pounds, I lose my will to go on. She says she can't trust my judgement under 142 pounds. I don't want to eat anymore and my energy level drops through the floor, so all I want to do is sleep. Therefore, Julie has set a new goal for me to never drop below 142 pounds.

I've been a Burger King guy ever since I tasted a Whopper for the first time as a teenager. Up until high school, my family never ate at fast food restaurants. My mom cooked every meal for us: breakfast, lunch, and dinner.

I still remember my first Burger King Whopper. My dad and I had been out on one of our weekend father-son adventures, and we wheeled into the local Burger King for a quick bite to eat. I ordered a Whopper with everything on it, onion rings, and a chocolate shake.

I took a big bite of my Whopper, and it was heaven! I had never tasted anything so amazing. I was hooked.

Thirty years later, I'm still a regular at Burger King.

Now that I'm doing the "Big Guns," everyone at Lakeside is telling me, "It doesn't matter what you eat. Just eat as much as you can to try to maintain your weight. Your only goal right now is to keep from withering away to nothing."

That sounds like a license to eat more Whoppers and milkshakes. Works for me!

7

Lakeland Revival

I play Christian music on my laptop when I'm in the hospital, and I always put my Bible in clear view on the bedside stand. The music settles me down, and I'm encouraged when I open my Bible and God leads me to a passage that speaks directly to me. But there's another reason why I leave my Bible in clear view and keep the praise music playing. I'm sending a message to the hospital staff that I am a Christian.

We've learned that in a secular hospital setting, like Lakeside, the doctors, nurses, and staff are strictly prohibited from initiating any discussion about faith with their patients. They can engage only after a patient initiates it, and even then, they have to be very careful.

Over the past few hospital stays, Julie and I have had some great conversations with the staff about our faith, and they've shared their stories of faith and healing with us. We've even prayed with some, but only after the hospital room door was shut to protect them from the possible consequences of breaking policy.

One night, about halfway through a one-week stay at Lakeside, our nurse Linda walks in and shuts the door behind her.

"Dan and Julie, I've been led by God to share something with you. May I bend your ear for just a few minutes?" she asks.

"Of course, Linda," Julie says. "Please do!"

"Have you heard what's been happening in Lakeland recently?" Linda asks.

"No," we answer together. "What's happening?"

"There's an amazing revival going on and people are being healed there every night," Linda says. "This thing started out as a one-week revival in early April and it's still going, six weeks later. The preacher is Todd Bentley, and he is amazing. Have you heard of him?"

"No, we haven't," I reply.

"You guys, I wasn't even supposed to be on duty tonight, but I was called in on short notice. As soon as I arrived, I heard God tell me to come into your room tonight and tell you that you need to go to this revival. I've been there several times in the past few weeks, and the preaching and healing power of this man are incredible. Hundreds of people are being healed. I've seen several cancer patients get healed instantaneously, right there on stage! Bentley lays his hands on them, and most times the people fall right to the ground because of the power that God is channeling through Bentley's hands. I've never seen anything like it!"

"Wow! That does sound amazing," Julie says, looking over at me to see what my reaction is.

"Yeah, it does," I say, trying my best to appear like I'm buying any of this. Inside, I'm thinking, *Man, what a ridiculous and cruel hoax,* but I don't want to be rude, so I keep it to myself.

"They're broadcasting live every night on the internet, so you can check it out for yourselves tonight if you want. Here's a link to the website." Linda hands me a slip of paper with the website written on it. "I encourage you to check it out. Then, as soon as you get out of here, go to Lakeland."

"Thanks so much for letting us know about this," Julie says. "It is so encouraging to know there are believers around us who care enough to follow what God has told them to do. Thanks for being obedient to God's instructions. Linda, before you leave, would you pray with us?"

We all join hands, and Julie leads us in a short prayer thanking God for bringing Linda into the room tonight, and she also prays for my healing.

At this point Linda is crying. "Guys, please consider going to Lakeland," she pleads. "You won't regret it."

We thank Linda again, exchange hugs, and she leaves the room to continue her rounds.

That night we watch the revival on my laptop. It's an impressive event with easily five thousand people under a huge circus tent. The band is pretty good, and Bentley is a super high-energy speaker, but he's covered in tattoos and piercings. He looks like he just got out of jail. Later in the hour, he starts healing people, and now he's beginning to sound like every other TV evangelist I've ever seen, with people falling to the ground and being healed on stage.

Julie and I are skeptical at best, but we're both wrestling with the question: Was it really God who sent Linda into our room tonight? And if so, does He want us to go to this revival to be healed? We agree to sleep on it.

Two days later we complete our one week stay at Lakeside and head home. Meanwhile, the question about the revival is still looming. Do we go to Lakeland or not?

The week of chemo treatment has kicked my butt and I'm feeling worse than ever. Bad chills, horrendous nausea, and I am reduced to crawling to the bathroom, too tired and weak to stand and walk there under my own power.

Then, out of nowhere, I sense this calling to pick myself up and get to Lakeland. "Is this You, Father?" I ask. I reason that if there is even the slightest chance this is God telling me to go to Lakeland, I cannot ignore it. If it's the devil talking to me, I'm praying God will forgive me and protect me.

I call to Julie and ask her to come into the master bedroom where I'm lying on the carpet, next to the bathroom door. The way I feel right now, I can't afford to get too far from the commode. I tell her I think God is telling us to go to Lakeland.

"Okay," she says. "If that's what you think God is telling you, we'll go. When?"

"Tonight."

"Well, okay then," she says.

Julie heads to the kitchen to pack a soft-sided cooler with some food and medications for the road.

My aunt Eileen has been staying with us for the past few weeks. She's my dad's much younger sister. In fact, she's only five years older than me, so she feels more like a cousin than an aunt. She has that wonderful gift of being an awesome listener, not to mention being an outstanding cook. Eileen is the kind of person you feel like you can tell anything to, a very accepting lady. So I'm not at all uncomfortable telling her that we're going to a healing revival in Lakeland, and she's invited.

"Count me in!" Eileen says. She's always up for an adventure, and this should be an interesting one.

Julie loads the food in the car, and we all hop in and head toward Lakeland.

I very rarely let Julie drive me anywhere. I guess it's my way of demonstrating that I'm okay. But tonight I am feeling extremely tired and miserable, so I relinquish the wheel to her.

About an hour later, we arrive at the River of Life Church in Lakeland, where the revival is already in full swing. We're a good hundred yards from the big white tent, but we can already hear the music rocking and the singers in the band wailing away.

As we enter the tent, I'm looking for the ticket booth, expecting that we'll have to pay to get into the main tent. But there isn't one. Amazingly, no one asks for money. Even the parking was free.

By now, the music is pounding, and we can hear the hoots and hollers of the crowd. Julie, Eileen, and I exchange one last pensive look before we go in. And I think, *What on earth are we walking into here?*

"You ready?" Eileen says.

"Let's do this," I tell her.

Inside the main tent, it is sheer bedlam. Five thousand people are screaming, shouting, singing, waving their hands in the air, and jumping up and down. People are lying on the floor convulsing. Some are babbling incomprehensibly, as if they're speaking in tongues or something. I've never seen anything like it.

I shout over the music to Julie, "We're not in Kansas anymore, are we!" Julie shakes her head in agreement as we make our way through the crowd to find a place to stand.

I'm trying my best to keep an open mind here. I'm sure I felt God leading me to come here tonight, so I've got to give this a chance. But man, this is way outside of my comfort zone. I'm particularly nauseous tonight, but I want to stay and experience this to the best of my ability. So I swallow hard and fight back the urge to throw up.

After about thirty minutes, the band finishes their set and Bentley steps up on the platform. He starts shouting and yelling. "I'm not satisfied until I see the miraculous! Let there come an anointing here tonight! Some of you have faith, but what you need is the power of God and your faith to mix together! People are going to be healed tonight and the power of God is going to be revealed! Is your faith up to it?"

Then he starts calling groups of people up to the stage to be healed. "I want everyone who is blind to come up to the stage right now. I want everyone who is paralyzed and in a wheelchair to be brought to the stage right now. Come on. Keep on coming. Tonight you will be healed. Take a bold step and have faith, and you will be healed by the power of Jesus."

In no time, there are at least a hundred people on the stage. And the healing session begins.

He lays his hand on the forehead of the first person in line and yells, "In the name of Jesus, you are healed!" The person immediately falls backward into the arms of two stagehands who were standing behind the person, as if they expected that to happen.

Then Bentley moves to the next person, and the next, putting his hand on their forehand and yelling, "Bam!" as another person goes down.

"Chacka! Hah! Hah! Hah!" And three more go down.

"Bam! Bam! Bam! Bam!" And four more people drop to the floor.

"Drink it up! Hah Ho! Ho! Bam! Boom! Boomba! Seega Baba Santa!" (Or something like that.)

People are dropping right and left on stage. This looks more like a circus than a church service. This guy has the crowd worked up into an absolute frenzy.

Then suddenly Bentley gets quiet and says, "There is a man here in the audience tonight who has cancer in the abdominal area. It is stage four cancer and the doctors have told you that you won't live much longer. You haven't come up to the stage yet, but you've come hoping to be healed nonetheless."

I glance over to Julie and Eileen to see them looking at me with eyebrows raised. Could he be talking to me? In a crowd this large there has to be several people here who have stage four cancer. After all, this is a healing revival, and folks are coming from far and wide to be healed.

"My brother, I say to you right now that you are healed by the power of Jesus! Amen! Hallelujah! Bam!"

At this point the nausea overtakes me, and I feel the need to make a speedy exit or throw up right there. I spot an exit door at the back corner of the tent, motion to Julie and Eileen that I'm leaving, and make my way back there as fast as I can.

I make it out the door just in time to lose my cookies.

I'm the only one outside the tent, which is great since I'm still dry heaving to beat the band. In times like these I'd rather be left alone. After a while, the dry heaving subsides for a bit and I sit down at a picnic table bench to catch my breath and gather my senses.

Just then a lady appears from seemingly nowhere and approaches me. I assume she's one of the volunteer staff.

"Are you all right?" she asks with a warm smile and a soothing voice.

"I'm okay," I tell her, but judging from the look of care and compassion I'm getting from her, she doesn't believe me.

"Is there anything I can do for you?" she asks.

"No, but thanks very much," I answer, staring down at the ground, trying to keep from dry heaving anymore. "I just need to sit here for a few more minutes."

By the looks of me, I don't figure I need to tell her why I'm throwing up. I think most people know what a chemo patient looks like. I lift my head to look at her and she's still just standing there with a look of deep compassion on her face.

"May I pray with you?" she asks.

"I think that would be good," I reply.

So she kneels in front of me in the dirt as I'm seated at the picnic table and reaches out for my hands.

As she begins to pray, I'm not listening to her words so much as I am sensing something, or someone, very special. I mean, this lady came out of nowhere. There is not another soul in sight, and she has no reason to be out here that I can see. Then it hits me. Is this an angel praying with me right now? Suddenly a deep peace falls on me as I listen to her praying earnestly for my healing and my faith.

The prayer ends, and she rises to her feet. "Are you gonna be okay?"

"Yes. Thanks for stopping to check on me."

"Take comfort in the fact that God is always with you and He will never leave you," she says.

"Thanks again, and God bless you," I tell her.

With that, she smiles, waves goodbye, and continues on her way, with seemingly nowhere in particular to go.

I gather myself as best I can and head back into the tent to rejoin Julie and Eileen. Their curious looks ask if I'm okay, to which I nod and begin singing along with the crowd. Julie and Eileen lean into each other and decide it's time to go. When we get to the car, I tell them about what just happened at the picnic table, and I sleep all the way home.

Getting to the Point

It's now May 2008, and I've completed two rounds of the "Big Guns." I am mostly losing the battle to keep weight on. I simply cannot eat enough to gain weight, let alone maintain what little weight I have left. The "Big Guns" are kicking my butt, and I am losing my ability to think rationally. Julie says it's called "chemo brain."

This morning Julie asked me if I would go and see an acupuncturist. She's been doing tons of research ever since this battle ensued and she read that acupuncture can help you recover quicker from chemo treatments.

Acupuncture? Seriously? Sounds like voodoo to me. I mean, I put acupuncturists and chiropractors in the same category. They're both quacks as far as I'm concerned. Besides, I hate needles.

The trouble is, I promised Julie that I'd try to be a good patient for her and do whatever she asked me to do. I'm feeling particularly lousy today, so if acupuncture stands any chance at all of helping, I'm ready to give it a shot. Besides, what do I have to lose? Seventy-five dollars, that's what. Acupuncture isn't covered by our health insurance plan, so this is coming out of our pocket.

Julie already has an appointment scheduled for me this afternoon with the acupuncturist. "Her name is Lela," Julie says, "and she's helped me a lot with my sciatica. She's a really nice lady. You'll like her. Tell her I said hello."

I shuffle to the garage and pour myself into my car. I'm extremely nauseous, and I'm just hoping to make it the acupuncturist's office without having to stop on the side of the road to puke. Thirty minutes later I pull into the parking lot of her office. So far I've not lost my breakfast, but the intense nausea persists.

I struggle to climb out of my car and make my way inside. The office opens directly to the parking lot, and there's a nice coconut fiber welcome mat on the landing in front of the door. As I grab the doorknob to walk in, I get a sudden strong urge to throw up. I'd rather not make a mess on this women's welcome mat, so I choke it back and swallow hard several times. After a minute or so, the urge subsides enough for me to think it's safe to enter, so I swing open the door to go inside.

Inside the office, it feels like I've stepped into some kind of weird parallel universe.

Outside, the world I've come to know and love goes on. It is a bright, busy, and sometimes noisy place, but that's how we in America get things done, and I will never apologize for being ambitious and productive.

Inside, the lighting is low and warm. Soft music is playing. Over in the corner, a small tabletop water fountain gurgles as the water rolls over the rocks. The furniture and wall decorations appear to be aimed at soothing office visitors and setting them at ease. They're clearly going for a comforting feel here, which is understandable, considering the fact this woman sticks needles in people.

After a minute or so, a lady quietly enters the room and smiles at me. She looks to be a few years younger than I am.

"Hi, are you Dan?" she says in a soft-spoken voice. I assume Julie has told her to look for the guy who resembles an Auschwitz prisoner.

"Yes, ma'am," I reply. I'm very suspicious of her practice and her motives, and I'm trying to send her the message that I'm not just another lemming who will blindly accept and pay for anything she wants to do to me.

"Well, Dan, when you're ready, you can come back to the second room on the right. Take your time," she says.

After a minute or so, I amble on back to the second room on the right, where she is quietly waiting for me.

"Welcome, Dan," she says. "When you're ready, you can take off your shoes and lie down on this massage table right here."

"Okay," I tell her.

"Take your time," she says.

I take off my shoes and lie down on the table. At this point we stop sharing any more words.

Being a regular at Lakeside, I've been stuck by countless needles, so I'm not stressing over the thought of more of them today. I'm just having a hard time seeing the point of this.

Meanwhile, the acupuncturist starts inserting needles in what appear to be very strategic locations ranging from my forehead all the way down to the tops my feet. What's weird is that I can't even feel the needles going in.

Finally, my curiosity gets the best of me and I have to ask, "What are you doing exactly?"

"I'm working on your digestive chi," she says. "Chi means energy, and if we can boost your digestive chi, it will help you get your appetite back so you can eat and recover more quickly from the chemo treatments."

That's exactly the kind of weird answer I was expecting. Whatever. It'll be over in an hour and I'll be out of here.

She finishes putting in the needles, about ten in all, then tells me to relax. Now there's an irony for you. I have ten needles in me and I'm supposed to relax.

"I'll be back to check on you in about thirty minutes," she says.

Strangely enough, after a few minutes of lying there and listening to the soft music, I close my eyes and eventually fall off to sleep. I'm awakened by the sound of the doorknob turning as she comes back into the room.

"How are you doing?" she asks.

"Fine," I answer. "I got a nice catnap in. I guess I didn't realize how tired I was."

"That's good," she says in a small, quiet voice as she takes out the needles.

"Okay, Dan, we're all done for today. You can put your shoes back on and come on out to the front desk whenever you're ready. Take your time," she says.

As I'm putting on my shoes, I realize I am absolutely famished. I mean, starving.

I pay the bill and head to my car. I'm so starved I don't think I can make it home, so I stop at Taco Bell on the way and order two of the biggest, nastiest burritos I can find on the menu. I devour them like someone who has just been released from solitary confinement.

Then it hits me. Lela told me she was working on my digestive chi so that I could eat. I walked into her office today nauseous and nearly puking, and I walked out famished.

As of this moment, I'm a believer!

New Perspective

It's mid-summer, 2008, and we're at Lakeside, waiting to be discharged so we can go home. I've just completed another round of chemo. I feel like vomiting, but I'm afraid if I do they may not let me go home, so I swallow hard and try my best to act natural.

Mom and Dad came over this morning to visit, as they often do, so they are waiting in the room with us.

Around 10 a.m. the shift nurse enters the room and lets me know I can go. While I'm waiting for someone to bring me a wheelchair, Julie goes downstairs with my parents to get their cars.

As they wait for the valet to bring their cars from the garage, Dad notices a man sitting in a wheelchair, waiting for his car. He is looking extremely poorly. Dad leans over to Mom and whispers, "That poor guy looks like he's knocking on death's door." Just then the man's vehicle arrives. He is clearly needing assistance to get into his car, so Dad runs over to help.

Overcome with gratitude, he says to Dad, "I'm Jeff. What is your name, sir?"

"I'm Vern Floen," Dad says. "My son Dan is undergoing cancer treatments here as well."

And at that moment Jeff steps outside of his impossible circumstance, smiles at Dad, and says, "Vern, how can I pray for you today?"

A few minutes later I arrive at the valet station and Dad tells me about his experience with Jeff.

Wow. Now there's a man I've never met who has changed my perspective forever.

Notes to self:

- In tough times, when it is tempting to dig a moat around your castle, you need to be building a bridge.

- Focus outside and above your own circumstances. Just love on someone, and God will bless you and protect you as you do that.

Healing Prayer?

Today is acupuncture day again, so I'm in Lela's office getting more needles stuck in me. I'm a converted believer in acupuncture, and Lela knows it, and we're making small talk as she inserts the needles.

"How is your family doing?" I ask.

Just then a somber look comes over Lela's face. "Our fifteen-year-old daughter, Ariel, has been in the hospital for six days with excruciating abdominal pain, to the point of vomiting, writhing in pain, and asking to die. We are at our wit's end."

As she explains the situation, she's getting more distressed and agitated. "She's been six days in the hospital with no relief, and no one can settle Ariel down from her writhing discomfort. Medications were not even phasing it," she says, on the verge of tears.

"I will pray for her," I say.

To be honest, I've told people I'll pray for them before and I rarely follow through with it. I say it just to be polite or make them feel better. I was lying, pure and simple, and now I've just told Lela that I will pray for Ariel.

Suddenly I get this undeniable feeling I'm being told to pray for Ariel aloud, right here, right now. Oh man! Really? I mean, I've prayed aloud with my family around the dinner table or with my Christian friends during C12 meetings or Sunday school, but Lela doesn't know me well. I'm guessing she knows I'm a Christian, but I'm not sure if she is. How will she respond if I start praying out loud? I've never prayed with someone this way before, and I'm trying to think of excuses why I don't need to pray now. Meanwhile, the undeniable calling to pray aloud for her gets even stronger.

I close my eyes as Lela continues to work on me, and I begin to pray aloud. Amazingly, it feels perfectly natural. The words come easy, like they are somehow being given to me. First, I ask for Ariel's pain to leave her body so she can get some rest. Then I pray that the medical process would accelerate to make the testing and diagnosis go faster.

When the prayer is over, Lela and I exchange no words, just a kindly glance. She finishes putting in the last few needles and leaves the room.

Thirty minutes later Lela comes back into the room, and her first words are, "I have just spoken with my husband, and after hours of writhing in pain, Ariel is now sleeping comfortably. And we are next up for an MRI scan."

And we both begin to cry.

As I begin to collect myself, I wonder what just happened here. Do I even dare think this was God instantly healing someone in direct response to my prayer?

Taking Waves Over the Bow

It's July 2008. I finished my fourth round of chemo a few weeks ago. The "Big Guns" have really taken their toll on me. I am battle worn, gaunt, and gray, struggling to walk under my own power. Judging from the way Julie looks at me, she knows I'm just about out of fight. The light in my eyes has long been extinguished.

Through this battle, I've made a special effort to make it to church every single Sunday, no matter how bad I felt. After all, church is where our support network is. Many people are praying for us, so I feel like I need to let them see how I'm doing every week so they can pray more specifically for us.

Recently I've been too weak to sit up for very long in church, so I've taken to lying down on the pew and resting my head on Julie's lap.

Last Sunday at church was the hardest one yet. It took all the energy I could muster to pull myself out of the car and scrap my way across the parking lot to the front door. Once inside, Pastor Dave happened to be walking toward me down the main corridor leading to the sanctuary. (Our congregation calls it "the love tunnel.") Dave took one glance at me, and immediately a look of great compassion and deep concern came over his face as he continued toward me. Never uttering a word, Dave met me with arms wide open. As we embraced in the love tunnel, Dave let out this guttural groan, as though he could actually feel my pain. And I thought of how the Spirit of God "intercedes for us with groanings too deep for words" (Romans 8:26).

Today we're back at Lakeside to get the results of the latest CT scans and learn what's next.

I was originally scheduled for six rounds of the "Big Guns," but I honestly don't know if I'll survive another round. As we sit in the examination room waiting for Dr. Blake, Julie, too, is wondering how much more of this I can take.

Even though this ride has been a terrible one, I feel certain the chemo is having a positive impact and that the tumors are shrinking. I can't explain it. I'm just sure of it. I guess I would call it the Spirit of God speaking to me.

After a few minutes, Dr. Blake makes his entrance. "Hello, Mr. Floen. How are you feeling?"

"Not so good," I reply.

Knowing how I look, I'm sure he's not at all surprised by my answer.

"I think it's time for us to discontinue the 'Big Guns.' We should have seen some kind of response by now if there was going to be one and we have not seen it." Looking at Julie he says, "I don't think it's prudent to subject him to anymore of this."

Julie nods in agreement, and my heart sinks.

I was so sure the tumors would be shrinking. I thought I had been spoken to directly by God on this. Did I hear Him wrong, or did I just conjure that up on my own? Something doesn't feel right, and I'm having a hard time letting this go.

"So what's next from here?" Julie asks.

Dr. Blake sighs and waits a moment to respond. "Well, a new trial has just become available that I think we should take a look at."

I get the sense that Dr. Blake is running out of cards to play, but he continues, explaining the details of the new trial, what the regimen will be, the side effects, etc.

"I need you to sign a release for the new trial," he says. "So, Mr. Floen, why don't you get back into your street clothes, and I'll get the clinical trial nurse to bring you some paperwork to look at." Then Dr. Blake leaves the room.

The China What?

As we sit in the exam room, waiting for the clinical trial nurse to bring us the release form, I am having serious doubts about the state of modern medicine in our country. I mean, based on my experience with the "Big Guns," I think I may be more likely to die from chemo than from cancer. Are chemo and radiation seriously all we have to fight cancer with? Is this really the furthest modern medicine has brought us in all this time? This is nothing short of brutal and barbaric. There has to be a better way.

I look over at Julie with a pensive look on my face. "What?" she asks.

"What else can we try?" I ask her. "With all the research and reading you've been doing, has anything sparked your interest? Is there anything you think might be worth a try?"

A very pensive look comes over her, like she's trying to decide whether to tell me something or not.

"What?" I ask.

She pauses for another moment. "Well," she says, guarding her words, "I've just started reading this book called *The China Study*."

"The China what?" I ask.

"*The China Study*."

"Okay. What does it say?"

"I don't know yet. I've barely gotten into it, but I felt led to read it after it was presented to me for the third time. I've learned that when God wants me to pay attention to something, He presents it to me three times. First, I read about the book in my cancer research. Then my friend Holly called me from the airplane on her way to China and told me about it. When Aunt Dot sent me a copy, I took the hint and started reading it."

"So you think God wants you to read this book?"

"Yeah, I guess so," she says.

"Well, can you tell me the general gist of it?"

"Honey, I'm only at the very beginning of it, so it's hard to say."

She wants so much to help. I can see it in her face. But she doesn't want to give me misinformation either.

I ask, "You believe God brought you to this book, right?"

"Yes," she says, with more certainty this time.

"Okay then," I tell her. "If it's good enough for God, it's good enough for me. Just skip to the back of the book and tell me what it says. I mean, what have we got to lose at this point?"

Julie starts flipping the pages, skimming as she goes. "It looks like the bottom line is that they're saying a vegan diet can help cure cancer."

"Okay, let's start today," I tell her, not having any idea what being a vegan means.

"Well, okay then!" she says.

Goodbye to the Whopper

Evidently Julie took me seriously when I told her I was going vegan. She's been buying vegan cookbooks and all kinds of weird stuff from Whole Foods Market that I've never seen or heard of before. I've been eating a Whopper almost every day for as long as I can remember, but I see those days coming to an end very soon.

Julie's been reading more of *The China Study,* and she's been sharing some snippets with me.

"Dan," she says, "the book tells about how the emperor of China died of cancer and his last order was to conduct a nationwide study of the occurrence of cancer in China. The study lasted for many years, and what they ultimately found was that there was a direct correlation to the occurrence of cancer and the amount of animal protein that the various people groups in China ate. Basically, the poor rural communities who ate little or no meat had nearly zero occurrences of cancer. On the other hand, the wealthier people living in the cities ate more meat and these people accounted for nearly all cancer occurrences in China."

"Interesting," I say.

"The book goes on to say there is a very clear threshold for when cancer grows, and when it recedes, that is directly affected by the amount of animal protein you eat. It's like a light switch," she says. "If over 10 percent of the food you eat comes from animal protein, cancer grows. Between 5 and 10 percent, cancer growth stops. Under 5 percent animal protein in your diet, cancer recedes."

"Really?" I reply.

"Think about this," Julie says. "Historically there has been a lot more cancer in the West than in the East. Why do you suppose that is? Take a look at our Western diet: meat, cheese, and tons of sugar. Now compare that to the traditional Eastern diet of rice and vegetables. But now look what's happening in the East. Today, cancer is on the rise in the East ever since McDonald's and Burger King arrived."

"Hmm. That's compelling," I reply.

Here's one thing I know for sure. No one in Western medicine ever talks about curing cancer. They only talk about "extending life." I think something is inherently wrong with this thinking. I mean, when we get scan reports that show "stable disease" (not growing or spreading) we celebrate, like that's a victory. I guess it's better than the alternative, but is this as good as it gets?

Recently I was walking through the Atlanta airport and a poster on a wall caught my eye. It showed a young boy about ten years old in a baseball uniform holding a bat over his shoulders, and his left leg had been amputated. The poster read, "Josh Wilson threw cancer a curve ball."

Seriously? Is this what we call beating cancer in America? They hacked this young boy's leg off!

As I walk down the corridors of Lakeside Cancer Center, I'm often met by some poor soul who's had some part of his face or body surgically removed. This place is a war zone. If there is the slightest chance that being a vegan will help, I'm in, a hundred percent.

Julie found a quote today on the internet from Ann Wigmore, author of *The Wheatgrass Book and The Healing Power Within*:

"The food you eat can be either the safest and most powerful form of medicine or the slowest form of poison."

Now, I'm a pretty black-and-white thinker, and I like to keep things simple. So from now on I'm going to think of the food I eat as either medicine or poison. It's one or the other.

From this day forward, every bit of food I put in my mouth is a life and death decision. No room for error.

Goodbye to the Whopper! And good riddance!

A Hill Too High

If you had told me I would ever be a vegan, I would have laughed in your face. But here we are. And of all times to start a vegan diet, doing it in the middle of heavy chemo treatments seems preposterous. I'm having difficulty keeping on weight as it is. And now I'm going to eat nothing but vegetables? I'm going to shrivel up to nothing. I mean, seriously, have you ever met an overweight vegan?

"How can I possibly do this on a vegan diet?" I complain to Julie. "I mean, exactly how many heads of lettuce a day is that?"

Julie smiles patiently. "Dan, I need you to trust me and give this a try. You promised me you were going to do whatever you could to stay here with me and Laurel. We can do this together. Just try it. You'll see, darlin'."

Great. She used the "you promised" line on me again. So I guess that settles it. We'll give this a try.

After a long day in my office of trying to breathe life into PM2, I get up out of my chair and wander toward the kitchen down the hall. With each step I take, an unfamiliar but very interesting sort of Caribbean smell is getting stronger and stronger.

Julie knew where the vegan diet conversation would wind up, and she's been cooking all day. Admittedly, it does smell pretty good. Julie knows I love spicy and hearty foods, and she's got a big pot full of interesting stuff bubbling on the stove.

"Dinner is served," Julie announces.

Laurel and I look at each other like, "What have we gotten ourselves into?" as we take a seat at the dinner table.

Julie takes the pot off the stove and brings it over to the table, smiling the whole way.

"This is Moroccan stew," she says. "It's got sweet potatoes, raisins, and all kinds of other healthy stuff in it. It's packed with calories and it's nice and spicy, just for you, darlin'. If you want to make it hotter, I got you a bottle of Sriracha," she says with a huge smile, like she's trying to sell me something.

"Thanks, sweetie," I tell her as genuinely as I can, and I take a bite.

Julie is watching me intently to see what my reaction will be.

"Wow, this stuff is awesome!"

Laurel is not nearly so impressed. "Mom, may I have some mac and cheese?"

"Sure, honey," Julie says. "That is pretty spicy, isn't it?"

I eat a huge plate of Moroccan stew and go back for seconds.

In the following days Julie keeps adding to her repertoire of interesting and tasty dishes. And I begin to think this vegan thing isn't going to be so bad.

Every morning she makes me a big protein shake with soy milk, vegan protein powder, and frozen strawberries, blueberries, and bananas. Sometimes she puts a little kale in there too. Then she tops it off with this stuff called Udo's Oil, which is like rocket fuel for weight gain at 120 calories per tablespoon. Julie puts several tablespoons of Udo's Oil in my shake and she also sprinkles it into most of the other dishes she's cooking throughout the day.

To get 3,200 calories in every day, I essentially have to eat constantly. This is a big mental shift for me. I mean, I have never lived to eat. I eat to live. Skipping a meal was never a problem for me . . . until now. These days I bring food with me everywhere I go. Nuts mostly because they're packed with calories. I especially like shelled pistachios and sunflower seeds.

I can hardly believe it, but yesterday I ate 4,147 calories on a vegan diet. I am gaining weight and I feel good.

Today I got out of my car without using my hands or arms. This is a far cry from where I was a few weeks ago. It's the little things I'm thankful for.

A few days pass, and I've been on the vegan diet for a week now. I never thought it possible, but I have gained weight on a totally vegan diet while doing heavy chemo treatments. Never say never!

8

Redefining Priorities

I'm lying in bed, awake, worrying about our financial situation. I roll over to look at the clock. It's 3 a.m. This is becoming a nightly thing lately.

The trouble is, I've been largely out of the PM2 picture this year, trying to stay alive, and I am the primary seller of our services. Now we find ourselves coming to the end of our biggest project ever and we have no new projects in the pipeline to keep us going. Julie and Eric have done a great job of keeping the wheels on operationally, but they've had little time for selling.

Lying there, I begin to pray. "Lord, I'm not sleeping at night, worried about our financial future. Here I am, fighting for my very life against cancer, and now we've added impending financial ruin to the list. Jeez, God, I just want off this train. Please help us!"

Through this ordeal I've learned it's a whole lot easier to give something to God that you have no real control over. The hardest things to give to God are those things we think we can control. I succumb to this delusion of control more often than I care to admit. But if I truly trusted God with every outcome, I'd surely be sleeping better at night.

I lie there a while longer, switching between praying and freaking out, and it becomes clear that no more sleeping will be happening tonight. So I roll out of bed, throw on some shorts and a T-shirt, and head for the kitchen to start the coffee maker.

I pour my first cup of coffee and go to my office. I start writing in my journal, but mostly I'm just sitting there, paralyzed with worry and fear. The hours drag on like a long slog in rough seas until I see the rising sun peek through the windowpane.

Around 7 a.m. I hear Julie rustling around in the kitchen, so I walk that way to get my morning hug, but mostly to vent on her about all my financial worries.

"Well, good morning, darling," Julie says with her usual bright smile, and she greets me with a peck on the lips and a hug. "Did you sleep?"

"Not so much," I reply with a furrowed brow, trying to let her see my deep concern.

Julie raises her coffee cup to take her first sip of the morning and says, "What's wrong?"

I look down at the floor as I let out a long sigh. "Julie, we are in deep financial trouble. I've been watching our cash flow dry up for the last several weeks, and I'm not sure if we're going to be able to pay ourselves for quite some time. I just don't know how much longer we can afford to sustain this lifestyle."

Julie puts down her coffee cup and comes over to wrap me in her arms. Speaking softly into my ear, she says, "Sweetheart, I've been watching you as you slide deeper and deeper into depression over this. You've become short-tempered and moody. You don't laugh anymore. If I need to go out and get a job to help us out, I'm ready to do that. If we need to sell this house, so be it. If we can't afford to keep the boat, that's okay. I've been watching the stress you're under and it is going to kill you. So from my perspective, we need to do whatever is necessary to free ourselves from this burden. I love you, darling. It's going to be all right. God will guide us through this just like He's guiding us through our journey with cancer. You know I'm right, Dan."

"Yeah, I know. I just don't like it," I reply.

Julie loosens her arm hold on me a bit and leans back just enough to look at me, face-to-face. "Honey, we need to sell the house and the boat as soon as possible, before it kills you," she says with eyes of unwavering certainty.

"In my gut, I know you're right, but I need some time with this. I mean, didn't God bless us with our house and the ability to have a boat? If He gave them to us, why would He want us to sell them? Why wouldn't He just bless the business and pull us through this financial valley? On the other hand, what if the house and the boat were never ordained by God? What if it was all our doing? What if the house and the boat are encumbrances that God wants us to be free of?"

"It's time to let them go," Julie repeats with even more certainty.

I look away from Julie to process her words for a bit, and my eyes are drawn outside, through our breakfast nook windows, to the backyard. A new day is dawning. The sun is just starting to peek over the rooftop and casts a warm glow over the boat, which is hanging on the lift out back. Julie's words begin to sink in, and a feeling of great impending loss comes over me as I stand there, in silence, gazing out the window at the *Floen Bayou*.

A minute or so goes by as Julie patiently waits for me to formulate a response. Still looking out the window, I begin.

"We've had so many great times in this house and on our boat. Living on the water and going out on the boat every weekend is the only life Laurel has ever known. She calls our house 'the party house.' Think of all the visitors we've entertained over the years. Laurel loves being the girl who spends her weekends on the boat. She's not alone. I mean, I'm a boat guy."

I turn from the window and focus on Julie. "We've built our life and family identity around being on the water. How can we throw that all away? I guess selling the house is one thing, but how can we seriously consider selling the boat? That boat defines who we are."

Julie doesn't skip a beat. "That's exactly the point," she says. "The boat defines who we are, and that's the problem."

Light bulb!

Have You Just Lied to Me?

Today I'm meeting Scott Hitchcock at Panera Bread for our C12 one-on-one. We meet here for lunch once a month. As I walk in through the glass double doors, I spot him in the corner near the window. He's beaten me here, as usual, and he appears to be going over some notes, presumably from our last one-on-one session.

"Hey, Scott."

"Well, hi there, young man!" he says with his usual high level of energy and stands up from the table.

"How are you doing, man?" I ask.

"Much better, now that you're here," he says and gives me a big "Scott Hitchcock hug." I get the same greeting every time we meet, but I never get tired of it.

After we get our food, Scott says the blessing and we dig in to eat.

We exchange the usual updates on how our families are and what God has been doing in and through the business. Then Scott pauses and says, "Dan, today I want to offer you a practical tool to help you stay on track in your Christian walk. I want to encourage you to join an accountability group," he says.

"Hmm. What is that exactly?" I was part of an accountability group in Atlanta years ago, but I'm curious to know what his version of this looks like.

"An accountability group is a small group of Christian men or women who meet regularly for the specific purpose of holding one another accountable in various areas of their Christian walk. Now, this is typically an all-male or all-female small group, because the kind of questions guys need to ask one another are different from what ladies need to ask each other, and you probably aren't gonna feel as comfortable cleaning out your closet in front of a member of the opposite sex, and definitely not your spouse. I think a good group size is two to four people. Any more than that, and it becomes harder to manage, harder to form strong bonds and to build trust."

I nod and take another bite of my sandwich as he continues.

"I suggest meeting sometime in the middle of the week, because that's usually when our memory wanes from the message of grace and rescue that we heard the previous Sunday. You might meet somewhere for lunch, or breakfast, as long as you can find a quiet and private setting to talk openly."

Scott takes a bite of his cobb salad, then continues. "The format of the meeting is essentially a list of accountability questions that the group agrees on and asks of each individual. Each member of the group answers the same questions. And depending on an individual's answers, the members may congratulate the individual for showing marked improvement in a particular area or offer encouragement and suggestions to help the person do better in that area the next time. I'm in an accountability group with two other C12 members myself."

"What kind of stuff do you ask each other?"

Scott reaches into his satchel, pulls out a well-worn folded up piece of paper, and hands it to me. I carefully unfold the paper.

Accountability Questions

1. Have you fulfilled the mandates of your calling?
2. **As seen through God's eyes,** have you been involved in any action (looking , lustful thoughts, etc.) with or about any woman, since you were last here, that could have been seen as compromising? Have you had victory over anxious thoughts?
3. Would God be happy with the way you spent your money?
4. Have you spent adequate daily time in the Bible and in prayer?
5. Have you given priority to your family and their spiritual needs?
6. Have you remembered what God has done for you every day?
7. Have you just lied to me?

"Wow, those are some pretty heavy questions, don't you think?"

"Yes, they are," Scott says, "and that is precisely the point. The thought of answering these questions may strike fear in your heart. But here's the thing, Dan. Fighting sin and death is a messy business, and sometimes we need help from our Christian friends."

"Well, I guess it's hard to argue with that," I admit.

Scott adds, "My accountability group helps me keep the memory of my salvation fresh in my mind, which in turn improves my outlook, and thus my behavior. So, Dan, I encourage you to consider becoming a part of an accountability group. You'll be glad you did."

As I drive home from lunch, I know Scott is right. Lord knows, I need all the help I can get to stay on the path. I figure I better do something about this before I reason my way out of it, so I dial Eric's cell phone as I drive home.

Eric answers.

"Hey, man," I tell him. "Got a question for you."

"Yeah, man. What's up?" he says.

"Well, maybe it's more of a request," I tell him.

"What is it?" he asks.

"Would you consider being my accountability partner?" I ask.

"What's that?" he says.

"Well, it kinda goes like this . . ."

A Test of the Heart

It's New Year's Day, 2009. The latest drug I'm on, and there's a long list of them by this point, is called IL-2. I go into the hospital once a month for a two- or three-day stay, depending on how quickly I recover. This experimental drug can have dangerous effects on your vital organs, so I have to be closely monitored. They give me a huge dose of IL-2 in the hospital, and in between hospital visits, I go to a different clinic, closer to home, for a daily IL-2 shot.

I'm driving home from my daily shot and notice players on the golf course just down the street from our neighborhood. I effectively traded in my golf clubs for a fishing pole when we moved to Florida, but sometimes I think it would be fun to get back out there. I used to be a pretty good golfer. But then I remember how painful and disappointing my last golf outing was a few months ago, when my friend Kevin from Chicago came to visit. Heavy chemo does terrible things to your golf swing.

"Nope," I say to myself, "I think we'll stick to fishing."

I drive to the end of Independence Parkway, running along the golf course, and roll up to the stop light in the left turn lane. I'm about a block from home now, and my mind is mostly on fishing as I sing along to "The Life" by Kenny Chesney.

As I sit there in my own little world, singing away, I suddenly become aware of someone staring at me.

I glance to my left to see a haggard middle-aged man standing on the curb next to my car. He's a gaunt man with dark, tanned skin, like leather. His blond hair is all askew and it looks as brittle as dry grass. His face is pitted and full of sores. His staring eyes are bloodshot and tired, and he's holding a sign that says, "Homeless. God Bless."

I'm tired from the constant chemo I have coursing through my veins, and I just want to go home. I begin to think of all the reasons why it doesn't make sense for me to help this guy.

I figure he must be a meth addict. He looks doped up to the hilt. I look away and decide not to make further eye contact. If I had anything in my wallet, I might be inclined to help, but I never carry much cash, and today my wallet is bone dry. Besides, he looks too far gone. What good is there in giving money to a guy who is clearly going to use it to buy more meth?

The light turns green and I make the left turn to head for home, just a few blocks down the road. As I drive, I begin to hear a small voice that feels like it is emanating from my soul.

"Are you seriously going to leave My child standing back there and not help him?" the voice asks.

I know who it is, but I don't like it.

"Awe, man! I'm tired and I want to go home, Lord. Can't You just let me go home please?"

"Dan, I am healing you and have provided for you so richly," He says.

I let out a heavy sigh and slowly drag my palm down my face in great displeasure.

Again, I hear, only louder this time, "Dan, are you seriously going to leave My child standing back there and not help him?"

As I turn into our neighborhood, I press my remote to open the gate and I roll through the entrance.

"Really, Dan?" He says in a loud, clear voice.

Suddenly some words from the Bible hit me like a two-by-four: "Truly I tell you, whatever you did for one of the least of these brothers and sisters of Mine, you did for Me."

I turn the car around behind the guard shack and drive back out of our neighborhood. There's a drive-up ATM across the street, so I pull in to get forty bucks, twenty for me and twenty for the homeless guy. Normally I give a dollar, or whatever loose change I have, to a panhandler, but suddenly I'm feeling like a big spender. I'm sure it has nothing to do with the fact that God guilted me into this.

I wheel out of the ATM and turn onto the street headed toward the intersection where the guy was standing. As I go, God says one more thing.

"Don't just throw a twenty at My child as you drive by. Get out of your car and talk with him. I want to speak to him through you."

"Seriously, God?" I shout as I bounce my skull off my headrest in disgust.

I gather myself and let out another long sigh. "Fine, I'll do it, but what do You want me to say to him?"

"'Tell him that I love him," He says.

As I roll up to the intersection, I see that there are now two panhandlers, one on each opposing corner.

"Naturally. I guess I deserved that, huh?" I tell Him.

Then, in a moment of clarity, I realize how selfish and stubborn I'm being. I feel completely convicted. "I'm sorry for being so difficult, Father. You can count on me to deliver Your message."

There's a small parking lot near the corner where one of the men is standing, so I turn into it and park the car. I get out of the car with the two twenty-dollar bills in hand and head toward the first man. As I approach, the look on his face says he's not sure what to expect from me.

"Hey, man, my name is Dan. What's yours?"

"Darrell," he says.

"Well, Darrell, I just wanted to stop by and let you know that God loves you more than you could ever know and He will take care of you."

I put a hand on his shoulder and hand him one of the twenties.

"Oh, thank you!" he says. "God bless you!"

"Darrell, I have stage four cancer and I'm supposed to be dead by now, but God is healing me. He's taking care of me, just like He's taking care of you," I tell him.

"I know that's right," he says. "Thank you so much."

"Darrell, you take care now, and God bless you."

"God bless you, and thanks again," Darrell says.

We wave goodbye to each other as I start toward the second man on the opposing corner.

The second man is the one I saw originally on my way home, and he's not looking any better at all. I find out his name is Justin, and our conversation goes much like the first one, but it's mostly one-sided, with me doing most of the talking. His eyes are glazed over, and his speech is slurred, and I sense that the words I'm saying are not registering with him. Then I realize that my job is simply to deliver the message. I figure, if God wants Justin to understand what I'm saying, He will clear his brain and the message will make it all the way to Justin's heart.

We part ways and I head back to my car. It's the first day of the new year, and it started right off with a test. I'm happy to have had this experience, but not at all proud of what it took to get me there. I know God expects better of me.

9

Out of Cards

I had a terrible pain in my side at dinner the other night, so Dr. Blake suggested a CT scan to see what's going on. Today we're in an exam room at Lakeside waiting to get the results.

"Hi, Mr. Floen," Dr. Blake says with a sort of half smile. I've seen this look several times before. It means bad news.

Dr. Blake opens the blue file folder he's holding and begins to look over the CT scan results. "Mr. Floen," he says, "yesterday's scan shows that you have a new tumor in your gallbladder, which explains the discomfort you were experiencing in your side. The good news is that you don't need your gallbladder to live, so we can remove it, and the tumor, with no problem."

"That sounds easy enough," Julie says. "Let's get it out of there."

I nod in agreement.

"We can certainly do that," says Dr. Blake, "but the scan also shows that regression has ceased in all the other tumors, which would seem to indicate that the IL-2 has reached the end of its effectiveness. I'd suggest getting you scheduled for a gallbladder resection in the next three weeks or so, and then you'll need four weeks to heal before we can introduce any new chemotherapy. At the end of those seven or eight weeks, I'll order a PET scan to restage you at that point."

Julie and I turn to look at each other. We both know that seven or eight weeks is an eternity in the world of stage four melanoma. Things could go really far south in that amount of time. In eight weeks I may be too far gone to qualify for any new clinical trials.

"Okay then," Julie says. "We need to get this show on the road as soon as possible."

"Very well, Mrs. Floen," says Dr. Blake. "Actually, let me see if Dr. Wilson is in the clinic today. He's the surgeon who would perform the resection. I'll be right back."

A few minutes pass as we wait in silence; then in walks Dr. Blake with another man in tow and introduces us to Dr. Wilson.

"Dr. Blake tells me he'd like to schedule you for a gallbladder resection, so I've asked my assistant to check my schedule for you. I do know it's going to be at least three weeks before I can get to you, though, maybe four."

I look at Julie. Her brow is furrowed, obviously not happy with that answer.

"Isn't there any way to get Dan in quicker than three weeks?" she asks. "Three weeks is a long time, and then we have to wait another four weeks beyond that. That just seems too long, doesn't it?"

Dr. Wilson just looks at her and shrugs his shoulders. He's obviously not getting what the big hurry is all about.

Julie picks up on his lackadaisical attitude immediately. Then she stands up, steps toward him, and says in a strong voice, "See, the thing is, Dr. Wilson, I don't want *a* husband. I want *this* husband. So I'd appreciate your help to make that happen."

I don't think Wilson is used to being spoken to that way, especially not by a woman. In general, I think doctors are used to having people blindly accept whatever they tell them. After all, they're the doctors. Julie's view is that she's the customer, and Wilson's sole purpose is to serve us to our satisfaction. He doesn't appear to be enjoying this exchange very much. It's kind of fun to watch.

Dr. Wilson pauses for a minute, still not visibly motivated to speed things up one iota.

"This is palliative care," he says.

Then silence.

Wow, I've never had it put to me that way before. He doesn't think I'm going to make it much longer. So, from his perspective, what's the big hurry? I'm dying soon anyway.

At this point Julie is infuriated and has no more words for Dr. Wilson. I think she just wants him to leave the room before she kills him.

After a moment of silence, Dr. Blake pipes up. "Okay, well, Dr. Wilson will let you know when the very first surgery date is available, and I'm sure he'll contact you if he has any cancellations."

"Thanks, Dr. Blake," Julie says. She crosses her arms and sighs after Dr. Wilson leaves. "What's the plan again after the PET scan?"

"Well," says Dr. Blake, "we'll have to see what Dan qualifies for after he has been restaged. I don't have any other treatments to offer him other than a few miscellaneous trials, which would all have a very low response rate. One potential option may be to go to Riverview in Houston to see what they may have to offer. I have a colleague there who is doing some very interesting things."

So there it is. Dr. Blake is out of playing cards. I must say, he's been a masterful strategist, being very careful to leave as many options open to us as possible throughout this process. But now the game appears to be over.

The next morning I'm up before dawn. There's not much sleeping going on, so I go out to the kitchen to start a pot of coffee. As the coffee is brewing, I walk into my office to see if there are any good devotions in my in-box this morning. A little encouragement would be nice right now.

Just then I hear the familiar *ding, ding* indicating a new email has just arrived. It's from Dad. Mom and Dad moved down to Tampa from Minneapolis last August, just in case.

> *Dear Dan,*
>
> *Trying to put myself in your shoes this morning, I think I can appreciate just a little how you might be reacting to Dr. Blake's comments. I had hoped for more options in his quiver. At any rate, I am here to help in any way that I am able in carrying this burden.*
> *My love to you always,*
> *Dad.*

My response:
> *Thanks, Dad. Just one thing. No matter what happens, continue to love my wife and my daughter as your own.*

Dad emailed back:
> *Done! Love,*
> *Dad*

The Snake Oil Peddler

Julie's still fuming over Dr. Wilson's "palliative care" comment and his unwillingness to schedule the gallbladder surgery any sooner.

She picks up the phone and calls our primary care physician, Dr. Shilpa Sharma, and asks if she knows anyone who can do a gallbladder resection on short notice. Julie continues to explain the situation and the urgency of it all.

After a few more words with the doctor Julie hangs up the phone and heads to the coffee machine for another cup. "Shilpa's husband has a surgeon in his practice and she's going to see what she can arrange with him. She should be calling us back shortly."

Just then the phone rings. It's her aunt Dot. Julie rolls her eyes at me.

Aunt Dot is a little bit "out there," you might say. She's been pestering Julie unmercifully, pushing her to try all sorts of weird stuff that are all "sure to heal Dan." However, it occurs to me that Dot survived stage four melanoma years ago, and all she did was the weird stuff, no chemo or traditional medications whatsoever. So far, besides going vegan and working out more, I've done nothing but chemo. Right now Dr. Phil's famous words, "How's that working for you?" are ringing in my head. Based on yesterday's experience at Lakeside, I'd say, "Not so good."

Part of Julie's assumed role is to be my blocker as she sorts through the myriad of miracle cures that well-meaning friends and relatives are constantly offering. Only a select few people are allowed direct access to me when it comes to the topic of cancer treatment. Julie sees herself as my protector, and she's been blocking Aunt Dot for weeks.

Julie's been on the phone with Dot for a good thirty minutes, and whatever they're talking about, it doesn't sound like Dot is taking no for an answer from Julie.

"Well, okay, Aunt Dot. I really don't think he'll be interested, but if you insist, here's Dan," Julie says as she hands me the phone.

"Hi, Dot!"

"Oh, hi, Dan! I've been talking with Julie about a special treatment that I just know is going to help you, but I haven't been making much headway with her, so I thought I better ask for the man of the house."

Dot is an old-style Georgia belle, and the way she was raised, it's a bold step to speak directly to the man of the house, maybe even rude. So I know this is very important to her.

"My dearest Dan, I need you to know that God told me He would not let me sleep until I share King Institute with you. So I surely hope you'll excuse my boldness, but I'm just trying to do what God told me to do. I do hope you understand."

"Absolutely, Dot. I certainly don't want you to lose any more sleep, so you better get this off your chest."

Dot proceeds to tell me about King Institute and a man named Jim Robertson who runs the Sebring location.

"Sounds interesting, Dot, but what does King Institute do exactly?" I ask.

"Now, Dan, I need you to trust me on this. If I try to explain how it works, I won't do it justice, and you'll think I'm really off my rocker," she says with a laugh in her voice. "Here's my offer to you. If you and Julie will go and see Jim Robertson, I'll pay for your appointment."

"My goodness, Dot. That's a very generous offer. You certainly don't need to pay our way."

"I insist," she says. "Please allow me to do this for you. Will you go?"

I pause for a moment.

"Count me in."

Voodoo Training

Two days later, on a Saturday, we drive to Sebring, Florida, to consult with Jim Robertson of King Institute and learn about this thing they call "The King Method®," or TKM® for short.

At 11 a.m., Julie and I wheel into the parking lot of Jim Robertson's office. His place appears to be an old house that's been converted into a clinic. It's a very modest building but clean.

"This should be interesting," Julie says.

"Yep," I reply, thinking this is probably going to wind up being some kind of voodoo. But I promised Dot I'd give this a try, and we're already here, so we might as well check it out.

"Well, hello!" says a female voice as Julie steps inside. "You must be Julie."

"Yes, and this is my husband, Dan." I smile and wave.

"Hi, Dan. I'm Melanie, Jim's wife, and we're so glad to meet you. Your aunt Dot has told us so much about you two, and we are really glad you're here. Oh, and here's Jim," Melanie says as he walks into the room.

I'm guessing Jim is around sixty years old. He's very fit for his age, with good muscle tone, bright eyes, and a warm smile. He seems to be very joyful and content, without a worry in the world.

"Why don't you both follow me back to my office and we'll get this show on the road?"

We go into Jim's office and we all take a seat.

"I'd like to start off just talking with you both for a bit to understand where you are now in Dan's treatment, and then I'll give you an overview of TKM. After we talk for a bit, we'll head over to the treatment room and I'll do some sequences on Dan. Sound good?"

"What's a sequence?" Julie asks.

"We'll get to that," Jim says. "But first, I'd like for you two to share with me what your journey has looked like so far."

Julie tells Jim every gory detail of my diagnosis, the pin in my femur, and the names of all the chemo drugs I've been given. She also explains that I've recently started eating a vegan diet and that I work out regularly.

Julie continues. "Our urgent problem right now, Jim, is that Dan has a tumor in his gallbladder, and others growing elsewhere. His gallbladder needs to come out right away so he can have four weeks to heal and start whatever the next chemo trial there is available for him. And speaking of the next chemo drug, Lakeside can't offer him anything else, so our oncologist has recommended we go to Riverview in Houston to see what they might have. To make matters even worse, the surgeon at Lakeside can't do the gallbladder resection for at least three weeks, so that means Dan could go seven to eight weeks with no treatment at all. As I'm sure you know, that's a really long time in the world of stage four melanoma."

Jim nods.

Julie continues. "Meanwhile, I called our primary physician yesterday to see if she can arrange a gallbladder resection any sooner than three weeks, but I haven't heard back from her yet."

Jim pauses briefly, then looks at me.

"Well, Dan," Jim says. "I must say, considering all you've been through, you look remarkably healthy."

"God has been protecting me," I tell him, intentionally mentioning God because I want to see what his reaction will be.

"Amen to that, Dan!" he says, nodding in agreement.

Okay, he passed the "God" test, so I decide to stay engaged a little while longer, just to see what else this guy has to say.

"Now that I have a good understanding of where you've been and where you are now, let me explain what King Institute's TKM is about," he says. "Julie, Dan, TKM is based on the premise that God created our body to heal itself."

As Jim continues to explain, he talks about energy spheres and how it's important to maintain a smooth, unobstructed flow of energy throughout your body. If an obstruction exists, energy gets dammed up at that point in the body where the obstruction is and bad things start to happen, like cancer or other ailments. He talks about how you can control the flow of energy with the touch of your hand on these energy spheres, and he demonstrates a few places where one might put their hands during the course of a sequence.

To me, this sounds like acupressure, or laying on of hands, from the Christian faith. From what little I know about acupuncture, the energy he's describing sounds a lot like chi (Chinese for "energy force"). Based on my firsthand positive experience with acupuncture, I guess this doesn't sound too far-fetched. But all the acupuncture did was help me with my nausea. Can this TKM stuff seriously have any effect at all on cancer?

We follow Jim into the treatment room, and Jim directs me to lie down on the massage table that's sitting in the middle of the floor. On top of the table is a pad of egg crate cushion foam cut to the exact size of the massage tabletop. Two narrow white sheets are stacked on top of the foam pad, presumably to give you a double layer of breathable cotton between you and the plastic foam cushion.

"You can leave all your clothes on," he tells me, "but please remove your watch, your belt, and your shoes. Are you wearing any other metal?"

"Just my wedding ring," I reply.

"Please take that off too," he says.

Reluctantly I take off my ring and lie down on the table. There is a stool on either side of the massage table, and Jim directs Julie to sit on one of them at my right side and Jim sits on the other stool to my left.

"The reason for the foam and the double layer of sheets," he says, "is so I can easily slide my hands into position underneath your body without causing you or me any discomfort."

Then he slides his left hand under my right hip and puts his right hand on my sternum.

"An easy way to think about what we're doing here is to say that we are completing electrical circuits," Jim says. "As I move my hands from one energy sphere to the next, I am directing your body's flow of energy and helping that energy flow more smoothly. Julie, when you're doing treatments on Dan, you will leave your hands in each position for at least five minutes, or until you feel that Dan's energy pulses are steady and in sync on both of your hands for one minute."

This is getting weirder by the minute.

"Okay, Julie, now you try," he says. "Put your left hand on Dan's pubic bone, like this. Now put your right hand on Dan's right side underneath his bottom rib, like this."

"Like this?" she says.

"Yes, that's it. Pretty easy, right?" he says.

"What are the pulses you're talking about?" Julie asks. "Do you mean his heart rate?"

"No, you're looking for electrical pulses, not Dan's heart rate. When you feel them, you'll know what I mean. Try leaving your hands in place for a few more minutes and see if you can feel them," he says.

"Okay," Julie says.

Jim continues. "When energy flow is stagnant or dammed up, bad things tend to happen in the body. TKM is all about breaking log jams and maintaining the body's healthy flow of energy. We call the various hand positions in a treatment a 'sequence,' and there are sequences for every part of the body or ailment you are trying to address. To make things easy, we've developed a book of sequence sheets that clearly tell you where to put your hands, step-by-step. It's basically an instruction manual. Let me show you what a sequence sheet looks like."

Jim picks up an eight-by-eleven sheet of paper to show to Julie and I catch a glimpse of it as it goes by. It appears to have an image of the anatomy of the body on one side and some sort of list down the other side that looks like a recipe. He lays the paper on my chest and turns it toward Julie so that she can read it.

"Take a look at this, Julie," he says. "Each sequence sheet tells you exactly where to put your hands, and in what order; hence the name *sequence*. Each energy sphere is clearly marked and numbered on the anatomy that's pictured on each page, and the numbers correspond to the procedures for this particular sequence. Notice, too, that there are left-side and right-side procedures for every sequence. You see, God made our bodies to have a left side and a right side, and our body energy pathways mirror this same design. So it's important to work on both sides of the body to encourage an even and steady flow of energy."

"Hey, I think I feel something," Julie says.

"What does it feel like?" Jim asks.

"It feels like a water current whooshing through my fingers."

"That's it," he says. "Those are Dan's pulses you're feeling."

"This is so cool," she says and smiles.

Voodoo is more the word I'm thinking of.

"Yeah, it's pretty neat, isn't it?" Jim says. "What's really interesting is that God designed these energy pathways to be fully intact, even if a part of the body is missing. For example, I was doing some sequences about a year ago on a woman who lost her left leg and hip to cancer. As I worked on her through a few sequences, the instructions called for me to place my hand on the bottom of her left foot, which of course did not exist. So I placed my hand where her left foot used to be, and I felt the very same pulses that you're feeling now, Julie."

"Wow, that's amazing!" Julie says, all wide-eyed.

It looks like Julie is drinking the Kool-Aid. As for me, I'm trying my best not to react visibly, but inside I'm thinking this guy is a complete nut job. On the other hand, it's not like I've got anything else going on that's healing me right now. Besides, Dot said that God told her to send us to Jim, so I guess that counts for something.

In all, Jim spends four hours with us, teaching us about TKM philosophy and training me and Julie how to do the treatments. Julie completes the last of the sequences and then Jim leads us back to his office for a little debriefing session.

"How long does it usually take to begin seeing results?" Julie asks.

"Great question," he says. "Typically, we start seeing results in about six weeks. If your primary physician can arrange for surgery next week, and you have four weeks to heal after that, you wouldn't get six weeks of treatments in before starting whatever the next chemo trial is. If it were my decision, I would delay the gallbladder resection until after the first six weeks of treatments. In fact, I wouldn't do it at all."

"Really?" Julie says. "That seems risky to me to wait that long, especially when the surgery is guaranteed to remove the cancer."

"Are you sure it's cancer?" Jim asks.

"Well, Lakeside seems to be sure it's cancer," she says.

"Maybe you can ask Lakeside to do a biopsy to find out exactly what it is," he says. "Do you think they would do that?"

"I don't know," Julie says. "I guess you don't get what you don't ask for, but I rather doubt it."

"I understand how you must feel," Jim says. "This is all very new to both of you, and you feel like time is of the essence to move quickly to the next chemo trial. I just wish we had six weeks."

I've heard a lot of pretty wild stuff today, and at this point I just have one question for him. If this guy is truly an instrument of God's healing, I want to know who gets the credit if this stuff actually works to heal me. I lean way forward in my chair, putting my elbows on my knees, and look very intently at him. "Jim, I've just got one question for you."

"Fire away," he says.

"If I am healed using TKM treatments, who did the healing?" I ask.

"God did," he says without skipping a beat. "I don't heal anyone. God does the healing, plain and simple."

"Thanks, Jim. That's good to hear. Well, let's see what God does with this."

"Exactly," he says. "Let's see what God's going to do to arrange for those six weeks we need."

As we wrap up our time together, Jim invites us to join hands, and he leads us in a prayer, thanking God for the healing He is already doing in my body.

As we're leaving Jim's clinic, walking to our car, Julie's phone rings. It's Dr. Sharma. After a brief exchange, she hangs up the phone and looks at me.

"Let me guess," I say. "He doesn't want to do the surgery."

"Nope," she says. "He's not an oncology surgeon. If he gets in there and the cancer has spread outside the gallbladder, he wouldn't be able to help, so he would simply have to close you up. He thinks we need Lakeside to do this."

"Well," I tell her. "It looks like we're going to get those six weeks Jim is hoping for."

I turn the car out of the parking lot, and we head for home.

Jim sent us home with a stack of sequences and other instructions he calls the "cancer pack." He said we need to "take out the trash" (remove toxins) as soon as possible so we can start building on a clean and sturdy foundation. He wants me to continue the vegan diet and be sure to get plenty of exercise. I also need to find a non-metallic wedding ring. He suggested a ceramic one. No more wristwatch either. In fact, nothing metal on my body whatsoever. I told him during our visit about the titanium rod in my left femur, and he understood why it needs to be there, but he sees it as an energy obstruction we'll have to work around.

Julie says, "I'll order a massage table online when we get home. In the meantime we can do your treatments on the couch in the family room."

Two hours in the car pass quickly as we continue to process what we've just heard. As weird as this stuff sounds, I must admit, it feels good to be able to take some action instead of waiting around to see what the next drug is going to be, if there even is one.

Some Gall

Ever since our training session with Jim Robertson four weeks ago, Julie and I have been very diligent in doing TKM treatments every day. One unexpected benefit has been that Julie and I are spending a lot more quality time together. Granted, some of the treatments put me to sleep because they're so relaxing, but I appreciate the time with Julie, nonetheless.

Dr. Wilson took out my gallbladder two weeks ago, and it went smooth as silk. I had asked God to protect me, and He most certainly did, just like when they put the rod in my femur. Once again I didn't touch any of the pain meds they gave me after surgery.

"Man," I say to Julie, "what if God chooses to heal me using this TKM stuff? Wouldn't that be amazing? I mean, then there would be no doubt about who healed me. What a glorious thing that would be. Dr. Blake is a really smart guy, but wouldn't it be great to see him completely dumbfounded when the PET scan comes back with tumors shrinking or gone? What an awesome day that would be! Lord Jesus, let it be so!"

"Amen to that!" Julie says.

Getting Uncomfortable

It's 4 a.m. Friday morning, and I've been lying in bed awake for hours. I feel like an elephant is sitting on my chest as the reality of my situation takes its toll on me. No more sleeping will be happening this morning, so I get up. I'm going to Friday morning men's group today, but I don't need to leave for another hour, so I grab a cup of coffee and head into my office.

I sit down at my desk and begin to type.

> *Sometimes I feel so foolish.*
>
> *I mean, I'm in a raging storm at sea here and things look really bleak! My entire being strains as I grapple with the boat wheel against the tremendous force of each crushing wave. My hands are clamped to the wheel like a vice and they hurt from holding on so tightly, and for so long.*
>
> *"Never let go!" I shout to myself.*
>
> *Between the high wind, the pelting rain, and the saltwater spray, I can't see past the bow of the boat. I blink my eyes as seldom as possible for fear of missing that one huge wave that would capsize me and seal my fate in an instant. My eyes burn from staring into the weather. My body shakes fiercely as adrenaline puts all bodily systems on emergency alert. Thoughts begin to creep into my head that my doom is near.*
>
> *Suddenly, I realize that Jesus is going to have to pry my cold dead hands off this wheel unless I let go of it, right now! Immediately, my hands fly off the wheel as though it were a red-hot branding iron.*
>
> *And then, Jesus calms the sea.*

Writing down these few words is hugely therapeutic. The weight on my chest is already feeling lighter.

I look up at the clock. It's time to go. I pour some coffee into my travel mug and leave for church.

I arrive at church and walk into our meeting room, but the normal jokes and jabs are strangely absent this morning. The guys are all just sitting there in silence, and I know right away there's trouble.

David breaks the silence. "Jim, how are you doing?"

Jim's eyes are bloodshot. He looks like he hasn't slept in days.

"Not so good, David," he says. "We got Carol's test results back on Wednesday. The doctor says it's Alzheimer's."

My heart sinks. These are two of the most special people in my life.

More silence.

Jim's best friend, Bill, puts his hand on Jim's shoulder. "Guys, I think we need to put Jim in the middle this morning. Would that be all right with you, Jim?"

"Sure," he says softly.

Jim stands up and Bill grabs his chair from behind him and puts it in the middle of the circle.

Jim puts his hands on his knees for support as he slowly lowers himself to sit down in the chair. As Jim sits, every man stands to form a tight circle around Jim, laying one hand on Jim and the other on a neighbor's shoulder to form a continuous bond around Jim.

Bill starts to pray. "God, we so love our friends Jim and Carol. They have made such a tremendous impact on all of us, and they are such faithful followers of Your Son, Jesus. So now, Lord, we ask that You heal Carol completely and fully. Father, You are the great physician, and it is in Jesus' name that we pray."

One by one, each man offers a few words of prayer as the Spirit leads them. After every man has spoken who is led to, David concludes the prayer and says at the end, "And all the men of God said . . ."

"Amen!"

As the group is breaking up, Jim and I walk out of the parlor and down the hallway with one arm on each other's shoulder. We stop in front of the exit door just as Bill catches us from behind.

"We love you, Jim," he says as he wraps his arms around our necks and pulls us into a tight huddle. "Let me pray for you both."

As Bill prays, I'm thinking how thankful I am to know these two men. I count them among my very best friends, and I would do anything for them.

"And we ask all these things in the powerful name of Your Son, Jesus Christ!" Bill says.

"Amen!" we all say.

Still in the huddle, Jim looks up from the ground as tears are welling up in his eyes. Just then I realize there is something I can do for him.

"Jim," I tell him, "today a pebble is going into my shoe for you. Whenever I feel it in there, I'll be praying for you."

Jim puts his head back down, obviously impacted by this gesture.

Still standing in the huddle, I pray a silent prayer. "Father, what a privilege it is to be included in this Christian brotherhood. Help me look beyond my circumstances and minister every day that I have remaining, whether they be few or whether they be many. Amen!"

As Jim taught me so well, a true friend is willing to be uncomfortable for you.

Daring to Ask

For some time now, there has been a lesion in my right femur about ten inches above my knee that Lakeside has been watching. My left femur already has a long rod in it, and now they're looking at doing some radiation on my right femur to see if that will help.

Throughout this journey I've been surrounded by maimed and traumatized people. Lots of bandaged wounds and battle-worn faces in wheelchairs. And I think, *Is this the path I am supposed to be on?* Since starting TKM treatments and the vegan diet, I feel and look so healthy. Just today someone else at Lakeside had to ask which one of us was the patient. Using only Western treatment methods just isn't making sense to me anymore. Maybe my tune will change if the PET scan comes back with bad news in the coming weeks. But as I stand here, I believe that as long as I glorify God, all things are possible.

With all of the carnage around me, I find myself wandering along the continuum between shear panic and unwavering faith and peace.

Then the words of Psalm 91 come to my mind.

Do not dread the disease that stalks in darkness,
nor the disaster that strikes at midday.
Though a thousand fall at your side,
though ten thousand are dying around you,
these evils will not touch you. (NLT)

"Darn right!" I say to myself, and my faith and peace quotients go up immensely right away.

I recall our Sunday school class yesterday, where we watched a DVD, and the speaker was using the analogy of life as a chess game. "When we think it's checkmate, God always has one more move," said the speaker. I disagree. I think God has infinite moves. God doesn't play on the same flat plain that we do. God's moves are four dimensional, and it's always thrilling to see Him in action.

Sometimes I look at our dire situation with health and finances, and I think about the odds that I will die and leave a healthy insurance policy for Julie and Laurel. I think about how me dying may be the simplest solution to our financial troubles. And then I think, no, God is going to make me do this the hard way and live through this trial and learn from it. And while I cannot possibly imagine how He's going to do it, I have renewed certainty that He will make a way.

I've heard it said that you should beware of any Christian leader who does not walk with a limp. Well, I don't know about me as a leader, but I think I've got the limping thing down.

The latest X-ray showed that the lesion in my right femur is shrinking on its own, so there's no need to do radiation. The radiologist who gave us the results seemed a bit confused, considering I'm not doing any chemo right now, but he was happy for us nonetheless. Woohoo!

Today I'm feeling emboldened by the news of the shrinking lesion and encouraged by what looks like progress resulting from this TKM stuff and the vegan diet. And I begin to consider asking God the one question I have feared asking Him since the start of this journey.

I think sometimes people don't ask questions because they're afraid of what the answer might be. Just ask Julie. She knows she better not ask me how her dress looks on her unless she's ready for an honest (and sometimes not very delicate) answer. I justify my often ruthless honesty with, "Hey, I'm just telling it like it is, honey. If you don't want the truth, don't ask me." For some reason that never seems to make Julie feel any better.

Now it's my turn to get told the way things are. But unlike Julie, who will lovingly season the truth to make me feel better about myself, the person I need to ask this question of is God, and He always tells me straight.

At least for now, I'm feeling strong enough to hear the answer, so I go into our family room to spend some one-on-one time with God. As I go, I remember the book Scott Hitchcock had given me called *God Guides* where the author talks about listening prayer. So I resolve to do less talking and more listening than I usually do. Scary as it is, I really do want to hear God's answer.

With knees and elbows on the floor, head in my hands, I ask as humbly as I know how, "Lord, what words do You have for me today?" And I wait. Facedown on the floor, I'm trying my best to keep my mind clear of distractions so as not to miss His response.

And I wait.

And I wait.

Then He says, "I will take care of you."

And I wait.

And I wait.

"Trust in Me," he says.

Encouraged by His responses, I muster the courage to ask Him the one question I have feared asking.

"Where will You heal me, Father, here or in heaven?"

Immediately His answer comes, and in a strong and clear voice. "It's here, Dan. It's here."

Faith and Obedience

It's Friday afternoon, and I'm sitting at my desk looking over my business calendar when Julie walks into the room.

"I spoke with Lakeside a few minutes ago. Since we won't have time to get back there to have the PET scan results read to us before we leave on Monday, they have agreed to email the results to us as soon as they get them so we'll have them to show the doctors at Riverview on Tuesday."

We are going to Texas for a consultation at Riverview and decided we would go a day earlier to visit King Institute in Carrollton, Texas.

"It's already four o'clock, so I expect they'll be sending them soon. Sound good?"

"That works for me," I tell her, trying to appear not to be in a hurry. The truth is, I'm wound up tighter than a Penn Senator fishing reel with a hundred-pound tarpon on the hook. I desperately want to know if this TKM stuff and vegan diet have had an impact.

I nonchalantly go back to work, acting like I've got some things to wrap up before the close of the business day. And I start hitting the Send/Receive tab on my Outlook about every fifteen seconds.

At 4:17 p.m. I get an email from Lakeside.

My heart races, and my body tenses up.

Every time I get new scan results it feels like I'm playing Russian roulette. I see myself taking a nickel-plated revolver in my hand and loading one bullet in the chamber. I spin the cylinder and lift the gun to my head.

As I prepare to pull the trigger, I'm wondering if this is the day my luck runs out.

I gather myself for a moment and take a deep breath. Then I open the email to see if there's a bullet in the chamber or not.

Woohoo! No bullet! The report says that the right-side adrenal tumor is dead and the left-side adrenal tumor is shrinking significantly! One down, one to go! Woohoo! Thank You, Jesus!

As I sit at my desk and think about how long the odds were that the PET scan would reveal anything good happening, I can only draw one conclusion. God responds positively when I follow His instructions in faith. It occurs to me that faith and obedience are what this entire journey is all about. It's never been about cancer.

So here's what we know:

- I've had no chemo treatments going on in my body for eight weeks. In the eyes of traditional medicine, this is not good. Tumors should be growing and multiplying in this time.

- Julie and I did TKM treatments for eight weeks and maintained a vegan diet during this time.

- Tumors either died or shrunk significantly.

Note to self: The next time God tells you to do something, no matter how ridiculous it sounds, do it immediately and without question.

"Hey, Julie!" I call out.

Julie answers from the kitchen, "Yes, darlin'."

"Can you come in here for a minute? I've got something special I want to show you!" which usually means, "I cordially invite you to come and get naked with me in bed."

"Really? It's almost dinnertime and I'm trying a new vegan recipe for you. Can I get a rain check until after dinner?"

"No," I reply, playing along. "You really need to come and see this right now. I'm in my office."

"You're in your office? Wow, that's a new twist. Interesting!" she says.

"Yeah, I'm a rebel that way!"

Julie rounds the corner from the kitchen and comes down the hall to my office. "Whatcha got going on in here, darlin'?" she says in her flirtiest voice.

I give her a devilish grin. "I've got scan results going on here, baby!"

"Oh, honey," she says. "Show me! Show me!"

Festus

The following Monday Julie and I are sitting in a treatment room at King Institute, waiting for Dr. Glenn T. King. After a few minutes, Dr. King steps into the room with a male assistant in tow.

"Good afternoon," he says. "I'm Dr. Glenn King, and this is Dr. Andrew. He will be assisting me today."

"Hi," Julie says. "It's very nice to meet you both. We're headed to Riverview tomorrow, and we're so glad your schedule allowed for us to come over and meet you in person while we're out here in Texas."

"That worked out well then," he says. Shifting his attention to me, Dr. King asks, "So, how are you doing?"

"I am great!" I reply with a big smile.

"That's good to hear. Tell me about it," he says.

Julie pipes up and gives him a quick summary of how things have been going since we began TKM treatments.

I chime in, "The tumor on my right adrenal is now dead, and the one on my left adrenal has shrunk by 50 percent."

"I wonder why the left side tumor didn't die as well. It's as if there's some sort of blockage on that side that's keeping your body energy from moving freely on your left side. Do you have an artificial knee or hip?"

"No," Julie answers, "but he does have a titanium rod that goes all the way down his left femur. Early on in Dan's treatment, Lakeside put it in to reinforce the bone because he had a lesion in the neck of his femur. The rod's been in there for almost two years now."

"Well, that explains that," he says. "Clearly the rod is an obstruction to your body's ability to heal itself. Notice that the rod is on your left side and so is the adrenal tumor that is still alive. The rod is damming up your energy flow. Can it be removed?"

"Is that even possible?" Julie asks.

"It does happen," he answers. "But, no worries, God can work around that too."

Dr. King continues. "Cancer is almost always a result of holding on to sadness and grief. That being the case, the central truth in the healing process is that you have to let go and let God. So, Dan, have you let go of your sadness and grief and given it to God?"

His question catches me off guard. Sadness and grief. Really? That's a new one. Nonetheless, his question prompts me to seriously ponder it for a moment.

"Well, yes, I believe I've let go of my sadness and grief and given them to God. That said, I think the hardest things to give to God are those things I think I have control over, and I am constantly trying to claw back the controls from Him. The thing is, what I'm beginning to realize is that I never had control of anything in the first place."

"Now that's an honest answer," he says.

While we've been talking, Dr. Andrew has been working on my left side. After an hour or so, Dr. Andrew finishes the sequences Dr. King had told him to do on me.

"I think that should do it," he says. "So you're headed to Houston from here, right?"

"Yep," Julie says. "I can't wait to see the look on the doctors faces at Riverview when they see these awesome scan results!"

"Well," he says, "it was a pleasure to meet you both. I'm sure Jim Robertson will keep me informed on your progress. In the meantime, God bless you and heal you."

"Thanks so much, Dr. King," Julie says.

"Yes, thanks a lot," I add as Dr. King and Dr. Andrew leave the room.

Now it's just Julie and me in the room. "Wow, that was interesting, huh?" Julie says.

"Very," I tell her.

"Maybe one day you'll get that rod out," she says. "With God, anything is possible, right?"

"Darn right!" I reply.

At 8:05 p.m. that night, our flight arrives in Houston. As we walk through the terminal toward baggage claim, I notice Julie is looking at me weird.

"What?" I ask.

"Do you know you're limping?" she says.

"No, but now that you mention it, my left leg is a little sore where the rod in my femur is."

"We have done a lot of walking today," Julie says. "Don't push it, okay?"

"I'll be fine."

By the time we reach baggage claim, my leg is doing noticeably poorer.

"Honey, your limp is getting worse. Do you want to sit down for a minute?"

"No, I'm fine."

In a few minutes our luggage comes around to us on the baggage claim belt. We gather our things and start out for the Hertz rental car counter. As we walk, my leg gets worse with every step I take. Finally we arrive at the Hertz counter.

"Dan, you're limping like Festus from *Gunsmoke*. Are you sure you don't want to sit for a minute?"

"No, I'm fine. Besides, we'll be sitting in our rental car in a few minutes."

"Do you want me to drive?" Julie asks.

"No, I'm good." (To me, letting Julie drive would be admitting defeat to whatever is going on with my leg, and I absolutely refuse to concede.)

Our hotel is just a few miles from the airport, about a ten-minute drive, and it sure feels good to sit for a while and get the weight off that leg. I'm sure the pain will subside by the time we get to our hotel.

Wrong!

As we bring our bags from the car to the hotel lobby, I'm having difficulty putting any weight at all on that leg. I've had some bad ankle sprains from my pole-vaulting days in high school, but this pain is sharper than that.

We check into our room at the front desk, and I'm happy to learn that our room is very close, just a few doors down the hall. By the time we reach the door of our room, I'm hopping on one leg. Putting any weight at all on my left leg gives me searing pain.

"Honey," Julie says, "do you want me to call a doctor for you?"

"No, thanks. Let me just hop over to the bed and get horizontal."

"How about some Advil?" she says as I dump myself onto the bed.

"No, thanks. Let me just lay here for a minute."

The next morning my leg feels perfectly fine when I wake up. But I wonder what's going to happen when I try to put weight on it.

No time like the present, I figure, so I sit up in bed and swing my legs over the side to stand up, gingerly.

Hmm. That's weird. No pain at all. In fact, my leg feels better than it has felt in quite some time. Ever since the rod was installed, I've felt a faint discomfort. Not today, though. I feel like I could go out and run four miles with no trouble.

Julie comes out of the bathroom to find me standing at the window, watching the sunrise.

"How's your leg this morning, darling?"

"Perfect."

"Really? That's amazing, seeing how much pain you were in last night."

"What the heck do you think that was?" I ask.

"I don't know," Julie says. "Maybe we should call Jim Robertson."

"Good idea," I reply.

"I'll call Jim right now," Julie says.

Julie proceeds to give Jim the blow by blow of how our meeting went with Dr. King and how my leg went downhill so quickly last night. Meanwhile, I'm walking around in circles in the hotel room, making sure my leg is still good. When she hangs up the phone I ask what he said.

"Jim says that when Dr. King and Dr. Andrew were working on your left side, the pent-up energy around the rod was evidently released. In other words, the dam broke, and that sudden release of energy manifested itself as pain in your leg. As you slept last night, the energy flow evened itself out and the pain subsided accordingly."

"Hmm," I reply, "I guess if you think about it from the perspective of energy flow, that makes sense."

"Yep," Julie says. "It makes perfect sense to me. And who knows? Now that the dam is broken, maybe the healing will speed up on your left side."

"Absolutely. That's our story and we're sticking to it!"

Who Are You?

It's Tuesday morning, and Julie and I are sitting in an exam room at Riverview Cancer Center in Houston, waiting to see one of their oncologists. After a few minutes, a young Indian woman in a white lab coat walks into the room. I'm guessing she's an intern or a physician's assistant.

"Good morning," she says. "I am Damini and I work with Dr. Lundstrom."

"Nice to meet you, Damini," Julie says.

"I'd like to ask you a few questions for our records, okay?"

"Sure thing," I reply.

She looks at my file for a moment and then looks up at me. Then back down at the file again. She seems a bit puzzled.

"Are you in any pain right now?" she asks.

"Nope."

"Any sudden loss of weight?"

"Nope."

"How is your energy level?"

"I'd say very good."

"How far could you walk right now?"

"Indefinitely."

She proceeds to ask a few more questions, makes a few notes on her clipboard, flips back through the many pages of my very thick file, then looks back up at me. "Can you verify your name and birthdate once again for me please?"

"Sure thing. Dan Floen," I answer and then recite my birthday.

Damini's forehead is furrowed as her eyes are laser focused on my file. "Okay, thanks so much. Dr. Lundstrom will be in to see you in just a few minutes."

"Thanks, Damini," Julie says with a smile.

About one minute later a young black man comes into the room. "Hi, I'm John, one of Dr. Lundstrom's PA's, and I just want to verify a few things with you, okay?"

"Sure thing," I reply.

John goes through the very same list of questions Damini asked me. "Thanks, Mr. Floen. Dr. Lundstrom will be right in."

About another minute passes, and in walks a middle-aged gentleman in a white lab coat. He's wearing a nice blue shirt, a gold tie, and a freshly shined pair of Johnston & Murphy dress shoes.

"Good morning," Julie says. "You must be Dr. Lundstrom."

"Actually, no," he says. "I'm Dr. Greg Davis, one of Dr. Lundstrom's colleagues, and I just wanted to come in and introduce myself."

"Well, it's very nice to meet you," Julie says as she stands to shake his hand.

"You've got quite a medical record here, Mr. Floen," he says.

"Yeah," I reply. "I guess you could say I've seen a thing or two."

"You certainly have," he says, flipping through the pages of my file. "Guys, I know you've been asked this already today, but would you mind confirming your full name and date of birth for me?"

I give him this information and then ask, "Is there a problem, Doc?"

"Well, to be perfectly honest," he says, "the medical history depicted in this file does not look at all like the man I see sitting before me right now. You look way too good. We're just trying to make sure we're talking to the right patient."

"Well," I reply, "that's very flattering of you to say. But, let me assure you, I'm Dan Floen, all right."

"Yes, you are, and I am so happy for you," he says. "Thanks for your patience with us this morning, and congratulations on your amazing progress. I promise Dr. Lundstrom will be the next person to walk through that door," he says as he smiles and leaves the room.

About thirty seconds later a very tall, distinguished man enters the room. "Hi, I'm John Lundstrom. It's a pleasure to meet you."

"Good to meet you too," Julie replies.

"I must apologize for the fifty questions this morning. It's just that you look nothing like the patient described in this file. I see from your most recent PET scan that things are certainly moving in the right direction, so that's great to see. Congratulations!"

"Thanks, Doc," I say.

"So, according to your file, you've had no chemo treatments or medication of any kind going on for almost three months now. Is that right?" he asks.

"Yep," I answer with a smile.

"Well, as long as things continue to move in the right direction, I'm not sure I'd recommend starting anything new. That said, we do have a very interesting new trial available right now called the TIL study. We take a piece of a tumor and grow cells in the lab to combat the cancer and then reinject the cancer fighting cells back into the tumor. The problem, if you can call it that, is that none of your remaining tumors are large enough to resect a workable sample from them."

"That sounds like a good thing to me," Julie says.

"Oh, it most definitely is. Just know that if the tumors do start growing again, the TIL study may be a viable treatment option for you. Until then, whatever you're doing is obviously working. Just keep doing it."

I stand up to look him in the eyes and give him a firm handshake. "Yes, sir!"

I Surrendered

It's been three months since we put our house up for sale, but we've had only two showings. Shirley, our real estate agent, says we've priced it right to sell, but so far we've received no offers. It's almost as if our home listing is being cloaked by God, like He doesn't want us to sell.

Meanwhile, we've burned through all our cash at PM2 and our credit is maxed out. So, given our financial situation, with no significant new business visible on the horizon, it's hard for me and Julie to imagine any outcome that doesn't require us to sell this house.

I had a dream last night about the financial mess we're in. In the dream I'm tandem skydiving with God. He's my instructor and I'm harnessed to

His chest. God is strapped to my back as we stand up together to make our way over to the door of the airplane.

God says, "Okay, Dan, on the count of three, we're going to jump out this door together. One . . . two . . . three . . . jump!" And out we go. Suddenly I've got a front-row seat as I stretch out my arms and legs, and I'm staring, wide-eyed, at the ground fast approaching below.

Fifteen seconds pass, and I'm beginning to wonder when God is going to pull the rip cord.

Another ten seconds pass, and I'm not wanting to appear concerned, but I glance back behind me, just to make sure He's paying attention to how close the ground is getting.

Another five seconds pass, and the ground is getting terribly close. Now I'm worried, so I tap God on His shoulder behind me and yell, "Lord, the ground is approaching! Don't You want to pull the rip cord now?"

I get no answer as we continue to plummet toward earth.

"Lord, what are You waiting for?! Don't You see we're going to die here?! Pull the rip cord!"

All I hear is the thunderous buffeting of the wind racing by my ears. Not a word from Him.

Then something strange happens. A feeling of peace and acceptance comes over me. All goes silent around me, and I begin to wonder, *If God never pulls the rip cord, will I be okay with that?* I process the question in silence as the ground continues to approach. And then I make my decision.

"I surrender," I tell Him in a low, calm voice. "I trust You, Father. No matter what happens, I'm going to do whatever You say and leave the outcome to You."

"Dan. Dan. Wake up, honey," Julie says, nudging me gently on my shoulder. "Are you okay? You were calling out in your sleep. Did you have a bad dream?"

"Yeah. I'm okay."

I usually don't remember my dreams, but I vividly remember this one, especially the decision I made and what I told God in my dream as we were plummeting to our death: "I surrender."

Awake and fully conscious now, I whisper to God, "Lord, I surrender."

Ever since that day back in '07 when I told my C12 brothers I had been given eight months to live and they immediately laid hands on me and thanked God for healing me, I've been trying to wrap my head around whether that was actually what God had done. On that day, for the first time, I began to consider the notion that maybe God had already delivered the antidote and it would just be a matter of time before the physical healing would manifest itself in my body. And lately there has been some great healing going on. Heck, even the lesions in both my femurs are shrinking, which the doctor said is nearly unheard of. He said that regeneration of bone is highly unusual, and even more rare in metastatic cancer cases.

Jesus said in Mark 11:24, "Therefore I tell you, whatever you ask in prayer, believe that you have received it, and it will be yours." Or, as my friend Isaac likes to put it, "Pray for things that are not as though they are."

So even though I am not fully healed yet from a strictly medical perspective, I am trying to maintain the belief that God has already healed me. Some days are harder to do that than others, but I guess that proves I'm human.

Toward the end of the business day, I sit down and start writing in my journal:

April 27, 2009

Father, I know from recent experiences that Your name is most glorified when all else has failed, when You are my only hope. Then You step in and do something amazing, just so I'm sure of who was responsible for it. I look forward to what You will do for your business and for Your people of PM2. Are we ready to receive Your blessing yet, Father? Are our people fallowed ground?

As I stare down the very real possibility that we will have to discontinue paying our mortgage soon, I know this is not what You have in mind about being good stewards with what we are given. We have promised to pay these bills. We've also promised to give 10 percent of our earnings to the church. But there are little or no earnings, and haven't been all year.

And yet You brought us here. You healed my body. You are the source of my hope and strength. So, knowing Your MO, and having seen what You've done so recently in my life, I can't wait to see what You have in store. Things are getting ugly financially, and I know that Your provision must be coming soon. It always does, just in time!

HOLD!

As I stare into the haze and smoke on the blood-soaked battlefield before me, I hear Your strong voice in my ear over the thundering hooves of the oncoming onslaught. "Hold! Hold!" You urge. "Remember how I delivered you from cancer and certain death? How I looked after your family and took care of PM2 while I tempered you in the fire? How I watched over you and protected you from countless perils since your first days on this earth. Why would now be any different? Dan,

trust Me. Have faith! Move on My command! Only on My word!"
And so, I hold. I hold!

I came across a quote by Alan Redpath that goes like this: "When God wants to do an impossible task, he takes an impossible man, and he crushes him."

I think I resemble that remark.

10

Farewell to the Floen Bayou

The next morning Julie meets me in the kitchen as I pour my first cup of coffee.

"You look like you've been up all night," she says.

"Yeah, well, I've got a few things on my mind," I reply.

"Like what?" she asks.

"Seriously?" I ask as I look at her in disbelief. "Jeez, Julie! If it's not about my health, it's about money. Look at us. We're not even out of the woods yet with this cancer thing, and now it looks like we're headed for financial ruin too. Is this really God's plan? I mean, we realized we were slaves to this house, so we offered it for sale to get out from under it, but it's not selling. Nothing seems to be enough for God."

"What about the boat?" Julie asks.

I snap back, "What about it?"

In a calm voice, Julie continues. "Well, darling, we hardly ever use it anymore. We can't afford to put gas in it, so it's been hanging back there on the lift for eighteen months now. Maybe the boat is the last impediment God needs to take away. Honey, we agreed months ago that we would no longer be defined by this house or by that boat, remember?"

"Yeah," I admit.

"I think it's time we put our actions where our mouths are," she says.

I don't respond. I know she's right. I really hate it when she's right. She's just standing there patiently, waiting for my response.

"Okay," I reply.

Later in the day I list the boat for sale on Craigslist. Man, that was hard. But if this is what's standing in the way of God blessing us, then let the boat sell quickly!

Three weeks later . . .

We got an offer a few days ago on the *Floen Bayou*, and this morning I'm delivering her to the buyer's hauler at the Courtney Campbell Causeway boat ramp. I will miss her; I can't lie. But I love God more than I love that boat, no doubt about that.

As I fire the engines and prepare to leave the dock, Julie is there to see me off. "You gonna be okay?"

"Yeah, I guess," I reply. "Just trying to do what God wants, ya know?"

"You're doing the right thing, Dan," she says.

"Well, I don't have to like it," I retort.

It's a cool and drizzly morning, befitting of my somber mood.

"Lord, I release the house to You. I release the boat to You. Take it, Father. I am letting go of it all."

I give!

A Fate Worse Than Death

Today Julie and I are meeting with Rick Denison. Rick's in our C12 group and he owns Family Life Resources, a credit counseling company. We shared our financial troubles in our group meeting last week, and Rick suggested we meet with him. Rick is such a godly man and so good at what he does. We're thinking he'll be able to help us get out of this mess.

"Are you ready?" Julie asks.

"Let's do this," I reply.

Hand in hand, Julie and I walk through the front entrance door of Family Life Resources.

The receptionist, Claire, leads us down a short hallway and invites us to take a seat in a small conference room.

"Rick will be right in."

We take a seat around a three-foot diameter circular table and I begin to survey the room. The room is unassuming, nothing fancy, like the rest of the offices: clean and comfortable. There's an acrylic sign hanging beside the door that has Family Life Resources' mission statement on it.

Committed to the Financial Well-Being of God's People

That's comforting because we see ourselves as God's people. I guess we're in the right place.

Then I notice a small framed saying on the wall just above the table we're sitting at. It says,

O God of second chances,
Here I am again.

That one hits close to home.

Just then Rick comes through the door. "Hey, guys! How are you doing?"

"Well, I guess we've been better or we wouldn't be here in your office today," I tell him with a smile.

"It's always a pleasure to see you, my friend." Rick gives me a big hug.

Rick sits down at the table with us. "Well, guys, let's see if we can figure out where we are. But first, let me pray for our meeting today."

Rick prays a wonderful prayer for us. It sets us at ease and makes us feel confident that we've come to the right place for help. Then he begins to interview us about past circumstances and how we wound up where we are financially. As we talk, he's taking notes and writing down some numbers.

"Guys, talk to me for a minute about what's important to you. I mean, as it relates to your current lifestyle, what are your priorities? Owning a house? Living on the water? Owning a boat? Private schooling for Laurel? Traveling?"

Julie starts first. "For me, keeping Laurel in her current school is our top priority, no matter what the cost. She's had a tremendous amount of turmoil in her life with Dan's illness, and the last thing she needs is to change schools in the middle of all that."

I nod in agreement.

Julie continues. "Dan and I have decided we're over the house. The stress of carrying that financial burden is killing Dan, quite literally. So we simply want out from under the house, which is why it's for sale."

"Same for the boat," I chime in, "which is why we sold it."

"That's right," Julie agrees. "We don't need to own a house on the water, or a boat, to be happy. The house and the boat don't identify us anymore."

"We simply want to be identified as followers of Jesus," I assert.

Julie looks at me and smiles in agreement.

Rick asks a few more interview questions and continues to write in his notebook. "So, just to confirm, neither of you have taken a salary from the company in a year, correct?"

"That's right," Julie answers.

"What about the house? Are you still paying the mortgage payments?"

"Yes, but we won't be able to for much longer, unless God blesses us significantly, and soon," I retort.

"We've been trying to sell the house for quite a while," Julie explains, "but we haven't received any serious offers yet."

He asks us several more clarifying questions, taking more notes as we respond. "Julie and Dan, would you say you're open to all options at this point?"

His question makes me nervous. How many options are there, and exactly how ugly is the worst one?

Reluctantly, I begin, "I suppose we're open to whatever God presents to us." Julie nods in agreement. "Why do you ask?"

Rick looks down at his notebook and pauses for a moment, like he's mustering the courage to say something unpleasant.

I'm thinking, *Dear Lord, how bad can it be?* Surely we're not in that bad of shape. Surely Rick has some strategy in mind that will help us out of this financial pickle.

"The reason I ask is that based on what you're telling me, and looking at the numbers, I really think your best option is to file for chapter 7 bankruptcy."

Julie and I just sit there, shocked.

My heart is racing, and deep anger begins to rage in my mind. Bankruptcy? "Seriously, God? Is this how the story goes? Is this the way You're going to glorify Yourself? Where is the miracle in bankruptcy? Bankruptcy sounds like a copout to me, a defeat, certainly not a victory! I mean, did You heal me from cancer just so we can go bankrupt? You could have let me die last year and then Julie and Laurel would have been well provided for from my life insurance policy. But no. Instead, we're going bankrupt! What the hell are You doing, God?"

"Bankruptcy," Julie murmurs. "I guess we didn't realize how dire our situation is."

I'm still pissed, so I'm not saying a word. My mom always said, "If you can't say anything nice, don't say anything at all."

"Guys, I know this is a shock, and you need to do whatever God leads you to do, but let me explain what this option would look like." He rotates his notebook on the table so we can read the numbers he's been writing. "Here's how the numbers work out." We both lean in to see what Rick has for us.

We arrive home around noon, and Julie heads into the kitchen to rustle up something for lunch. I need some time to process what we've just heard from Rick, so I go out to my favorite place: the swing on the end of our dock.

When we first moved into this house, it didn't take me long to buy a windsock and hoist it out on the dock above the swing. I used it for years as a telltale to show me how windy it was, and from which direction, but it also served as a flag of sorts. I was proud to see it flying. I guess it fed my ego to have it there, as though I had hoisted the flag after taking this fort, or something like that. I never consciously thought of the windsock this way until the reality set in that we would probably have to sell or lose the house because of our financial train wreck.

Windsocks wear out fairly quickly in the Florida sun, so it's never very long before I need to put a new one up on the pole. But now that selling or losing our house seems imminent, I don't feel like replacing the worn-out one. So I walk out to the dock and take down the half-inch conduit pole that it flies on.

No more windsock. No more flag.

No, Not My Friend!

Ever since receiving that death sentence two years ago, there's been an ever-growing network of people following my progress and the things God has been doing to heal me. It's humbling to think about how many people have been praying for us all along. No doubt, their prayers are the reason I'm still here.

As the crowd of witnesses has grown, more and more people are calling me, asking me and Julie to talk with their friend or loved one who has cancer. I'm guessing they want to hear our story because they see that God is healing me. I'm sure they're looking for any shred of hope and encouragement they can get.

It's Thursday night. I've been in Connecticut on business and I'm changing planes at LaGuardia Airport, headed for home. As I'm walking down the concourse toward gate C12 (go figure) to Tampa, my cell phone rings. It's my old buddy Marc.

Marc and I were both branch managers in Dallas before I moved to Atlanta and met Julie. We hit a lot of golf balls together and drank our share of beers back then. Since my diagnosis, he's been keeping tabs on me, checking in from time to time.

"Hey, Marc! How are you doing, man?"

"Well, Dan." I hear him take a deep breath and let it out. "Not so good."

"What's up?" I ask, walking briskly down the concourse.

"Dan, I am in the hospital and they are doing emergency surgery on me first thing in the morning to remove a ping-pong-size tumor in the back of my brain. It doesn't look good."

I stop in my tracks and all seems to go silent around me. "What happened?"

"It came on really quickly," he says. "This morning I had a really bad headache, so I took some Tylenol, but it didn't faze it at all. By noon, I was having trouble with my balance, and I figured it might be an inner ear thing, possibly associated with the headache. By dinnertime, I could barely navigate, so Paige decided to bring me to the emergency room to get checked out. By seven, they had done an MRI and found the tumor. The surgeon says it's in a dangerous place and it needs to come out immediately. He's preparing us for any number of outcomes, including death, but none of them sound good."

Still processing, I have no words to give him right now, so I just stay with him on the phone.

After a moment of silence, he says, "I believe God led me to a special

Bible verse tonight. Do you know what Joshua 1:9 says?"

"I don't remember, Marc. What does it say?"

"'This is my command,'" Marc reads with fervor. "'Have I not commanded you? Be strong and courageous. Do not be frightened, and do not be dismayed, for the Lord your God is with you wherever you go.'"

"Wow, that is powerful! Be strong and courageous. Amen to that!"

"That's right!" he says.

Then a thought occurs to me. Thus far, God has been using cancer as leverage to get me to make the changes He sees necessary in my life. Maybe the same is true for Marc. "Marc, may I offer you a perspective from a guy who has walked this road?"

"Please. By all means!" he replies.

"I believe this experience you're going through is not about cancer. This is about a journey God is bringing you on. From my vantage point, I can see that He must have big plans for you or He wouldn't be giving you this big assignment."

"A journey, huh?" Marc says. "That's a new one. I'm not sure what to do with that."

"I think you'll have to trust me on this," I tell him. "You'll see."

The following afternoon Marc calls me on my cell. "Dan, you're not gonna believe what happened this morning!" and he tells me all about it.

Early this morning Marc was in his hospital room, waiting for the surgical transporters to come and bring him into surgery. Marc's wife, Paige, and Paige's good friend from church, Laura, were there with him. Laura was praying aloud as they all held hands. As Laura prayed, Marc saw a vision of a large black chalkboard and an eraser wiping the chalkboard clean.

When Laura concluded the prayer, Marc told the ladies about the vision he just saw.

"Maybe it's God's way of telling you everything is going to be okay," Paige said.

"Yeah, that sounds good," Marc agreed. "Let's go with that! I think I'll head to the restroom before they show up to get me."

Marc got out of bed and walked to the restroom. He had been having trouble navigating since yesterday, but that didn't happen this time and he counted it as a happy coincidence, not giving it another thought.

Moments later the surgical transporters arrived to take Marc into surgery.

A few hours later Marc was in the recovery room, with Paige at his side. Marc was still groggy, but he felt okay, considering a surgeon had just carved around in the back of his skull.

"Marc, honey," Paige said. "Are you awake?"

As Marc slowly opened his eyes, Paige's blurry image came into view. *Well,* Marc thought, *that answers the first question. I didn't die. Praise Jesus!*

"Do you feel alert enough to talk yet?" Paige asked.

"Yeah," Marc replied, working hard to swallow after having a ventilation tube down his throat.

"Honey," Paige said. "I've got some amazing news for you."

"What is it?"

"They couldn't find the tumor!" she said, beaming with joy and excitement.

"What do you mean they couldn't find it?"

"I mean, when they opened your skull and went to where it should have been, all they found was the residue of where a tumor once was! God is so good, isn't He?"

"He sure is!" Marc replied.

Obviously that eraser Marc saw was more than just a figment of his imagination. It was real, and Marc knew it the moment he woke up and Paige told him the news.

The next time I see Marc in person is several months later. Marc lives in Tennessee and he travels a fair bit for his job, as I do. And just by chance (or is it?) I run into him in the Charlotte airport.

Marc's face is aglow, like Charlton Heston's in the movie *The Ten Commandments* as Moses comes down from the mountain after having spoken with God Himself. His eyes absolutely sparkle, and he has a joyful and happy countenance about him that I've never seen before. He talks differently.

He tells me that from that moment he found out God had healed him, Marc's outlook on life changed. A grenade had just exploded in very close proximity to him, and he'd been spared, with little more than a scratch. Believe me, Marc knew exactly whom to thank for that.

He now speaks of the things of God, right out in public. He's anxious to share with me what he's been doing at his church, how he's been pursuing the lost, and how God has told him to write a book entitled *What Did Jesus Say?* This is most definitely not my old beer drinking golf buddy. Marc says he sees himself as being on a "Journey for Jesus" and that he just wants to be more like Jesus. Marc has been changed completely from the inside out, and it shows in every fiber of his being.

Some students are faster learners than others. Marc got it the first time out. I, on the other hand, need lots of repetition.

The Gift

"Consider it a sheer gift, friends, when tests and challenges come at you from all sides. You know that under pressure, your faith-life is forced into the open and shows its true colors. So, don't try to get out of anything prematurely. Let it do its work, so you become mature and well-developed, not deficient in any way."
James 1:2–4 (THE MESSAGE)

I'm running and lifting weights five days a week these days, and I'm feeling stronger and healthier than I have in many years. I think the vegan diet is doing great things for me. People often tell me my color is better and my eyes are brighter and bluer than ever. Folks are starting to call me "Miracle Man." Sometimes I have doubts, so I think it's a little early to claim the victory, but it sure feels good to hear it, nonetheless. "Miracle Man" does have a nice ring to it.

Healthwise, things seem to be moving in the right direction. I just wish I could say the same for our financial situation.

I guess I'm not accepting this bankruptcy thing like a man who truly doesn't care which way God chooses to lead him. Every morning I wake up and the weight drops on my chest again as I realize this is not a dream, not a drill. This is very real. It's a familiar feeling because it's like the way I felt when I woke to experience the weight of my probable death. Only bankruptcy is heavier and harder than dealing with cancer. There's a stigma that comes with bankruptcy that doesn't exist with cancer. It's embarrassing, to say the least, and I'm sure people are talking about what financial failures we are. I fear that I will fear myself to death. If I die, all of Julie's financial problems are solved, but I really don't believe that's God's plan for us. I figure, where's the miracle in that?

Every morning my fervent prayer and desperate cry for help is that God would spare us from this tragedy. But no rescue comes.

A few days ago we took $10,000 from our IRA to live on as we prepare for bankruptcy. What's weird is that I never saw the money disappear from the account. I mean, it's as if God replaced it immediately using an uptick in the market to increase our account by exactly $10,000. What is God doing here?

After months of agony, today is our day to appear before the bankruptcy court downtown. It looks like God is going to allow us to walk down this dark alley.

I've been watching intently as God makes things happen at just the right time. I see that He is showing me just enough evidence of a brighter future so as not to crush my spirit. I see that He is holding His blessings until this thing today is done.

Julie and I are seated in an unadorned forty-by-forty room at the county courthouse. At the front of the room is a wooden desk with an empty high-back office chair behind it and two gray folding chairs in front of it. Roughly sixty more gray folding chairs fill the room, and they're arranged in six neatly spaced rows, with an aisle down the middle.

Today we're scheduled to meet with the county trustee to learn what our fate will be regarding our bankruptcy filing. As our attorney explained, the trustee receives a fee for examining our file, and they will also receive a percentage of any of our assets that are sold. So, naturally, the trustee is financially motivated to carefully scrutinize the debtor's property. Although they are supposed to treat debtors fairly, their financial interests are not always in line with that directive. For this reason, our attorney, Susan Baker, had advised us to dress very simply today, nothing fancy, and not to wear any expensive jewelry, other than wedding rings. As a part of the filing process, we were required to detail all our assets, valuables, and jewelry, so it's all in the file anyway. It's just not a good idea to wave it all in the trustee's face at your hearing, she says.

There are roughly forty other debtors scattered around the room in the chairs. Nobody seems very happy. Go figure. It appears we'll all be watching each other's hearings. Oh joy! You evidently sacrifice your privacy when you file for bankruptcy. Julie and I are seated about halfway back on the side nearest the door, so we figure we're close enough to hear what's going on and yet not appear too eager to be at the front of the class.

A few minutes pass, and then a red-headed woman in a blue pinstripe suit enters from the door at the front of the room carrying a stack of manila file folders and sits down at the desk. The deep lines on her face tell me she's been at this for a long time. I mean, it must be hard listening to sad tales of woe, day in and day out. It has to wear on a person.

We've been told this lady is the toughest trustee in the county, so we're bracing ourselves to see how she handles the other cases leading up to ours. Susan is seated at the front of the room with a handful of other attorneys. She approaches the trustee's desk and gives her a handshake and a friendly greeting, evidently trying to put the woman in a good mood.

The trustee is shuffling her papers and then opens the first manila file folder on her stack. "Mr. Randolph Jensen."

"Yeah, that's me," says a man sitting right behind us.

"Please approach the desk, Mr. Jensen."

"I'll be right there," he replies nonchalantly. He's been talking on his cell phone since we got here, which is explicitly forbidden in this room.

As he walks by us toward the trustee's desk, I quickly conclude that he was not prepped for this day as Susan prepared us. He's got a gold ring on every finger and gold chains dangling from his neck. He strolls by us and takes a seat in front of the trustee.

"Mr. Jensen, I reviewed your file in my quarters prior to this hearing, and I have some questions about the assets you have documented here."

"Okay," he says, fidgeting in his chair.

I sense that he's getting uncomfortable. Is he hiding something? The trustee senses something too, and she looks like she's getting ready to pounce.

"Mr. Jensen, why did you fail to mention that you actually own a house on 2534 Crawford Lane? Did you not realize that this is a matter of public record? Were you intentionally trying to hide this property from the county, sir?"

"Oh, no, ma'am! I just thought that—"

"Where is your attorney, Mr. Jensen?"

A tall, slick-looking man rises from the front row. "I'm Mr. Jensen's attorney, ma'am."

"What's your name, sir?"

I can feel the heat going up in the room.

"Gerald Long," the man replies.

"Mr. Long, was it not your job to inform Mr. Jensen of his obligations under the law here?"

"Yes, ma'am."

"Well, you didn't do that, did you!"

"Ma'am, I can explain," he replies.

"Save your breath, Counselor," she rumbles back.

By now, the trustee is visibly fuming. "Mr. Long, it seems your client has perjured himself on his filing, so you'll want to advise him of his options at this point. As for me, I'm done wasting my time on this file." She closes the manila file folder with fervent attitude.

I lean over and whisper to Julie, "That's just perfect! Now that she's all worked up, I'm sure our day will get even better from here."

The trustee opens the next manila file folder in her stack and reads the names of the next unlucky souls.

"Mr. and Mrs. Daniel and Julie Floen."

My heart sinks, and I feel that familiar heavy weight fall onto my chest. But then suddenly, I feel a sense of peace and calm come over me. It's hard to explain, but I can sense that people are praying for us right now. (I will find out later that back at Family Life Resources, Rick Denison and ten of his employees have been praying for us that morning.)

As I look at Julie, her eyes are calm and she appears relaxed as she puts her hand in mine. She senses the prayers too.

"It's going to be all right," she says, smiling at me.

As we walk toward the trustee's desk, Susan is approaching from our left, and she's staring at us with a concerned look on her face. As we take a seat in the chairs before the trustee, I see the anger in her eyes melting away. In a matter of seconds, her whole demeanor changes from anger and frustration to peace and calm, almost friendly.

"Good morning, Mr. and Mrs. Floen," she says warmly.

"Good morning," Julie replies with a smile.

"I think we can make this pretty quick and painless," she says. "I've reviewed your file and I see that you've completed your file completely and accurately. I really appreciate that. Do you have any questions for me at this time?"

"I don't think so, ma'am," Julie says as she turns to me for confirmation. I shake my head slightly. "Is there anything else you need from us?" Julie asks.

"No, I think everything is in order here. I don't have anything further. I will sign and stamp your file to show that your chapter 7 bankruptcy filing has been fully discharged with no other incumbrances. Ms. Baker," she says, looking at our attorney, "do you have anything else?"

"No, ma'am. Thank you," she replies.

"Okay then," the trustee says, "I think we're done here. Enjoy the rest of your day, and I wish you both the best of luck in the future."

"Thank you, ma'am," Julie says. "We hope you have a blessed day."

Back at home, the reality of what happened is starting to set in. There's a lot of downside. For starters, our credit score is now trashed, and we may never be able to buy another house, or at least not for many years. We'll have to move into a rental house, not on the water. With no boat, I'm going to have to fish from shore or a pier.

There is one big upside, though. We are free! Free from disease (or almost), free from debt, free to live and serve God and other people.

Here's what I've learned:

On the road of life, God sometimes allows you to come upon a pothole. Your faith is your shock absorber.

11

The Faith Promise

One weekend a year our church hosts a Global Mission Conference, where we invite twenty to thirty missionaries from all over the world to come and share what they are doing and invite us to join them in the mission field. The missionaries stay for the weekend and various church members open their homes to them. Then each missionary is assigned a booth at church in a kind of "mission fair" that goes from Saturday morning through Sunday at noon, with other events and activities mixed in.

It's Saturday night, and Julie, Laurel, and I have come to church to experience International Feast Night, where each missionary cooks a favorite dish from their native country and we all get to taste them. Laurel, now eleven, is a very finicky eater, so this should be interesting.

Julie and I take a seat at a table and Laurel takes off to explore the mission fair.

After thirty minutes or so, Laurel comes briskly walking into the room with a short black man in tow.

"Mom, Dad, I want to introduce someone to you," she says, grinning from ear to ear. "This is Mr. Yvan Pierre, and I'm going to Haiti with him!

Mr. Yvan, this is my mom, Julie Floen, and my dad, Dan Floen."

The man reaches out his hand to greet us. "It's a pleasure to meet you, Mr. and Mrs. Floen," he says in a heavy Haitian Creole accent. "Miss Laurel is a very special young lady, but I'm sure you already know that. She told me she had stopped by all the other missionaries' booths and asked if they would take her on a mission trip, but they all said she is too young. Then she came to my booth and she asked me if she is old enough to go to Haiti with me, and I said, 'If you are old enough to ask for it, you are old enough to go.' But, of course, she would have to ask her parents. So here we are," he says with a big grin.

"Well, Mr. Yvan, thanks for being willing to take her," Julie says. "I think I'll need some time to consider this. Won't you please join us for dinner so we can talk about it some more?"

"It would be my honor and privilege. Thank you!" he says, and he and Laurel sit down at our table.

Dinner arrives, and it is a Haitian specialty, rice and beans with chicken and goat, according to Mr. Yvan.

All Laurel hears is "goat" and her eyes get wide. She sits there staring at it and then tries picking around the goat without being too obvious. All the while Mr. Yvan is watching her out of the corner of his eye.

"Miss Laurel, may I tell you something?" he asks.

"Yes?" Laurel says with a worried expression on her face, like something is coming that she's not going to like.

"Miss Laurel, if you lived in Haiti with the children in my school, you would be most happy to get this large plate of food and you would finish every single bite, without hesitation. In fact, many children in my country eat pies made of mud to fill up their little stomachs so they don't feel hunger pangs."

"Really?" Laurel asks in amazement. She stops for a moment and looks down at her plate full of food. "Those poor children. That is so sad."

With newfound courage, Laurel makes sure that she finishes every bite on her plate.

The next morning it's Mission Sunday at church, and Julie and I are sitting in the pews among our friends from Sunday school. Laurel is at kids' church in the Lighthouse building across the parking lot.

After the sermon, our mission director, Marsha gets up to address the audience.

"Today," she says, "we're going to ask each of you to make a faith promise for the coming year to support these wonderful missionaries. A faith promise is different from the commitment you make each year on your giving pledge card. When you fill out an annual pledge card, you are generally saying that you will meet your pledge commitment from out of your regular and current income. A faith promise is much different. With a faith promise, you are saying, 'God, I don't have the money now, but I trust You to provide it. And if it is Your will to provide it, I promise that I will make good on my faith promise.' Some faith promises can be quite large. After all, it depends on what God is going to provide. So, let me ask you: What is the Lord telling you about what He will provide? Each of you should have a faith promise card in your bulletin today. I'd like you to take it out for me. Now, I'd like each of you to spend some time with God and ask Him what number He would have you put on this card. If God were to provide it, how much would you give to support our missionaries? I invite you each to take a few minutes, right now, and let's see what God reveals to you."

Julie looks at me. Her eyes are saying, "We can't do this, can we? We just declared bankruptcy, for goodness' sake."

"Well, how about we just ask Him?" I tell her as I tear off a corner from the bulletin and hand it to her. "We'll each ask individually and then write down the number He gives us on these scraps of paper. Sound like a plan?"

"Sounds good," Julie replies.

We each take a few minutes in silence to pray and listen for God's leading. Immediately a number comes to my mind, but I think, *That's crazy, Lord! You can't be serious! No way! We just went bankrupt, and now You want me to put this number down?*

I pray and wait for another minute or so, but the same number keeps coming to me. I write down my number on the scrap of paper, fold it in half, and wait for Julie.

A moment later Julie writes her number, folds it in half, and puts it on her lap.

"What did He tell you?" I ask her.

"You have to promise you won't freak out," she says. "I simply wrote down the number God told me. Do you promise not to get mad?"

"I promise." If she thinks her number is crazy, wait until she sees what I wrote down.

"Are you ready?" I ask.

"Yes. You're not going to get mad, right?" she says.

"I'm not going to get mad, sweetie. Let's exchange scraps of paper and we'll open them together, okay?"

"Okay," she says.

We exchange our papers, then open them at the same time.

"Oh my gosh," Julie whispers. "He gave us both the same number."

Julie's card says $50,000, just like mine. We both sit in silence for a moment, absorbing what is happening.

"This is our faith promise," Julie says. "Right, Dan? This must be the number, isn't it?"

"It must be," I reply.

It's just a faith promise, I reason. If God doesn't provide it, we don't have to give it. So I write $50,000 on the faith promise card and we stand up together and walk to the altar with the other folks who are putting their cards in the offering plate.

When we arrive home after church, Laurel seems in a big hurry to eat a quick lunch and get on to her next thing.

"Mom, can I ride my bike around the neighborhood for a while?"

We live in a small, gated community, so Julie feels safe letting Laurel ride by herself around the neighborhood.

"Sure, just don't go outside the gate, okay?" Julie says.

"Thanks, Mom. See you later." Laurel takes off on her bike.

About fifteen minutes pass by, and the house phone rings. It's Debbie, a neighbor who lives a few houses down the street. "Do you know what Laurel is doing?"

"Well," Julie says, "she's supposed to be riding her bike around the neighborhood, but your question makes me wonder if I might be mistaken."

"Oh, she's fine. I just didn't know if you were aware that she's going door to door collecting money for the children of Haiti. She's raising money for vegetable seeds, so the children won't have to eat mud pies anymore. I just thought you'd like to know. She's an awfully special girl, that Laurel."

"Yes, she sure is," Julie says, tears streaming down her face. "Thanks so much for telling me, Debbie."

T-Boned

It's a beautiful sunny Thursday morning. The birds are singing, and the October morning air is fresh and crisp (at least for Florida). Julie has just dropped Laurel off at school. Maggie, our orange-and-white Brittany spaniel, is sitting in the passenger seat with a big smile on her face, panting happily. Maggie loves riding in the car, and she always insists on coming along to take Laurel to school.

Driving down Carrollwood Boulevard, Julie is singing softly along with the JOY FM Christian radio. Still singing, she reaches over and starts kneading the scruff of Maggie's neck. Maggie really likes a good neck rub, and she starts licking Julie's forearm in appreciation.

Julie rolls up to the intersection and stops at the red light behind a rust-colored Jeep Wrangler. The light turns green and she follows the Jeep out into the intersection and looks left, just in time to— *WHAM!* And all goes black.

Julie wakes up in a haze. Looking around, she sees that her Toyota minivan is sitting catawampus in the middle of the intersection and the sliding door behind her seat is pushed way into the passenger compartment. Out her side window, a badly crumpled black pickup truck is sitting about fifteen feet away with a disheveled-looking female driver at the wheel, holding her cell phone.

Is she okay? Julie wonders. *Am I okay?* Julie's neck and back are really sore, but no broken bones as far as she can tell.

Julie fumbles for her cell phone and attempts to call 911, but still dazed, she's having trouble figuring out how to do this. Finally, her call goes through to 911.

As she waits for the emergency vehicles to arrive, a man approaches her vehicle. "Ma'am, I saw the whole thing," he says. "You were in the right. I need to get to work, but here's my business card. Give my phone number to the police and I'll be happy to tell them exactly what happened."

"Oh, thank you," Julie says, still not fully cognizant. "That's so nice of you. God bless you!"

Suddenly she remembers that Maggie was in the car with her. She painfully turns around to see Maggie getting up from where she was thrown to the floor on the passenger side. She too looks dazed.

A fire rescue ambulance arrives a few minutes later, with a sheriff's squad car close behind.

By now, the other driver has gotten out of her truck. She's clearly shaken and in high defense mode. "The light was green! The light was green!" she insists to anyone who will listen.

Julie knows better, but she chooses not to argue with her. Then Julie calls my dad, who lives nearby, and my dad calls me.

"Oh my God," the lady continues, "I'm going to lose my job. I need my truck to do my job. There's no way they'll let me keep my job with no vehicle, and my truck isn't insured. Oh my God. What am I going to do?"

I roll up to the scene about twenty minutes later, and Dad is already there. Julie is being interviewed by a sheriff's deputy.

"Are you okay, sweetheart?" I ask.

"I think so. But I'm worried about the lady who hit me. She's very agitated and frantic that she's going to lose her job. She doesn't have anyone here with her, and she looks so sad and lost. I think we need to help her. At the very least, we should give her a ride."

I look over at the lady and she is sobbing bitterly, head in her hands.

"You got it. We'll take her anywhere she wants to go."

One week after Julie got T-boned, her neck and back are still hurting her. If fact, the pain has gotten progressively worse, so Julie goes to see her chiropractor, John, for X-rays. Turns out she has two burst discs in her neck and other structural damage in her back. John recommends that she speak with an attorney who can help her negotiate with our insurance company to get this taken care of.

"Really?" she replies. "An attorney?"

"Trust me. You need an attorney," he says.

At 10:00 that night, Julie receives a call on her cell phone from an unknown caller.

Julie runs into the family room where I'm watching one of my favorite fishing shows. "It's Suzy, the lady from the car accident," she whispers, eyebrows raised.

I wonder what that's about, I think, then I go back to my fishing show.

About twenty minutes later, Julie comes bouncing back into the family room, almost levitating.

"You've got to hear this. This is such an amazing story! It turns out Suzy was more distressed than we knew over the accident. Her brother recently committed suicide. Her husband is on disability. She got laid off from her job and waited months to get the census job, and now she had no way to do it because it involves driving in her personal car.

"She had rejected God after her brother's death and had become a Wiccan. Suzy was suicidal the night of the accident. That evening she called her son, who is a youth pastor in Orlando, and he brought her to Christ that night!"

"Wow, that's amazing!" I reply.

"And her son baptized her over the weekend! Dan, she was literally choosing between life, which really wasn't working for her at the moment, and death. She chose eternal life! Isn't that awesome?"

Now crying, Julie continues. "She was allowed to keep her job and was given an even larger territory. Her mom gave her enough money to replace her truck. She was stunned by our offer to give her a ride after she slammed into me that day. She asked me for a church recommendation, and I told her about St. James because it's close to where she lives in North Tampa." (Our good friend, Steve, is the senior pastor at St. James UMC.)

"Okay, now God is just showing off!" I chuckle.

"You know what, Dan? This may sound crazy, but it occurs to me that the light may truly have looked green to Suzy because God wanted us to meet that day."

"Hmm. Maybe so."

Firsts

The past few months have been filled with several first-time experiences for Julie, Laurel, and me.

For the first time in I don't know how long . . .

We have zero debt. Throughout the pain of bankruptcy, I questioned God. In hindsight, I now realize He simply wanted me to be free. Free from disease. Free from debt. Free from my guilt and fears.

For the first time ever . . .

I prayed with a client at his place of business. I had spent several weeks working in a conference room alongside John, our client, so I got to know him pretty well. The pressures of his new role in the company seemed to be having a cumulative effect on him, until one day there was no more hiding it. The pain on his face was unmistakable. So, out of the blue, I felt a strong leading to ask him if he'd like to pray together. He agreed, and our friendship flourished from that day.

For the first time . . .

Dr. Blake called me "Miracle Man." This is a big deal. I mean, above all, Dr. Blake is a scientist, and a very good one at that. He deals in the physical realm, analyzing facts, causes, and effects, and he can always offer a very scientific explanation for everything that occurs with my prognosis. And, God love him, he's very quick to take the credit for any positive results that happen. So for him to call me "Miracle Man" is significant because he has not been able to explain my positive results any other way.

For the first time . . .

Julie, Laurel, and I went to Haiti on a mission trip. We saw firsthand what life is like in the poorest country in the northern hemisphere and were blessed and amazed at the joy we saw in their eyes, in spite of their meager existence. I never saw myself as a missionary, until now.

For the first time . . .

PM2 has record profits. I am not a believer in a prosperity gospel, but based on the way God has been developing and teaching me, I see an undeniable correlation between faithful obedience and God's provision and protection.

For the first time . . .

I prayed with a perfect stranger. I met Todd on an airplane, which is unusual in and of itself, because I never talk to anyone on airplanes, except to tell the flight attendant what kind of drink I want. But this time was different. Todd was clearly inebriated, which on any other day would have motivated me to avoid talking to him all the more. But as the two-hour flight continued, Todd began to share his gut-wrenching tale of woe with me. Todd had lost his children and his wife a year ago because of his drinking, and he had just lost his job that week. His eighty-seven-year-old mother had bought him a plane ticket to come and live with her in Tampa. As Todd told me his story, my heart broke for him. After two hours in flight, Todd's liver had just about worked through the alcohol and he was starting to sound better.

As the wheels touched down in Tampa, I heard that familiar small voice saying, "You need to pray with Todd." It took me a minute to make sure I had heard correctly, but I concluded that even if God had not told me directly to pray for Todd, it was still the right thing to do. So I gathered my courage and asked him. "Todd, I would like to pray with you right now. Would you be open to that?"

"You would really do that for me?" he said.

"Of course, Todd. It's my honor to do it. We all need help from the Lord once in a while. So let's ask Him for some help, okay?"

By now the plane had stopped at the gate and everybody was standing up to grab their bags, but not Todd and me. We stayed seated, arm in arm, praying to God for help, forgiveness, strength to persevere, and abundant provision.

We concluded our prayer with a big "amen" and Todd gave me a long hug.

"I think God put you in the seat next to me today," he said.

"Me too," I replied. "Here's my card. If you need anything as you're getting settled here in Tampa, don't hesitate to call me if I can help you in any way. And give me a call if you need someone to pray with sometime."

"Thank you, Dan. God bless you!" he says.

"God bless you too, Todd. He's going to take care of you, brother. Keep talking with Him."

"Oh, I will!" he replies.

I Remember

Fighting cancer is most definitely a team sport. The trouble is, in the heat of battle, with a continuous spray of bullets flying in your direction, the people closest to you are bound to get hit. It comes with the territory. So when Julie showed me this essay Laurel had written, my heart broke for my little girl.

From the start of this cancer journey, Julie and I promised Laurel that we would always tell her the whole truth and never keep secrets from her about my prognosis. We promised to share the good, the bad, and the ugly with her, no matter what. And we have always been sure to tell Laurel what God is telling us along the way.

No doubt, complete honesty and transparency has come with a cost. Laurel wears the battle scars to show it, but Julie and I wouldn't change a thing. As hard as it has been for the three of us at times, we're so thankful to have had Laurel walking right alongside us, every step of the way.

I remember. I [I remember] by: Laurel Flan
remember all the
shots he had. I remember staying
hear over night and hering him
not be able to fall asleep.
I ~~remr~~ remember when
I saw him in the hospital
bed. I remember all the times
I cryed. I remember how
I was only 9 when he foundout
the cancer had come back.
I remember how week and
pail he was. I remember my
mom having to leave me
to confert him. I remember
all my friends being nurves
to talk to me and acsedently
bringing up the subject. But
the one thing I will never
forget is the saying, "What dosint
kill you, makkes you stronger." I
remeber it all

For: Dana + Jule Flan

Laurel's right. What doesn't kill you makes you stronger, and we are all much stronger having walked this path together.

Landlubber

The house (the beautiful waterfront home we have enjoyed so much) was auctioned off a month ago. Two weeks ago we found an affordable rental house in Lutz, just north of Tampa. It is not on the water, or anywhere near it, and I fear I'll become a landlubber.

Dad bought me a fourteen-foot john boat after we sold the *Floen Bayou*, but I've intentionally not taken it out or been fishing in over a year. Expecting that we'd be leaving our waterfront home soon, I have been weaning myself off boating and fishing, so the letdown wouldn't be so hard when we had to leave.

Today is moving day.

As I stand in the kitchen of the rental house surveying our new surroundings, Julie comes in from the garage carrying a moving box.

"We're going to like it here, darling," she says with a smile, "don't you think?"

"Yeah, I guess this will be fine." In my head, I know God has freed us from insurmountable debt, and I should be happy right now, but in my heart, it feels like I'm losing a part of myself. I have long thought of myself as a fisherman, and a fisherman should live near the water.

Julie sees me struggling and comes over to stand toe to toe with me.

"Sweetheart, do you remember how we agreed that we would never again be defined by a house or a boat?"

"Yeah."

"Do you remember how God is healing you?"

"Yeah."

"Do you believe that God is for us and that He has guided us to this very place on this very day?"

"Yes, I do."

"Then I propose, starting today, that we think about our home in a new way. Let's pray that we have many opportunities in this house to share the story that God is weaving into our lives. Let's ask Him to free us, once and for all, from the notion that we would ever be defined by a house, or a boat, or any other worldly possession we might own."

Her words ring true to me, and she's smiling at me because she knows I think she's right.

"So, what do you say? Does that sound like a plan?" she asks.

"Yeah. That sounds like a plan."

As her words begin to sink in, the thought occurs that maybe God wants me to do a different kind of fishing. I remember there's a verse somewhere in the Bible where Jesus says, "Come and follow Me, and I will make you fishers of men." Maybe that's what I'm supposed to be doing.

Opening Remarks

It's Sunday morning, and Julie, Laurel, and I are walking down the hallway of the church, heading in for the 9 a.m. service. A lady I don't recognize is bounding toward me.

She introduces herself, then tells me all about how she's been following my journey and she just finished this amazing book called *The Last Lecture* and she wanted to tell me about it. "So many similarities," she says.

"What's the book about?" I ask.

"It's by Randy Pausch, a professor at Carnegie Mellon University, and he had pancreatic cancer. He passed away last year, but before he did, he gave a lecture at Carnegie Mellon, and that's what the book is based on. He shares so many encouraging words and life lessons. It's really powerful. And he's funny! I just know you'd like it. There's also a video of it on YouTube."

Back at home, I sit down at my desk and search for the video. I immediately notice it has over nineteen million views. *Wow! This is going to be good.* According to the video caption, Randy was only one year older than me, and he died on July 25, 2008. In my Google sidebar, I see that he'd even been on *Oprah.*

Right away I can see this is a high energy guy, and he's really smart. He looks healthy, just like me. Hard to believe he's got terminal cancer. He starts right off with what he's *not* going to talk about.

"We're not talking about cancer," he says.

That works for me. I'm tired of talking about that too.

"And we're not going to talk about things that are even more important than achieving your childhood dreams. We're not talking about my wife; we're not talking about my kids."

I'm okay with that too.

"And we're not going to talk about spirituality and religion," he says. "Although I will tell you that I have experienced a deathbed conversion. I just bought a Macintosh." The audience erupts in laughter.

He's an entertaining speaker and funny, no doubt. But as I watch, an uneasy, almost morose feeling comes over me. I mean, this man believes he's dying, and he doesn't want to talk about spirituality or religion? What does he think is going to happen when he dies, or does he care? I wonder where he stands with Jesus, but I can't help but wonder, how does a man who thinks he's facing certain death speak so flippantly about a deathbed conversion if he actually believes they happen?

He's such a gifted and smart man, and he's sharing such wonderful life lessons. Who knows? Maybe Randy Pausch knew Jesus intimately and he simply chose not to talk about it in his lecture. Maybe he finished the work the Lord had for him to do here on earth, and God brought him home. I prefer to think that.

Randy Pausch called his talk at Carnegie Mellon "The Last Lecture," and as it turned out, it truly was.

I guess if I were going to give a talk like that right now, I'd call it "Opening Remarks."

God's Money

We've been in the rental house for a few months now and we're pretty much settled in. The john boat is sitting on a trailer inside the garage, and it's been calling me to the water lately. I may ask Dad if he wants to take it out with me one of these days.

Meanwhile, I've been slipping up a lot on my vegan diet. I'm looking more and more like a carnivore. I don't do my KI treatments nearly as often either. That said, my CT scan results continue to come back moving in the right direction. All I can figure is that God is protecting me despite how I'm sliding off the straight and narrow path. I just hope God doesn't change His mind any time soon.

"Hi, honey. I'm home!" Julie says. "And I've got something to show you!"

She drops some grocery bags on the kitchen counter and turns across the living room toward my office. She's holding a white envelope and wearing a wide toothy grin as she practically skips toward me.

"Whatcha got there?" I ask.

"I think you should open this and see for yourself," she says, laying the envelope in front of me on my desk.

I open the envelope. It's a check for $64,000.

"The insurance settlement came in from my car accident," she says, giddy. "God is so amazing! I mean, we just came out of bankruptcy and now He has sent us a check for $64,000!"

Immediately my mind is racing with all the things we could do with this money. A new boat comes to mind. Maybe a new car. Maybe both!

"Now we can pay the $50,000 faith promise we made!" Julie declares, all excited. "Isn't that just so amazing?"

"Whoa, whoa!" I exclaim. "Slow down! We just came out of bankruptcy. Doesn't it seem a little irresponsible to give away $50,000?"

"Dan, I think you've got it backward. I think it would be irresponsible of us not to fulfill our faith promise. We made a promise and asked God to provide so we can fulfill our promise. God has kept His part of the bargain, so now we have to keep our promise. This money was never ours. It's God's."

Ugh! I know she's right. I just don't like it. Being married to Julie has taught me that when Julie receives crystal clarity from God, you gotta go with it and things will always turn out for the best.

"Okay. We'll keep our promise," I reply.

"We will never regret it, Dan," she says. "You know that, right?"

"Yeah, I do know that."

The following Monday night Julie brings a $50,000 check to the trustees meeting at church.

Play More

It's Labor Day, 2009, and our friends Scott and Tracy are throwing a party at their new house. Scott runs a commercial landscaping business. He's about my age, and I've always admired his love of life. He's always dreaming up new ways to have fun, or get hurt, and today is no different.

"Look, Dad!" Laurel screams as we turn into their driveway. "They've got a water slide!"

Scott has laid out a fifty-foot length of Visqueen black plastic sheeting that he uses for his landscape jobs, and it stretches from the middle of the yard all the way down to the pond in their backyard. And he's running a stream of water down the slide with a garden hose.

"Dad, you have to go on this with me! Seriously!" Laurel begs.

"Seriously?" I groan.

"Absolutely!" she says with a grin.

"Aw, shoot," I moan. "I didn't bring my swim trunks, Laurel," I say, hoping that excuse will suffice.

"No problem, Dad," she says. "I'm sure Scott will loan you a pair. So will you go with me? Please?"

As I formulate my response, it occurs to me that I used to be that adventurous guy, the guy who was always looking for new ways to have fun or get hurt. Where is that guy now? I seem to have lost him in the heat of battle. He's been fighting for his life, struggling for survival in business, and trying to hang on to what he's got.

It also occurs to me that God is healing me, the tumors are continuing to shrink, so it appears that He plans to leave me here for at least a little while longer. So what's my problem? You'd think I'd be jumping for joy all day long, but instead, I've been wallowing in stress and self-doubt.

Then I hear that still, small voice that says, "Dan, I am healing you. And yet you are missing out on the fullness of life I want for you."

His words hit me right in the gut, and a deep sense of guilt and loss comes over me. What the heck am I doing? This is insane! God is giving me extra innings here and I've been too busy worrying about losing to simply play and enjoy the game. I'm not doing that anymore!

I look in my rearview mirror at Laurel. She's still patiently waiting for my answer, sporting her best puppy dog eyes and expectant grin. "Do you have your bathing suit on, Laurel?"

"Yep!"

"Well, what are we waiting for?" I ask.

"Woohoo! Let's go, Dad!" Laurel shouts as she runs toward the house. "I'll ask Scott if he's got an extra swimsuit you can borrow!"

Before Julie and I reach the house, Laurel is back with a swimsuit for me. "Here you go, Dad. Put this on, and let's go!"

After I put on the swimsuit, Laurel grabs my hand and drags me outside to the waterslide. "Come on, Dad!" she says. "You first!"

This is a really long waterslide with not much of an incline, so I'll need a running start to slide all the way down to the pond. Go big or go home, I figure.

I back way up into the lawn and take off in a full sprint. As I approach the Visqueen slide, I dive headlong, hands outstretched in front of me, like I'm sliding in headfirst for home plate, and yell, "Cowabunga!"

As I come out of the pond, I look up to see Laurel's beaming face. "You're up next, sweetie!"

The next morning is a school day, and the three of us are getting ready.

As is typical, I'm the first one dressed, so I head into my office to see what devotions God has brought to my email in-box this morning.

As I begin to read, Laurel comes into my office. "Hey, Dad, would you do a braid in my hair for school please?"

"Where's Mom?"

"She's in the bathroom getting ready, but I want you to do it, Dad," she says, smiling at me.

"Laurel, what makes you think I can even make a braid?"

"It's easy, Dad. Here, I'll show you," she says and she starts to walk me through the steps. "Simple, huh?"

Suddenly it occurs to me. *Hey, stupid, your daughter is trying to spend quality time with you. Braid her hair!* Sometimes I'm pretty slow on the uptake.

I start braiding as Laurel tells me about her schedule for the day. It's fun spending this time with her, and I can't believe I don't do this more often.

"That sounds like a full day, sweetie. Have fun, and let me know how your day goes when you get home."

It strikes me that there have been many days Laurel has doubted whether she'd ever see me alive again when she gets home from school. The threat of my death has been constantly on her mind.

She gives me a big hug. "I love you! See you later!"

"I love you too, Laurel. Have a great day, and I'll see you later today. I promise."

Note to self: Play more. Live more.

12

Do What?!

For the past three years I've had no chemo treatments at all. Until recently, I have maintained the vegan diet and been doing TKM treatments religiously. And for three years the scan results have continued to show that things are moving in the right direction. It's Good Friday, April 6, 2012, and Julie and I are at Lakeside this morning, waiting to hear the latest MRI and CT scan results.

"You look pensive, darlin'," Julie says. "What's on your mind?"

"I guess I just wonder what these results are going to be. I mean, things are going exceedingly well. All the tumors have been shrinking for a long time, and God has really been blessing PM2. It's been so amazing to see what He's doing in our lives. But the truth is, I've been slacking off more and more in the last few months. I'm not as vegan as I used to be. I'm letting more and more animal protein into my diet. I'm not as disciplined on the TKM treatments either. And, well, I've been resting on my laurels at PM2. In general, I've not been as disciplined as I once was. I've been coasting. So I half expect to hear something not so good this morning."

"Oh, darling, don't borrow trouble," Julie says. "Whatever it is, we know that God has this well in hand, right?"

"Yeah, I just like to go into these things knowing I've done my part, that I've been disciplined and obedient. You know, Jesus said, 'Why do You call to me Lord, Lord, and not do what I say?' How long can we expect God to continue His blessing if I'm not doing what He told me to do?"

"It will be what it will be," she says calmly.

A few minutes pass and in walks Dr. Blake with a cordial "Good morning" and a handshake. He gets right to business. "Mr. Floen, the CT scan results show that several tumors are now growing, and we've detected a few new ones as well."

I'm not at all surprised. I figure I got what I paid for.

Just then I hear a clear voice emanating from the depths of my soul, and it drowns out whatever Dr. Blake is talking about right now. The voice says, "Dan, I want you to take out the rod in your left femur and get back to the things I brought you before."

Dr. Blake is still talking, but I can't hear him over the conversation going on in my head.

"Do what?" I silently exclaim. "You seriously want me to get the rod taken out? Doesn't that seem a little drastic, God? Dr. Blake would never allow it, would he? Starting today, I will double down on the vegan diet and TKM treatments, but I really don't know about getting the rod removed. Father, are You sure that is necessary?"

"Dan?" Julie says.

"Oh . . . yes," I reply, snapping back into the room. "I'm sorry. Where were we?"

"Mr. Floen, I have a new PD-1 inhibitor trial I'd like to start you on just as soon as we can. This is a controlled group trial, and I won't have a spot open for you for about six weeks. So let me get you some paperwork to sign so we can get you in the queue ASAP. I'll be right back."

"Sounds great," Julie says.

The door closes, leaving just me and Julie in the room.

I'm not nearly as sure about this new trial as Julie is. I mean, God has been healing me in His own way up to this point, and not with drugs. Why would I entrust my life now to a drug? On the other hand, I know my family will kill me if I refuse to do this trial. It's not available for six weeks anyway, so I've got time to decide whether I'm going through with it or not.

Julie sees my wheels spinning and asks, "What's wrong?"

I'm sure she's not going to like what I'm thinking about right now, but reluctantly I decide to share it with her.

"I'm not at all feeling led to go on this trial."

"Why on earth not?" she asks.

"I just don't think this is the way God is going to heal me."

A look of deep concern comes over Julie's face. "What makes you think that?"

"God spoke to me when Dr. Blake was in the room. He told me to get back to the vegan diet and TKM treatments and take out the rod."

"He told you to take out the rod?" she asks.

"Yes."

"Well, let's take it out then," Julie says. "But what does that have to do with the trial? Did He tell you not to do the trial?"

"No, but He didn't tell me to do it either. He gave me some pretty specific instructions on how He plans to heal me, and this trial was not part of them."

"Well," Julie says, "why don't you go ahead and sign the papers today so you can get in line for the trial? Then if you decide not to do it later, you can always cancel."

"Okay," I reply, knowing I have no intention of ever going on this trial.

Just then Dr. Blake returns to the room. "I'll have Jennifer bring in some papers for you to sign and we'll get you scheduled to start the trial as soon as it's ready."

"Okay," I reply. I reason with myself that simply signing the release doesn't mean I'm obligated to start the trial. I'll save that battle for later.

That Saturday morning I decide to record a video for our friends and family who are following this journey. The rental house has an upstairs room just above the family room where I keep my weight set and treadmill. There's even a pool table up there that our landlord left. I call this the "meeting room" because this is where I go every morning to meet with the Lord. I figure the meeting room is an appropriate place to record what God is doing in our life. After I finish and send out the video (which you can watch on my website: danfloen.com), I spend time with God and come up with a plan.

I've decided to double my run to four miles a day, effective immediately. Julie and I are also doubling down on the vegan diet and TKM treatments. This plan starts today. I'm still not sure about taking out the rod in my leg. It's poking me inside the bone at my knee joint, but I'm trying not to focus on that.

In the shower after my run, I notice a new lump just under the skin in my right front pelvic area. I guess God is leaving me a visible reminder of this test.

That night I head upstairs to have a little talk with God. I lie there, facedown, for a long time, trying to remove all distractions from my mind.

When I think my mind is clear and ready to listen, I pause and take a few deep breaths. Then I ask the question.

"Lord, You have brought me so much and You have healed me, freed me, and provided for us so amazingly. But now this. If I may ask, what are Your intentions here?"

I wait . . . and I listen . . . and I listen . . . and I listen.

"To heal you and glorify Me," He says.

Getting Dunked

My friend Marc (the miracle brain tumor survivor) called me a few weeks ago. "Dan," he said, "I feel God leading me to get rebaptized as a public reaffirmation of my faith and my journey with Jesus, and I want to know if you'll do it with me."

"That sounds like a great idea, Marc!" I exclaimed. "In fact, I think you should fly to Tampa and we can both get dunked in the Gulf of Mexico. What do you say?"

"Outstanding!" Marc howled. "If you'll coordinate a time and place to do it with your pastor, I'll book our flights."

"You got it, brother," I replied. "I'll let you know when we're all set. See you then!"

It's 6 p.m. on May 29, 2012: reaffirmation day. A group has gathered on the beach at Honeymoon Island State Park, which faces the Gulf of Mexico. Marc and his wife, Paige, are here with their three boys, Carson, Hudson, and Evan. Julie and Laurel and Mom and Dad are also with us along with about twenty of our friends from church. These dear people have walked alongside us every step of this journey. True prayer warriors. True friends.

A tropical storm has brought heavy rain all day, but the sun just broke through as we were pulling into the parking lot. (Marc calls those "God-incidences.") Even though the rain stopped, there is still a twenty-knot sea breeze blowing in from the Gulf that is producing a formidable surf.

Marc and I and the boys are wearing board shorts and T-shirts. Hey, it's the beach. What else would we be wearing? Pastor Chuck and his associate pastor, John, are dressed the same. (Pastor Dave retired recently.) We all came prepared to get wet.

Between the howling wind and the waves breaking on the shore, this is a noisy place. Undaunted, Pastor Chuck begins to speak in a loud, clear voice to our group gathered here. He starts off with some words to put this reaffirmation ceremony in biblical context. Then he wraps up with a reading from 1 Samuel 7:12: "Then Samuel took a stone and set it up between Mizpah and Shen and called its name Ebenezer, for he said, 'Till now the Lord has helped us.'"

Chuck continues. "So there's not going to be a monument left here, but the second pavilion"—pointing to the nearest beach pavilion—"will always be a monument of what God is going to do, and that He's been with us thus far, and He's not going to quit now."

Marc and I take position on the beach in front of the gathering with the wind and the surf to our backs as we prepare to speak.

I lead off. "One of the reasons I'm here tonight is because I'm thankful for what Jesus has done for me. He's protected me. He's healed me. He's guided me. And I feel like I've let Him down on more than one occasion. So today I'm here to draw a line in the sand. This is the line," I say as I drag my right toes to make a four-foot line in the sand.

"This line represents where Jesus has brought me in my life, today, right until now; the way He's taken care of me up until now. And I'm here to commit to you all, today, my brothers and sisters in Jesus, because we're responsible for each other, I commit to you that I'm going to stick close to Jesus. You know, it's funny how we only get really close to God when we're in crisis, and I don't ever want to leave His side, crisis or not. And I'm asking for your commitment to hold me accountable to that."

After looking at the crowd standing around me I continue. "So, that's what I'm here to do today. To promise that I'll just walk with the Lord, closer than ever, and stay there by Him; not wait for the next crisis, but just stay there by Him. And this too, that every opportunity I have to be bold and testify, that when God gives me an opportunity, I take it without any reservation. I don't ever have to apologize for my friend, Jesus Christ. He saved my life, and He's going to do it again. So thanks for being here tonight."

Marc turns to me with a look of deep solidarity and gives me a fist bump. He recognizes the significance of this ceremony, not only for him, but also for everyone here tonight.

After he speaks about his journey and the miracles God has done in his life, the crowd applauds. I give Marc a fist bump and a hug. Then Pastor Chuck turns to me and says, "Are you ready to do this?"

"I was born ready!" I reply.

So we turn toward the Gulf, and Chuck, John, Marc, and I wade out into the surf. As we make our way out, the sun lowering in the sky paints a spectacular amber tapestry casting brilliant rays of light from behind the clouds down to the water. Just for a moment, all goes silent, and I can no longer hear the wind and the waves. In this moment, I hear God say to me, "Dan, the storm has passed and today marks a new beginning." As His words sink in, I breathe deep and resolve to hold fast to the commitment I'm making today for the rest of my life.

We stop in about waist-deep water and turn to put the waves to our back. Each wave is trying to push us back to shore, and we lean into each one to avoid falling forward. It all just adds to the moment.

As I stand between Chuck and John, they both put one hand on each of my shoulders.

"Dan," Chuck says, "do you confess Jesus as your Savior?"

"Yes, I do."

"Do you put your whole trust in Jesus' grace and promise to serve Him as your Lord?"

"Yes, I do."

As they prepare to lower me back into the water, Chuck and John each put one hand on my shoulder blades and the other on my chest.

"Dan," Chucks says, "I baptize you in the name of the Father, and of the Son, and of the Holy Spirit."

With that, Chuck tells me to pinch my nose, and he and John lower me backward into the surf. My head goes under for a second or two; then they raise me up to a standing position.

"Praise Jesus!" Chuck exclaims.

"Amen!" I reply.

Marc wades over and gives me a high five and a big hug. "I love you, brother," he says.

"I love you too, Marc. You're up next, my brother!"

"Yes, sir!" he says as he wades over to get into position between Chuck and John.

Chuck asks him the same questions, and Marc answers with a huge smile. Then they dunk him in the Gulf. Marc emerges from the surf with his face beaming, like he just saw Jesus.

"Way to go, Marc!" I tell him. "It all starts from here!"

As I look toward the shore, I see that Paige and their sons and Julie and Laurel have waded out to join us.

"We'd like to be baptized too, if that's all right," Paige says.

"Outstanding!" Marc howls. "Chuck, do you and John mind dunking a few more?"

"Of course not!" Chuck replies. "The more, the merrier!"

Paige goes first. They dunk her in the water, and she comes up all smiles. Julie is next as she bounds toward Chuck and John, arms up in celebration.

The boys are next, and John invites Marc to stand in for him so Marc can baptize his sons with Chuck. Marc doesn't hesitate.

Laurel is next, and Marc motions for me to take his place so I can help to dunk my daughter. I jump at the chance. Then Laurel takes position between me and Chuck, and Chuck asks her the questions to confirm her faith.

Laurel answers, "Yes, I do."

Chuck nods at me, signaling that I should say the words as we baptize Laurel. I'm caught off guard. I didn't expect that. I assumed only pastors can baptize people. But I figure if Chuck is okay with it, then so am I.

So, with my right hand on her shoulder blade and my left hand holding hers, I take a deep breath and say, "Laurel, I baptize you in the name of the Father, and of the Son, and of the Holy Spirit."

As Chuck and I lower her into the water, the tears start to flow. I feel so privileged to be asked to do this for Laurel. Luckily, we're all soaked from head to toe, so Laurel can't tell I'm crying as my tears blend with the sea water on my face.

Laurel gives me a big hug and says, "I love you, Dad."

"I love you too, Laurel."

Several other friends are baptized with us and it strengthens my resolve to stick to the commitment I made in front of them on the beach. I will hold the line and never retreat!

(You can watch the video on my website: danfloen.com)

Best-Laid Plans

Six weeks have passed, and we're back at Lakeside today to get the results of the latest scans. I'm next in line to start the PD-1 trial, and they had to do a new set of scans on me to make sure I still qualify. For the past six weeks we've been doing TKM treatments religiously and I am back on track with the vegan diet. I'm hoping for good results. I mean, I've done what God told me to do (except take out the rod), but I figure two out of three ain't bad.

I've not heard a peep from God on whether to do this new trial or not since that day in the doctor's office six weeks ago. Today is the day I'm supposed to start, and I am not at all comfortable with it yet. So I just keep going through the motions, letting everyone think I'm starting the trial today. I'm still waiting for a word, any word from God on this, but none are coming.

"This is very interesting," Dr. Blake says as he looks at my chart. "Mr. Floen, what we're seeing is a mixed response, but what makes this so interesting is that you've had no medication in your system for the past six weeks, so I can only surmise that we are seeing residual effects from one of the previous treatments, which is highly unusual, but not unheard of. At any rate, the scans show that the tumors on your right adrenal, right lung, and right pelvic area are all shrinking. However, the large tumor on your left adrenal is still growing."

Just then it occurs to me that the rod is on my left side, and I wonder what the scan results would have been if the rod wasn't there.

"So based on these results, it's a good thing we're starting the trial today. We want to get ahead of this as soon as possible."

"Absolutely," Julie chimes in.

"They are waiting for you downstairs. Let's get going on this."

"Okay," I reply as we gather our things to make our way down to the infusion center.

I still have heard nothing from God on whether to do this trial or not. I mean, why should I? All but one tumor is shrinking with no medication at all, and the one that's still growing is right above the rod in my left femur, but if the rod were gone, would that tumor be shrinking too? By doing this trial, am I not willfully going against God's explicit instructions? By starting this trial, am I not saying that I don't trust God's plan to heal me? This whole thing feels like I'm hedging my bet. Where's the faith in this? How can God honor this?

As we walk toward the infusion center, every fiber of my being is railing against starting this trial. Julie can see it on my face.

"Julie, I can't do this. God gave me explicit instructions, and this trial was nowhere in them. If I do this, I'll be going against God's plan to heal me, and I simply won't do that."

"Has God specifically told you not to do this trial?" she asks, concerned.

"No. I've been asking and asking, but He's been silent on that question."

"Darlin', I'd suggest you take as much time as you need right now, just you and God, to talk this over and get some guidance from Him. The infusion center can wait for you. Will you pray with me?" Julie asks.

We embrace, and Julie begins, "Oh, Lord God, You have brought us so far, and we are trying to follow Your instructions to the letter. But today, Lord, Dan is struggling with the decision to go on this trial. Father, please speak clearly to him so that he can have peace about whatever path You have for him. In Jesus' name I pray. Amen."

"Amen," I answer.

"Why don't you find a quiet place for the two of you to talk?" she says. "I'll be right here. Take all the time you need."

The weight of this decision has me way too amped up to sit still, so I decide to take a walk.

As I wander down the halls, my mind blocks out all other inputs and all goes quiet. I'm asking, "How can I do this, Father? How does this honor You? How does this demonstrate faith and obedience? Please, Lord, tell me what I should do."

And I listen. And I walk. And I listen. And walk. And listen.

By now I've wandered the entire third floor of the hospital. Still nothing. Then, as I turn the corner to head back toward the infusion center, God breaks the silence.

"Dan, no decision of yours will ever negate My healing power."

I stop in my tracks and stand for a moment in the hallway as I try to take in what He just said. As it begins to sink in, I suddenly realize how utterly insignificant my decisions are to God's plan. He told me He is going to heal me, and that's the end of it. He wants to grow my faith and obedience, for sure, but His grace doesn't allow for His promises to be negated when I fail. So I can do the trial, or not, but God is going to heal me either way.

That's a load off my mind!

I walk back to the room where Julie has been patiently waiting. "Let's do this," I declare. And we walk hand in hand into the infusion center.

Even though God released me from the responsibility of this decision, I'm still not happy about it. It feels like a cowardly thing to do, but if I don't do this, my family will kill me. So onward we go.

I always bring my laptop with me to the hospital so I can take care of any business need that may come up. But today I'm using it to search the internet for orthopedic surgeons. I'm guessing it's going to be next to impossible to convince Dr. Lee to take out the rod so I'm looking for alternatives. I figure our health insurance won't cover it, so we need to find someone who will take it out on the cheap. After a few minutes, I narrow it down to a few preliminary candidates: one surgeon in Canada and two in Mexico. I dial the office line for the one in Canada, figuring they'll be most likely to speak English.

I explain what I need done and that we'll be paying for the surgery ourselves. They come back with a price tag in the range of $10,000. Suddenly I have a heightened motivation to figure out how to get the rod out and have our health insurance cover it.

Today is my next appointment with Dr. Blake, and after much trepidation, I've decided to talk with him about getting the rod removed.

Two quick raps on the door announce Dr. Blake's arrival. "Well, Mr. Floen. Once again we have some very interesting results here. The three tumors we're watching in your right lung, your right pelvis, and right adrenal are all continuing to shrink. However, the tumor on your left adrenal is now 50 percent bigger than just six weeks ago. Very interesting indeed. I suggest we keep doing what we're doing, and we'll hope the left adrenal mass decides to follow suit with the rest of them by your next set of scans. Sound like a plan?"

"Yes," I reply, "but I want to ask you something."

"Sure. What is it?" he asks.

I pause for a moment as I gather the gumption to ask the question. "Well, Dr. Blake, what if I told you I wanted to get the rod in my left femur removed?"

"Why would you want to do that? It's certainly not hurting anything, so what medical reason would there be for taking it out?"

At this point he already thinks I'm crazy, so I figure I might as well remove all doubt.

"I believe the rod is impeding my body's ability to heal itself."

His forehead is furrowed and he's rubbing his chin, clearly vexed. "Mr. Floen, the rod has absolutely no bearing on whether the trial is working or not."

"Dr. Blake," I reply, "as crazy as it may sound, I believe the rod does have bearing on my healing, but it goes way beyond what the PD-1 is or isn't doing."

He sighs and pauses for a moment. I expect he's seeing the futility of reasoning with a nut job. "Well, I'm not the surgeon who put the rod in there," he says. "If you can talk Dr. Lee into taking it out for you, be my guest."

"Thanks," I reply.

The truth is, I was not asking for permission. This rod is coming out one way or another. It will just be more convenient if Dr. Lee does it.

As soon as we leave the exam room, I'm on the phone to Dr. Lee's office, scheduling a consultation to pitch the idea to him of removing the rod. I set an appointment for a week from today. Julie and I have one week to perfect our argument on why we need him to take out the rod. We think of a list of things we're going to tell him, some true, some not so true. The rod hurts me when I run: true. Because the rod hurts me, I don't run as far or as often as I want to: not true. The rod keeps me awake at night: usually not true. My body is telling me something foreign is in there and it is affecting my attitude toward healing: true.

Julie's got a bunch more. Truthfully, we're prepared to stretch the truth to get it done. After all, God told me to do this, so I feel justified in whatever means we choose to achieve the desired outcome.

A week later we're in Dr. Lee's exam room waiting for him to come and speak with us.

"Julie, would you pray for us please?" I ask.

"Absolutely," she says.

"Dear Lord, You told Dan that You want this rod out, so we're asking for You to soften Dr. Lee's heart toward this idea and make him open to our reasoning for wanting this done. We love You, Lord. Amen."

"Amen," I reply.

A few minutes pass and Dr. Lee enters the room and asks how my leg is doing.

"Well, that's what we're here to talk with you about," I tell him.

"Okay," he says. "Tell me about it."

Suddenly I feel a very clear leading to simply tell him the truth, as near as I can. In that moment our long list of well-prepared arguments flies right out the window.

"Dr. Lee, I believe the rod is impeding my body's ability to heal itself," I tell him.

There, I said it. Sounds crazy, I know, but there it is.

"Let's take it out then," he says.

Huh? Did I hear that right?

"That would be awesome," Julie replies. "When can we get it scheduled?"

"I expect we can get this done in a week or two," he says. "I'll have you stop at the desk on your way out and they'll get you scheduled, okay?"

"That sounds great, Dr. Lee," Julie says. "Thanks so much for your help!"

We stop at the desk on our way out and schedule the surgery for August 22.

"Wow, that was way too easy!" Julie says. "Isn't it amazing how God made that happen for us?"

"Amazing," I reply. "Why do we ever doubt?"

Hot Potato

It's August 22, rod removal day, and Julie and I are in pre-op as the nurses are getting me ready for Dr. Lee. I'm sitting up in the gurney wearing one of those wonderful open-in-the-back hospital gowns when Dr. Lee stops by to talk with us.

"Looks like they've got you all set," he says. "Dan, that rod has been in there for a little over three years, so the bone has had a lot of time to bond itself to the rod. In other words, it's going to come out a lot harder than it went in. It will probably take us several hours to get it out."

"Okay," I reply. "But before you go, would you mind praying with us?"

"Not at all," he says.

The three of us join hands and I begin to pray. "Heavenly Father, You told me to take out the rod, so I'm asking You now to make it easy for this guy. Amen."

"Amen to that," says Dr. Lee. "We'll see you in there!"

A couple minutes pass; then the OR nurse arrives to wheel me into surgery.

"I love you, darling," Julie says. "We'll see you in a few hours."

Back in the recovery room I feel rested and refreshed, albeit a bit groggy, like I've been asleep for days. No pain whatsoever.

"There he is," says Dr. Lee.

"Hey, Doc," I reply.

"Dan, amazingly, the rod came out in just fifteen minutes," he says. "It's as if your body expelled it like a hot potato."

"Wow," I say. "I guess God answered our prayer, huh?"

"It would definitely appear so," he says. "How are you feeling right now? What is your pain level?"

"I feel great, Doc. I have virtually no pain. I feel like I could walk out of here right now."

"Whoa, slow down, partner," he says. "Let's give you some time for the anesthesia to wear off completely and then we'll see how you're doing. In the meantime, keep this rubber bulb handy and squeeze it as often as you need it to control pain."

After twenty minutes or so, Julie comes in and I am fully awake and clear-headed, at least as far as I can tell. I haven't touched the rubber bulb, and I don't plan to.

"Hey, darling, it sounds like it went really well, huh?" she says.

"Yep," I reply. "God did it again."

"Amazing!" Julie replies. "Have they got a room ready for you yet?"

"I won't be needing one."

"What do you mean?" she asks.

"I mean I'm walking out of here today. I'm not hurting much at all and the bleeding has stopped, so I think we need to blow this joint as soon as possible."

"Really?" she asks.

"Really," I reply, in full confidence.

"Well, okay then," Julie says. "Let's see what we can do about that." Julie walks over to the nurse's station to talk with someone in charge.

In a few minutes Dr. Lee is back in the room. "So they tell me you're feeling well enough to go home. Is that right?" he asks.

"Yes, sir. Without a doubt," I reply.

"How's your pain?" he asks.

"I am feeling just fine and I haven't touched that bulb since you gave it to me."

"Have you used a pair of crutches before?" he asks.

"Yep, I'm an expert from my days as a skier."

Dr. Lee laughs and says, "I can identify with that. Well, Dan, if you can show me how well you get around, I will consider letting you go home today. Let's get you some crutches and you can show me what you've got. In the meantime, you can go ahead and change into your street clothes."

In a few minutes Dr. Lee returns with crutches and I'm dressed, ready to go.

"Let's see how this goes." He hands me the crutches.

Without hesitation, I take off down the hall, around the nurses' station, then back, and I stop in front of Dr. Lee, with a big smile.

"Do I pass, Doc?"

"You pass," he says. "No pain?"

"Nope."

"Well, okay then. Let's get you out of here," he says.

"Copy that!" I reply.

Six weeks later, on October 5, we receive a fresh set of scan results. All the tumors on my right side are still shrinking, but now the large tumor on my left adrenal (the one above where the rod was) has shrunk by 56 percent.

Outstanding! I'm not at all surprised, though. Ecstatic, but not surprised. It's pretty simple, really. God told me to take out the rod and I took it out. Then God responded to my obedience by healing me further.

When we get home, I record a video to document the facts of the case and commemorate the miracle God has just done. (You can watch the video on my website: danfloen.com)

PTSD

Even as well as things have been going, miracles and all, this journey has left an indelible mark on Laurel's psyche that she will not soon forget. At fifteen years old, Laurel is exhibiting behaviors that look for all the world like PTSD. For years now, her closest friends and most trusted confidants have been telling her I am going to die. Even though Julie and I have been sharing God's promise with her, no one in her world is encouraging her that her dad surviving is even possible. In a very real way, she has already experienced my death. I feel terribly guilty for having subjected her to this agonizing experience. On the other hand, she has matured way beyond her years through this journey. Laurel has always been an old soul, but I think this experience has given her a new appreciation and perspective for living every day to the fullest and never missing a chance to say, "I love you." Or maybe that lesson was mostly for me.

The good news is, Laurel's teachers are encouraging her to write about it, which is very therapeutic for her. She wrote this about her experience when she was nine years old.

Being Left in the Dark: Laurel Floen 9/12/12

Why me? That was the only thing that came to my head as my dad first told me about the illness. I felt the kind of scared you get when the lights go out and you are suddenly in the dark. Why my family? Haven't we been through enough? I was still. I didn't cry. I didn't flinch; and I just stared at him. I was nine and in third grade, my first year at a new school. On my first day, the school looked colorful and bright, but now, everything was gray and meaningless.

The most horrible day of my life was when dad first got admitted to the hospital. We were on our way to visit him like I did every day after school. I was staying with my Grandparents at the time. I was tuned out in the back seat of the car, listening to hard rock music to drown out all life around me. Grandma and Grandpa kept looking back at me to make sure I was still there, I guess. Once we get there, I notice that the whole hospital looked like a spaceship. Dad refused to wear the gown the doctors gave him because it would make him look "too girly." I walk into the room and everyone is there, my whole family, watching, waiting, for something to happen. I'm not sure what, but it must have been important. They didn't talk. They didn't smile.

They just stared at my dad who was asleep in the bed. Everyone notices the awkward silence in the air, making the room feel icy cold. I sit next to my mom, who had slept there that night to make sure that Dad would be OK.

When you're nine years old, sometimes it's hard to distinguish between a nightmare and reality. This next part may be Laurel's recollection of a nightmare. Nonetheless, this is imprinted on her brain:

We stay there for a really long time before a doctor with brown eyes and brown hair comes in and asks to talk with me. Me? What would he want me for? I can't understand all the gigantic medical words he says. My mom gets up and starts to follow me out the door. Then, the doctor said that he wanted to talk to me personally. I felt like I was going to throw up. We get outside into the hall where you can see all the other patients through their open doors. They looked miserable, just waiting for someone to treat them like a person, not a patient. They were just waiting for someone to smile at them. I didn't; I was too scared to smile. Then I looked back inside the room one last time. I see my father, with his cute bald head. He didn't look in pain; he looked like he was happy. Not the kind of happy you feel when you find out what was inside the box on Christmas morning, but the kind when you know something bad is going to happen, but you enjoy the moment until it does.

The doctor looked down at me with pity. I was used to that look by now. He felt uncomfortable I guess so he bent down to my eye level. He said "Hello, Laurel. Do you know what type of cancer your dad has?" Come on, is that the hardest question you can throw at me? I say,

"Yeah, he has stage four melanoma," feeling very proud of myself for using such big words. I had overheard my mom say it so many times to her friends on the phone. He starts talking very slow like he was trying to talk with peanut butter in his mouth. "I don't know how to put this but there is no treatment for your father's cancer. I think he has eight months to live." He keeps going but I stop listening. All I wanted to do was tell him that he was wrong and that my dad is strong and that nothing can break him, not even cancer. I start to feel prickly in my feet, my knees feel weak like they are holding 300 pounds, my face starts to burn, and the tears feel like acid running down my face. I sink to the floor, not caring if people see me cry. Then I see my mom in front of me when I open my eyes. I don't know how she got there. She says, "It's OK. The doctors are wrong. Everything is going to be OK. Nobody blames you for crying. It's going to be OK."

For the rest of the day, I stay at my father's side, staring at him. He wakes up and turns to me, my face bright pink, and says, "Come here" in his silly voice and I smiled. I crawl up next to him in the bed, trying to not lay on his IV tubes. I talk, laugh, and smile with him until we have to leave.

He hugs me and I feel the stitch on his side, from where he had surgery. I get up and start walking out of the room. Dad says, "See you tomorrow." I say, "I love you, bye." He waves and says, "Bye honey."

Laurel continues . . .

No matter how much you prepare for death, it still hurts. You think that it is OK, but when it comes, all you want to do is trade places. The pain that they feel, you want to make it go away. Looking back, I know how the story ends, but I thought I was going to be left all alone. It is as scary as being left in the dark.

Two months later Julie, Laurel, and I are in church on Sunday morning and Pastor Chuck is just finishing up his sermon. Chuck continues, "I know some of you here today are carrying a heavy load. Maybe your finances are in ruin. Maybe you desperately need healing for yourself or a loved one. Maybe you've been having trouble in your marriage or you need help to mend a broken friendship. Maybe you just lost your job. Does any of this sound like you? Friends, I want you to know that Jesus is for you and He wants the very best for you. Jesus is inviting you to bring Him your hurts and your troubles, and He has promised that He will lighten your load. So let's take some time this morning to do that. The altar rails are open. Triss and I are here to pray with you. So come. Bring it to Jesus."

As the music plays, people begin walking down the aisle to kneel at the altar rail. Chuck and Triss, our director of adult education, are praying with each one as they come. Just then Laurel stands up and starts down the aisle toward the altar. This is highly out of character for Laurel. She's never done this before, and tears well up as I imagine the pain she must be in that would motivate her to go forward this morning. She arrives in front of Triss with tears streaming down her face. Triss would later tell us about what happened next.

Triss reaches over to hold Laurel as Laurel continues to weep. "How can we pray together today?" Triss asks.

"I think my dad is going to die of cancer," Laurel says, still sobbing.

"Oh, honey, I know that's a really heavy burden to bear. Let's pray, okay?"

Laurel nods.

As I watch from my seat, Triss prays for Laurel and rubs her back lovingly as she speaks to Jesus on Laurel's behalf. My heart breaks for Laurel, and the tears begin to well up in my eyes.

After Triss and Laurel finish the prayer, Laurel rises and starts back toward where we are seated.

I dry my eyes before she gets to our seat, hoping she won't see I've been crying. She sits down next to me, puts her head on my shoulder, and reaches for my hand. She's grasping my hand like she never wants to let go. Neither do I. "Please, God," I pray silently, "don't make me leave my little girl!"

Three months later, Laurel and I are driving in my truck, headed for dinner. When Laurel became a teenager, we started a new tradition. Once a month Laurel and I go out on a date, just the two of us. We call it "Daddy Date Night." Laurel has a learner's permit and she would normally be driving, but it's date night, so I'm at the wheel. We're going to Kobe Japanese Steakhouse, Laurel's favorite.

Laurel has come to expect heavy or deep questions from me when it's just the two of us on date night. I always start off with this verbal queue to let her know it's coming: "So, Laurel, I've got a question for you." It's fun to hear what she's thinking and learn about her view of the world. She is so wise for her years, and I often ask her advice on a broad array of topics. We have some great talks, just Laurel and me. I know she's struggled for a long time with me having cancer, but things are going so well lately. I want to give Laurel a chance to share her feelings about this journey we've been on together.

"So, Laurel, I've got a question for you."

"Oh, here we go. What is it?" she says, bracing herself.

"I know we've been doing this cancer thing a long time, and I'm just wondering, what do you think about my chances?"

Laurel pauses, like she's deciding whether to give me her honest answer or the one she thinks I want to hear. After a bit, she's made her determination to tell me her honest answer. I know because if it were the one I want to hear, it would have come much sooner than this. Laurel looks nervous, but she's determined to tell me the truth, because she loves me too much not to.

She sighs and then says, "I think you're going to die before my sixteenth birthday."

Whoa. I didn't see that one coming. Not sure how to respond, I simply ask, "What makes you think that, sweetie?"

"It's just a feeling I've had for some time now," she says. "It's hard to explain. I just feel it."

Julie and I have talked to Laurel about our belief in God's promise for my healing, but I also know she's struggling. In a rare moment of clarity, something occurs to me about trust and feelings, and I decide to share it with Laurel.

"Laurel, feelings can be very powerful, but they're just feelings. Feelings often cannot be trusted. Trust is a decision, not a feeling. Here's what I know. God told me He's healing me, and I've decided to trust His promise. And honestly, Laurel, I'll take God's promise over your feeling any day of the week. I look forward to going out on date night with you after your sixteenth birthday," and I give her a wink and a smile.

She smiles back and says, "Go for it! I really hope you prove me wrong."

"Just wait, sweetie. You'll see."

God Is Saying

The further along this journey I get, and the more time I spend with God, the more I hear from Him.

Go figure.

As I look over my journal entries for the last month or so, I realize I've been receiving a steady stream of messages from God lately. I figure He must be trying to make a point with me, so I decide to capture what I've heard on one sheet of paper so I can refer to it often. I'm a slow student, so if God is trying to tell me something, I figure I need it plastered right in front of me.

I open a new Word document on my laptop and start typing out God's messages to me. Then I print it, cut it out with some scissors, and tape it to my PC monitor on my desk.

There, that oughta do it!

God Is Saying

- *Quit trying to save yourself. Relax and I will take care of you.*
- *Peace is a weapon against Satan. Don't let Satan steal your peace and joy from you.*
- *Here's the secret to temptation: Don't fight it. Just refocus. Whatever you resist persists.*
- *Even in the black hole, I still protect you.*
- *Believe your beliefs; doubt your doubts.*

- *My provision comes from secret places.* "*I will give you the treasures of darkness, riches stored in secret places, so that you may know that I am the Lord*" (Isaiah 45:3 NIV).

- *Listen for my voice.* "*My sheep listen to my voice; I know them, and they follow me*" (John 10:27 NIV).

- *Choose to believe according to what I, the Lord, will do based on what I have said.*

- *Your success will be based on your obedience,* not your skill or your sweat and toil.

- *I have instructed you to do four things.* Be obedient in these and I will take care of the rest.

    1. **WRITE** the story I have given you.

    2. **LEAD** the people I have put in your care.

    3. **MINISTER** to them.

    4. **MENTOR** the leaders of tomorrow.

Keep Calm and Trust God.

Amid the many messages I'm getting from God lately, and the continued healing He is doing in my body, I've come to understand something about God's ways that I never fully believed before: *God heals imperfect people.*

See, for years I've struggled to control my lustful thoughts. Sometimes I win, but all too often I lose. I know a lot of men struggle with this, and I take some comfort in knowing I'm not alone, but I also know that doesn't make it right, or healthy. Throughout this journey, I can point to many instances where I missed the mark and then God immediately allowed me to suffer a consequence, usually some sort of physical or business setback. I can just about set my watch to it. As soon as I screw up, the consequence quickly comes. God's been consistent that way.

So, quite naturally, I had concluded God was going to withhold His complete healing of me until I stopped sinning, once and for all. The trouble is, I know I can never stop sinning completely, so I had pretty much accepted that God would always leave this cancerous thorn in my side until He decides to bring me home. After all, cancer is how God keeps my attention on Him, so why would He ever take this away from me fully?

But recently I've come to realize that this reasoning doesn't make sense. I mean, the more I understand who God is, and His MO, the more I realize the flaw in this cause and effect way of thinking about God.

Think about it. Jesus died for us all while we were still sinning. Being healed of some illness seems like small potatoes compared to being saved for all eternity. Jesus didn't wait for us to clean up our act before He acted. God's healing is no different.

On the other hand, Jesus did tell the woman at the well to "go and sin no more." Obviously Jesus couldn't reasonably expect her to never sin again. I think Jesus was specifically referring to the adulterous sins that He had called her out on. "Don't keep making those same mistakes," He told her, in effect. I think the same is true for me. Jesus has called me out on the sin of lust, so I need to stop making those same mistakes if I ever expect God to heal me fully.

What Matters to God

This week Eric and I are in Portland visiting our project team who has been at Boeing for the past several months. Tonight our Boeing team, Matt, Jason, and Tom, have invited us to go with them to a local church that has been serving the homeless. It is so cool to see our team beginning to embrace the idea of working for a greater cause than ourselves. I mean, if we all believe that God owns PM2, then we must act upon the things that matter to God. And we know that people matter to God.

As we walk toward the main building through the parking lot, Matt is leading the way, and we're all trying to keep up with him. I know Matt has had a long day, but he's got a spring in his step tonight. He is bright-eyed and visibly excited to be here.

"Every Wednesday night," he says as we're walking, "the church serves the people a hot meal and provides a bed for them to spend the night in a warm, safe, and dry place. The coordinators try to make it a good time for everyone. They play group games and do other fun activities to get everyone involved. It's a lot of fun, and it feels great to be here, just spending time with them. I really look forward to coming here every Wednesday night."

Just then we arrive at the entrance.

"Hey, Matt!" says the young lady at the door. She gives them each a warm hug as she greets them.

"Hi, Ashley!" Matt says. "I'd like you to meet my bosses, Dan Floen and Eric Eichelberger."

We both say hi. "It's a pleasure to meet you," I add.

"And you as well," Ashley replies. "Your guys have been such a blessing to the people here. It's been really great having them here every Wednesday night."

Matt explains, "Ashley is the program director. She's doing such an amazing job."

"Awe, thanks, Matt!" she says, blushing. "Well, come on in, guys!"

Matt steps through the doorway and into the main space where about fifty people have gathered. Eric and I follow them as best we can as our guys greet people all over the room, high-fiving and fist-bumping with them as they go. About halfway through the crowd, Matt stops to talk with a young woman.

"Dan, I'd like you to meet someone," he says. "Andrea, this is my boss, Dan Floen."

"Hi, Andrea."

"Hi, Dan," she says. "It's a pleasure to meet you. You've got some pretty special guys here."

"Thanks. We are blessed to have them."

"Andrea, would you feel comfortable telling Dan your story?" Matt asks.

"Absolutely," she says.

"I'd be honored if you'd share it with us," I tell her.

"Dan, six months ago I lost my job. I have two daughters. Anna is five and Megan is seven. I've always been the main breadwinner for our family, so when my company downsized and cut my position, we were in a pretty bad spot. I guess the stress of our situation got to my husband because one month after losing my job, he left me and the girls. I haven't heard from him since."

As she tells her story, I feel so inadequate. I have no words for this woman. What can I tell her that will encourage her and give her hope?

Andrea continues. "With my husband gone, it didn't take long for what little money we had to dry up. Our landlord evicted us after I missed our rent payment for the third month in the row. Now the three of us sleep most nights in my car, so we were really happy to learn about Wednesday nights here. These people are a godsend, and your guys have been such an encouragement to me. We started coming to church here on Sundays too, and the girls and I really like it. Pastor Jeff is so inspiring. I never went to church before coming here."

"I am so glad you found this place," I say, still searching for words.

"So, Matt, have I told you the news?" she asks.

"No," he replies. "What's up?"

"I got a job, and I start next Monday!" she says with a big smile.

"Andrea, that is fantastic!" Matt exclaims. "I need to give you a hug!"

"Now all I need is a laptop," she says. "I'll be working mostly from home, and they need me to have a laptop so I can dial-in to their system and work remotely."

"Do you have one?" Matt asks.

"No," she says, "but I'm planning a trip to Best Buy this weekend to see what I can find."

Matt glances back at me. I know what he's thinking. I nod at him in approval.

"How about if we buy the laptop for you?" Matt asks.

"You would really do that?"

"Absolutely," Matt replies. "We'd love to do this for you."

"That is so amazing!" Now she's crying. "Thank you so much!"

The next day after work Matt goes to Best Buy and gets Andrea a laptop with his own money. We had agreed the previous night that PM2 would buy the laptop, but we later realized we don't have a good way to account for donations of cash or merchandise that the IRS will readily recognize as tax exempt donations. So Matt took the matter into his own hands and bought the laptop.

Hopefully we would never let taxes stop us from being generous, regardless of whether we can claim it on our taxes or not, but this experience with Andrea has highlighted a barrier that we have in PM2's giving ministry. We have no simple way to spontaneously help someone in need. The next time God presents us with an opportunity, we want to be able to act on it, right then and there.

When I arrive home from Portland, I start researching and find out there is a special type of private foundation that allows you to write spontaneous giving right into the foundation charter. That's exactly what we need, I conclude. So the following week I hire a specialist to help us get our foundation up and running.

Six weeks later, the PM2 Foundation is born. We now have a sales tax exemption certificate and a separate PM2 Foundation bank account. The account has a debit card tied to it so we can purchase items to donate on a moment's notice or we can immediately reimburse generous team members using a cash app on our cell phone. We seeded the account with $1,000 for starters, and from now on the plan is to put 10 percent of PM2's cash profits into the PM2 Foundation account.

For the past five years PM2 has been chugging right along and my health has been steadily improving. It's now September 29, 2017, and Julie and I are in San Antonio attending C12's National Marketplace Leader Conference, called Current '17. Tonight I am receiving a "C12 Hero" award.

Here is how C12 describes the award:

> In 1999, Buck Jacobs instituted an annual award to recognize
> leaders who have been consistently faithful and courageous in
> their leadership over the long haul. These leaders may have been
> pioneers, opposed, and unsung champions of the faith in ways
> normal market recognition programs would never compute. He
> called them . . . C12 Heroes.

Me, a C12 Hero? I'm not so sure about that.

Death of the Glass-Half-Empty Guy

Yesterday Julie, Laurel, and I rented a boat and went fishing in the Gulf.
We caught three nice Spanish mackerel and two blacktip sharks. It had
been way too long since we'd been on the water. I guess life just gets in the
way sometimes. On second thought, no; that's a cop-out. The truth is my
worries got in the way, not life. Worries about the business. Worries about
whether God was going to keep healing me. Worries about worries.

But every time I go back and read in my journal about the many
challenges God has brought me through, and how He provided for me and
protected me *every single time*, the more I am ashamed by my lack of faith.

I mean, for a guy who God has done so many amazing things for, you'd
think I would surely be the most optimistic and joyful man on the planet.
And yet even my closest companions call me "the glass-half-empty guy."
It's embarrassing.

People who are pessimists don't often call themselves pessimists. "I'm just being a realist," they say. I've described myself like this many times over the years. But looking at where God has brought me, and the miracles He's done for me, can I seriously call myself a realist anymore?

Realists look at the numbers. They take things at face value. They only care about the facts. Realists don't believe that anything other than what is logical and expected will ever happen. Where's the faith in that?

Optimists often do things solely on faith. They have undying hope. They see the best in people. Their vision of the future is positive. They fear less. I think optimists make better leaders. I mean, I want to follow an optimist, not a realist. Oh, sure, any good leader has to have a grip on reality, but I want to follow the one who sees the potential to overcome and the power of God's hand at work in everything we do. I've observed that optimists are generally happier and more joyful overall. I want to live like that—happy and joyful.

I read a devotion the other day that talked about thanking God in advance. The point was, if you thank God after the fact, that's gratitude. If you thank God beforehand, that's faith. It reminded me of the time my C12 brothers laid hands on me and prayed, thanking God in advance for healing me. I was only six weeks into a stage four cancer diagnosis, and a certain death sentence, and I had never heard anyone pray so boldly and with such faith. At that moment I think I began to believe it myself, that God had already delivered His healing antidote but that it would take time for His healing to be fully manifested in my body. After all, God still has a lot of work to do on me, and cancer is how He keeps my attention on Him.

I am sick and tired of being the glass-half-empty guy. So today it stops! After all, faith is a decision, not a feeling, right? Today I decide to believe my beliefs and I will doubt my doubts. From now on, the glass is at least half full!

13

Am I Free Yet?

About eight months ago, we moved out of the rental house in Lutz and into another rental house in Apollo Beach. This house is on a saltwater canal—PRAISE THE LORD! For this fisherman, three years away from the water has been an eternity. We also bought another used boat that fits into our budget. This time around, Julie and I have committed to God that we will not let this home on the water, or the boat, define us, as we did the first time. This time God has told us to make our home a refuge for those He puts in our path, and that is precisely what we intend to do. Lord, let it be so!

It's November 2013, fifteen months since getting the rod removed from my left femur. Every three months since then, scan results have continued to show shrinking tumors. In fact, yesterday Dr. Blake told us he thinks both remaining tumors are now dead. The only way to know for sure would be to remove and biopsy them, which he won't do because it's too invasive a procedure to simply satisfy our curiosity about whether they are dead or alive. So I am wrapping my head around the idea that God may leave them there forever. But yesterday's news at least tells me that God doesn't want me burdened by them anymore. I recommit today that I will stay vigilant and remember the lessons God has taught me. And I'll leave the rest up to Him.

I wonder, was our last appointment at Lakeside the day God set me free at last? Could it be that God used Dr. Blake to send me a message of complete healing? Maybe I should be thinking of the dead tumors as battle scars. Surely lots of people who have been completely healed walk around with scars. I have several. Maybe I should think of these scars as a visible sign of a battle fought and won.

Understanding the Roadblock

In November of 2017, I hired my good friend, Marc, my fellow miracle survivor. He had recently retired from a thirty-year career at Grainger, and when his change in status showed up on LinkedIn, I felt strongly led to talk with him about coming to work for PM2. As it turned out, God had been speaking to Marc as well, so the decision to come and work for us was an easy one.

Since last November Marc and our sales team have made some great inroads with our partners and our client base. But all this work has not translated into enough revenue this year to float the boat, and we are sinking fast.

Now it's July 3, 2018, and PM2 is still in a nosedive. By the end of the first quarter, we had already lost $110,000. By the end of the second quarter, total losses exceeded $185,000.

I'm befuddled. I mean, we have an awesome team at PM2. We have great partners. We have lots of opportunities in the pipeline. And yet we are hemorrhaging money, and I see no end in sight. What is God waiting for? Why has He withheld His blessing from His company? I'm wracking my brain to figure out what on earth is going on here. What, or who, is the barrier?

I remember the story in the Bible where Joshua sent his army out to take the city of Ai. His spies had told Joshua that he didn't need to send out his entire army because only a few people lived in Ai. So Joshua only sent three thousand men, but they were soundly defeated.

Joshua was perplexed. *That should have been any easy victory,* he thought. Dejected and depressed, he got facedown in the dirt and went to God in prayer to ask Him why they were defeated. Here is what God said:

The Lord said to Joshua, "Stand up! What are you doing down on your face? Israel has sinned; they have violated my covenant, which I commanded them to keep. They have taken some of the devoted things; they have stolen, they have lied, they have put them with their own possessions. That is why the Israelites cannot stand against their enemies; they turn their backs and run because they have been made liable to destruction. I will not be with you anymore unless you destroy whatever among you is devoted to destruction." (Joshua 7:10–12 NIV)

Is that what's going on with PM2? Do we have evil in the camp? If so, what or who is it?

So far this year I haven't slept well. I lay awake many nights worrying.

Nonetheless, whenever I do get to sleep, it is a great escape from the constant weight of our impossible financial situation, so I spend a lot of time trying to sleep and napping throughout the day. As the pressure mounts, I spend a lot more time thinking about lustful things. Oh sure, I know this is not God's highest and best for me, but this too serves as a mental breather for me, so I figure the benefit outweighs the cost. In fact, thinking about anything other than our financial debacle right now seems like a good thing for my mental health.

Today I made the very painful decision to liquidate $150,000 from our IRA and convert it to cash in order to finance PM2 operations for another few weeks. If PM2 can't repay this amount within sixty days, we'll pay taxes on that money along with a 10 percent penalty for early withdrawal. I don't see us being able to get the money back into the IRA in time. Truthfully, I see us burning through it and needing to take out another $150,000 in a few weeks.

Later this week Julie and Laurel leave for three weeks to spend some time in North Carolina with Julie's cousin, Samantha, and Julie's sister, Diane. The prospect of Julie leaving me home alone in the middle of our financial crisis scares the crap out of me. I've never had a problem being alone, but Julie has always been the one who goes in after me when I go into my occasional funk. Without Julie here, I'm afraid of where my mind will go and the depths of depression and hopelessness I may descend to.

A thought occurs to me. Is it possible God arranged these three weeks home alone for me with a purpose in mind? Is this some sort of test? Maybe God arranged my own personal boot camp to see what I'm really made of. In military boot camp, they tear you down so they can build you back up. They get rid of your bad habits and replace them with personal discipline and obedience to a higher power. So what bad habit is God trying to get rid of?

Oh. Now I see.

It's my lustful thoughts. I've been fooling myself thinking my lustful thoughts are not damaging to me and that God is okay with them. God has been watching. He's not okay with this, and He intends to rid me of it once and for all.

Another thought occurs to me. In the Bible, one of Joshua's soldiers, Achan, had broken God's covenant, and God was not going to bless the Israelites until Joshua removed the evil. I now realize who the evil in PM2's camp is.

It's me.

Boot Camp

Julie and Laurel left for North Carolina this morning. Boot camp starts today. For the next three weeks, I believe God has set some very specific goals before me. During this time of testing, I will:

- Take control of my thoughts. If my mind starts heading toward the gutter, I will refocus on the things of God.
- Intentionally spend at least one hour with God every day, reading the Bible, writing in my journal, praying, and listening.
- Eat right and work out every day.

It starts now.

The next morning, as I'm reading the Bible, God leads me to Isaiah 43:18–19, which says,

But forget all that—
it is nothing compared to what I am going to do.
For I am about to do something new.
See, I have already begun! Do you not see it?
I will make a pathway through the wilderness.
I will create rivers in the dry wasteland. (NLT)

As the days pass, I begin to realize that God is trying to bring me somewhere I've never been before. Throughout this journey with cancer, bankruptcy, losing our house and the boat, there has always been one room in my house I have not allowed God to enter. It's a mess, even worse than Laurel's bedroom, and I'm sure God wouldn't like what He saw if I let Him in there. This room is where all my unhealthy thoughts live. So I've kept this room securely deadbolted, and only I can go in there.

But I now know this too is a ruse. The only person I've been fooling is me. God knows my every thought. So who do I think I'm kidding? I guess on some level I was always aware that God knows what's behind that door. I was just hoping He wasn't looking, or that He simply didn't care about it. I know now that I was foolish to think that. I mean, how can a person truly live out their calling from God if their mind is a cesspool? It's time for me to let God into this room and let Him help me take control of my thoughts. Philippians 4:8 says,

Finally, brothers and sisters, whatever is true, whatever is noble, whatever is right, whatever is pure, whatever is lovely, whatever is admirable—if anything is excellent or praiseworthy—think about such things. (NIV)

From God's lips to my ears. Lord, let it be so!

Ten days have passed since boot camp began, and I am now halfway through. PM2 is still in the ditch with no sign of relief on the horizon. Today is C12 day, and I'm hoping to gain some wisdom from my group to strengthen my resolve to complete this boot camp with flying colors.

Our day at C12 starts out as usual. We begin with a devotion and then spend the morning hours working through this month's business reading material. In the afternoon we work through the "business as ministry" material. The last two hours of the day are typically set aside for one of the members to present their core business review to the group, but today our chairman, Scott, doesn't have a core presenter on the agenda.

"Well, guys," Scott says, "today we've got some time to discuss any issues that you might be facing in your business or personal life. Does anyone have an issue they'd like to present to the group?"

As I look around the room, no one is clambering for the floor. My eyes land on Scott, and he's staring at me very expectantly. (I made him aware of PM2's struggles during our one-on-one last week.)

"I believe the floor is yours," Scott says, looking at me, smiling.

"If you insist," I reply.

"I insist," he says.

So I proceed to tell the guys about the terrible year PM2 is having.

I tell them how we're sitting on a $200,000 loss so far and how we just took $150,000 out of our IRA to fund the business. And I tell them how I believe God arranged this three-week boot camp for me, and that God is bringing me somewhere I've never been before. (I don't tell them about the deadbolted room. I figure that's between God and me.) And even though I'm holding true to the goals God set before me for this boot camp, PM2 is still losing money hand over fist and I see no end in sight.

"Well, guys, what do you think?" I ask.

Josh pipes up first. "Dan, I can clearly see that God has something special for you or He wouldn't have arranged this time alone. Your job is to complete the course, brother."

Others chime in and they all are encouraging me to complete the course.

Meanwhile, Dave is sitting at the far end of the table, soaking it all in. Dave is like E.F. Hutton; when he talks, people listen. After the guys have had their say, the room falls quiet for a moment.

Then Dave weighs in. "Behind this is the blessing," he says. "Stay obedient to the Father so He can complete His work in you, and then and only then will God release the blessing." Again, he says, "Behind this is the blessing. God has big plans for you and PM2. I'm excited to see it when God releases the blessing, and He surely will. Just hang in there, Danny!"

"Thanks for that, Dave," I reply. "I haven't thought of it that way before. Behind this is the blessing. But only after God finishes His work in me through this boot camp. I see that now. Thanks, guys. I'm gonna complete boot camp with flying colors and you all will be the first to know when God releases the blessing!"

"We look forward to that!" Scott says. "Let's pray for Dan right now, shall we?"

The guys all bow their heads.

The Last Holdout

It's been three weeks since Julie and Laurel left for North Carolina. Julie just got home last night. (Laurel stayed up there to attend a summer theatre camp.)

Boot camp is over now, and I feel good about how I did. My personal discipline was great, and even though God and I did some serious wrestling on the floor, I really value the time I spent with Him. I'm expecting God to release the blessing any day now.

A day goes by. No blessing.

No problem, I figure. God has a lot going on. I'm sure the blessing is coming soon.

Three days go by. No blessing. "Okay, Lord, where are You?" I ask. "I held up my end of the bargain. So where's my blessing?"

A week goes by. Still no blessing. "Lord, this isn't funny! Why have You not released the blessing yet? I did everything You told me to do!"

It's now August 24, 2018, and PM2 continues to bleed, with record losses now at $232,500. Julie is out running some errands and I am home alone. It's been three weeks since boot camp, and we are in worse shape than ever. I am completely frustrated and confused, but mostly I'm just pissed. "What the hell, Father? What was that boot camp all about? I've done everything You asked!" My complete frustration quickly boils over into hopelessness and despair, and I drop down on my face in the stairwell that leads to my office. Now sobbing, I shout in desperation, "Where are You?"

No answer comes. I guess He doesn't like being yelled at.

That night Julie is putting on her pajamas in the bathroom and I'm reading my Bible in bed. I've settled down from the height of despair I got to earlier today, but the question still burns. Why hasn't God released the blessing? What on earth have I left undone? "Lord, please speak to me. I am listening. What do You have to say to me?"

And I wait, and I listen. A few moments pass, and then He says, "There's one more thing." Immediately, I know exactly what "thing" He is referring to. "You need to tell Julie," He says.

"Oh no! No, no, no! Not that! Anything but that! Please, Lord, don't make me do that!"

Fifteen years ago, I found myself in the VIP room of a gentleman's club doing things no gentleman should be proud of, married or single. The term *gentleman's club* is a total contradiction. There are no gentlemen in those places, and I certainly wasn't one on that day. Anyway, I plan on taking this to my grave. Julie must never know.

I try to reason with God. "Lord, nothing good could ever come from Julie knowing this. All it would do is hurt her. Surely You don't want me to hurt Julie, do You?"

My reasoning falls on deaf ears. "You need to tell her," He says.

The idea of telling Julie makes me sick to my stomach. I can't think about this anymore tonight, so I get up and head to the refrigerator for a Guinness. I pour it into a pint glass and chug it straight down. I figure a beer will help me fall asleep faster.

The next morning I'm awake with the birds, and the first conscious thought that enters my head is, "You need to tell her." God is not letting this go. And it's clear to me that He is not going to release the blessing until I tell her. So the way I see it, I will probably ruin our marriage when I tell Julie, but the company will survive. Or if I don't tell her, we are sure to lose the company and we'll go broke and financial ruin will probably kill our marriage anyway. What a heck of a pickle to find myself in.

"Okay, God, I surrender. I just need some time this morning to work up the gumption to tell her."

I'm the first one out of bed most mornings, and today is no different. I get up, brush my teeth, and put on my clothes for the day. Then I brew a cup of coffee in the kitchen and head upstairs to my office to gather my thoughts in preparation for this message I have to deliver.

Facedown on the floor, I'm asking God, "Father, please help me. I don't have the words to say to Julie. Please help me, Lord. I see Your purpose in this. I know You want to set me free from this burden I've been carrying around for the past fifteen years. So I'm asking for Your help, God. Please help me to see this through. I pray in Jesus' name. Amen."

I gather myself up from the floor, take a deep breath, and let it out. Looking at my cell phone, I see it's 8:30 a.m. Julie should be up by now.

"Here goes nothing," I say under my breath.

I walk downstairs, through the kitchen, and into the family room. No Julie. But I can faintly hear the *Today Show* playing on the TV in the master bathroom. I walk through our bedroom and into the bathroom where Julie is in front of her make-up mirror, putting on some finishing touches.

"Good morning," she says as she turns her head to greet me. This would normally be when I give her a good morning hug, but this morning I'm keeping a respectful distance from her.

"What's wrong, darlin'?" she says, immediately sensing something is not right. I imagine she can see the extreme shame on my face and my humble posture. I take a position just inside the bathroom door about six feet from her. I'm too ashamed to come any closer.

"Julie, I need to tell you something this morning that will be hard for you to hear."

She pauses for a moment and turns to fully face me. "What is it, darlin'?"

"Julie, I made a terrible mistake fifteen years ago and I need to tell you about it."

Staring at the floor in shame, I proceed to tell her the gory details of where I went on that dark day fifteen years ago and what I did. As I'm explaining, my guilt and shame overpower me, and I begin to weep. I finish with what I have to say, and I slowly look up at her.

"Julie, that was such a stupid mistake, and I am so deeply sorry. Can you ever forgive me?"

Julie comes over and puts her arms around me. "Oh, darlin'," she says, "I already have."

Still holding me, Julie explains how she knew fifteen years ago what I had done. She knew way back then, and she had already forgiven me.

"We're gonna be okay," she says. "Dan, you need to forgive yourself, and let the past be the past. I've forgiven you. So now it's your turn. Forgive yourself, and then we can move on together. Will you do that for me?" she asks.

I collect myself for a moment and consider what Julie has asked me to do. I know she's right. I have to forgive myself.

"Yes, I will," I reply.

I am so unworthy of Julie. Thank You, Lord, for this wonderful lady, so full of grace. God knew that Julie knew all along, and I was dragging that boat anchor around for no reason. I was prepared to take that terrible secret to my grave, but the irony is, it was never a secret in the first place. I see now that this so-called "secret" was robbing Julie and me from ever having complete trust between us. It seems obvious to me now, but I know God's highest and best for our marriage is that there can be no secrets between us.

I feel like a prisoner set free. No more dragging the anchor. No more secrets to bring to my grave. No more uncomfortable questions to steer clear of.

Thank You, Jesus!

14

Dam Break

Ever since I confessed my transgression to Julie and God freed me from that burden, the dam broke and God has been releasing a flood of blessings on PM2. Massive losses have turned into respectable gains.

It's clearer to me now more than ever that I was the problem at PM2. My unconfessed transgression was the evil in the camp. I just can't see it any other way. Before God set me free from this burden and I knew that Julie had forgiven me, I saw no end to the bleeding in sight for PM2. But as soon as the evil was removed, God released the blessing. Just like my friend, Dave, said at C12, "Beyond this is the blessing." It most certainly was!

Restoration

It's April 17, 2019, and Julie and I are back at Dr. Blake's office to get the results of the last CT scans. We've been getting scans every six months for the last three years or so. Honestly, the last several visits have been more fun than tense. I mean, the news has been good every time. The tumors are now all believed to be dead and they continue to diminish in size. In fact, the remaining masses are of so little consequence that we usually wind up talking about which new restaurant Dr. Blake recommends for us to try. Man, this is a far cry from the nail-biter appointments of years ago. Still, I've pretty much accepted the idea that God will always leave a little something there for me to keep my attention. I guess I can live with that. As they say, it sure beats the alternative.

After a minute or two, those familiar two raps come on the door, and Dr. Blake enters the room.

"Hi, guys," he says. "How are you doing?"

"Hey there," I reply. "We're doing great."

"Well, I think you are too," he says with a smile. "The scans look great. Actually, we didn't detect any evidence of neoplasm anywhere in your body," he says. "In fact, your scans have been looking good for over five years now. So, Mr. Floen, I'm comfortable saying that you are 100 percent cured."

Cured? Now that's a term I never thought I'd hear in any sentence referring to me.

The conversation continues between Julie and him, something about a Broadway show, I think, but I'm still taking in what he just said to me. In the world of stage four metastatic melanoma, no one ever uses the word *cured.* They use words like *regression, remission,* and *extending life,* but never *cured.* This is a bold statement for any oncologist to make about a guy who wasn't expected to live past eight months.

As I sit there I begin to take inventory of the past several years, especially the last few months. Then it dawns on me. God has been waiting on me.

Since 2007, we've been doing this dance, God and me. It starts with me being in some sort of trouble and I sidle up to God. He always welcomes me with open arms, without fail. It is peaceful and safe being with God, and

He showers blessings on me when I'm with Him. But then, inexplicably, even as God is blessing me, I begin to believe the lie that the blessings are all my doing, and I scurry off to conquer the world. The devil tempts me unmercifully during these times. Inevitably I give in to the temptations and soon find myself dancing around the fire pit. God often allows me to suffer consequences, usually health or finance related, during these times. This is a very anxious and fearful time for me, which weakens my resistance to the devil's impulses, and I spiral down even deeper.

At some point, after things have gotten bad enough, I realize what I've done. So I go back to God, hat in hand, and ask Him to forgive me, yet again. He always does. And the cycle starts all over.

But ever since my personal boot camp with God and the breakthrough in the fall of 2018, the cycle has been broken, and God's blessings just keep on coming. Our marriage has never been stronger. Laurel sees how much more at ease I am. I'm not worried all the time. I enjoy life, love people, and have more fun. The business is the healthiest it's ever been.

People often tell me what a great fighter I am for having survived stage four cancer this long. I tell them, "I stopped fighting. I surrendered."

Now more than ever, I believe God loves fishermen. Case in point, our outboard motor blew this past summer, and it was going to cost $28,000 to replace it. We didn't have this kind of cash lying around, so I had been praying to God about what to do. I felt uncomfortable praying to God about something so materialistic as an outboard motor. But nonetheless, He was listening, and He responded. He said, "Wait, I have not acted yet." So I waited. And I waited. Then one bright day in September, our CPA called to say our tax refund for last year's return would be—you guessed it—$28,000. That message was clear enough, even for me!

Ever since our bankruptcy ten years ago, we have not owned a house. It's now the summer of 2020, and I have one more year of being cancer-free under my belt. Recently God made it possible for us to buy the house we had been renting for the past six years. When God first showed us this house for rent on a saltwater canal, Julie and I had some trepidation about moving back out to the water. We were determined never again to be defined by the house we live in, or a boat, or any other material thing. As we prayed about whether to move to this house on the water, God instructed us both to make our home a refuge for others. Since then, many people have come and stayed with us, and I think our home has been a place of peace and restoration for them. Julie makes sure of that.

Fish On!

A few weeks ago Laurel arrived home for the summer from the University of Alabama at Birmingham (UAB), where she just finished her junior year. It's Saturday morning and a beautiful sunny day is taking shape. Julie, Laurel and I are standing in the kitchen sipping on our coffee, just enjoying being together and making small talk.

"Dad," Laurel says, "I think the three of us need some boat time."

"I could not agree more," Julie says.

"Done!" I bellow, holding my right index finger to the sky as if a major resolution has just been made. "I'll load up the boat and meet you at the dock in fifteen minutes, OK?"

"Dad, you are such a dork," Laurel says, laughing.

"That's why we love him!" Julie chuckles.

So, I bring rods, tackle, and ice down to the boat and start the live well just to make sure the pump still runs. I've been caught out on the water too many times with a dead live well pump and a bunch of bait dying, so now I check the pump first thing every time I go out.

The girls bring towels, sodas, and bottled water with them as they board the boat, and Laurel is singing "Home" by Jack Johnson. I do love hearing that girl sing. It brightens my day.

We're all loaded up, so I start the engine and we ease away from the slip. It's a twenty-minute putt through no wake zone water to the end of our canal. Laurel has connected her iPhone via Bluetooth to the boat stereo and we're listening to her favorite Pandora station, Jack Johnson Radio. We reach the end of the no wake zone and I call out, "Is everybody ready?"

This new 300 hp Yamaha really blows your hair back, so you need to be ready when I give her the gas or you may wind up tail over teakettle, or overboard.

"Let's go!" the girls reply in unison.

I put the throttle down and we are quickly up on plane, headed out into the bay. We start out looking for bait at the range marker just north of Big Bend Channel in about twenty-five feet of water. We're looking for greenbacks (scaled sardines), and we're watching the sonar for a cloud of red marks near the bottom.

I'm at the bow, ready with the cast net, holding the lead line in my teeth. Laurel is at the helm, idling around the range marker.

"There's a bunch showing on the screen right now, Dad," Laurel calls out.

"Let's ease up to this side of the tower and I'll throw off the left side of the boat," I reply.

"Okay," she says. Laurel eases the boat into position, and I let the net fly. The net spreads out nicely and pancakes on the water.

"Nice throw!" Julie says.

"Thanks!" I reply.

As the net sinks down to the sea bottom, Laurel backs the boat off the range marker to give me room to pull it in. It's feeling pretty light as I pull in the line.

"Nothing," I groan.

"Really?" Laurel says. "Those marks were huge on the screen. How about we try it again, but this time throw your net on the other side of the boat."

"Really?" I say under my breath. I'm pretty sure this will be a big waste of time.

Laurel pulls back up to the tower, and I let the net fly, but this time on the right side of the boat. The net reaches the bottom and I begin to bring in the line.

"This feels heavy," I say in amazement.

"Cool!" Laurel says. "I told you so. You need to listen to me more often!" she giggles.

As I bring the net to the surface, I can see flashes of light as the sun reflects off the scales of a huge load of greenbacks. With the net at the surface, I realize I can't bring this huge catch over the gunnel by myself.

"Julie, I need your help! Come and give me a hand, would you?"

"You got it!" Julie says as she jumps into action.

Together, we haul in the huge catch. We have blacked out our bait well with just one throw of the net. That doesn't happen very often.

With a bait well full of greenies, we turn south toward our fishing spot.

Ten minutes later we arrive on a calm grassy flat. It's nearly high tide, plenty of water for our boat to get up to where the fish are. We have a light cool breeze to our back and the water shimmers as the sun dances on the surface.

"I see you're still wearing your necklace," Laurel says.

"Yep."

"I like it on you," she says. "I know you're not one to wear jewelry, but this one suits you."

"Thanks," I reply.

The necklace is a carved bone fishhook hanging from a braided cord. I bought it from a tabletop vendor on our vacation last year. To me, this fishhook necklace has a double meaning. I suppose the first one is obvious enough. After all, I'm a fisherman. The second meaning, however, is the more important of the two. I am a fisher of men in training: a fisherman's apprentice, as it were. Whenever I feel the rough braided cord around my neck, that is my reminder to always have a line in the water for God's children.

As the three of us stand there watching our bobbers, taking in this tranquil bit of God's creation, I think about the many rough seas God has brought us through. I'm not the man I was at the start of this journey. I know God has more work to do, but I'm thankful for the molding and shaping he's done so far.

"It is so beautiful here, isn't it?" Julie says.

"It sure is," Laurel replies.

Just then the line goes screaming off Laurel's reel.

"Fish on!" she yells.

Appendix

In 2017, our story made it to C12 headquarters, and they asked to shoot a video of Julie and me to share what the impact of our journey has been on our marriage.

This is the transcript of what Julie and I said in the video or you can watch it on my website: danfloen.com.

Dan:

"For PM2, how business impacted our marriage came through a trail of adversity. It came from a really rough start. The first three years were really hard. We decided to turn the company at that point over to God. We changed our mission statement and let all our employees and contractors know that they now work for a company that is owned by God. A few years later I was diagnosed with stage four metastatic melanoma and I was given eight months to live. And at that point, we were told we should make preparations for me to leave."

Julie:

"I had been in business all my life, but I had never run a company, and there were so many different things that I didn't know. I didn't know what I didn't know. And the people that were in our C12 group, as well as the other groups within our area all pulled together to help me and teach me what I needed to do—the questions I needed to ask, the things that I needed to be watching, and helped me keep things together during the time that Dan was absent. And I was preparing to run the company."

Dan:

"We were preparing for the worst, hoping for the best. God brings you to the valley because He wants you to get close, and I've never been so close to God than when I was right there in the desert with Him.

In the last few years, we've seen a huge transition in our marriage. And for me, it was based in seeing a side of Julie and a strength in Julie that I had never seen before. This is the most tenacious person I know. She was going to make sure that I stay here."

Julie:

"What I told the doctors was that I didn't want a husband. I wanted this husband, and what are we going to do about it. So, as we prayed about it, Dan got a very clear message that God was going to let him live. I mean, as he went through this diagnosis, and as he went through all the things that God took him through to prepare us for whatever it is He has for us, it got really ugly. And people outside of our little cocoon were saying, 'She's delusional because she's really not facing the

fact that he's dying right here, and she's not talking about it.' And I'm just saying, 'He's going to be fine. He's going to be fine. We just need to do what God brings us to do,' and that's what we did. And so, it was important for me to learn that obedience, which is not really in my nature."

(Dan looks at Julie and laughs.)
"Right!"

Dan:

"It was about a six- or seven-year journey, an up and down roller coaster, and as of about a year and a half ago, I've been declared in remission. It's the first time they ever used the r word. He has blessed PM2 in ways He's never blessed PM2 before. Our marriage has never been stronger. Julie and I have said it many times that for us, it was never about the cancer. It was about how He was going to change me and grow us through this experience. And He's used that for that very purpose."

Reader's Guide

Chapter 1

Dan's life seems to revolve around fishing. Let's be real for a minute, shall we?

- What does your life revolve around?
- Does the thing your life revolves around add to or detract from your calling?
- What adjustments would you make, if any, to put your priorities more in line with your calling?

Chapter 2

In this chapter Dan learns a lesson about who owns the company. How about you?

- Did Dan's revelation that God owns the company change your perspective about the things you own? If so, how?
- Did this chapter change your view of the influence you have over the things you control? If so, how?
- Do you work hard to control outcomes or are you more likely to let go and let God control the future?

Chapter 3

In chapter 3 Dan is presented with resources and people that prepare him to be a more successful fisher of men. Dan learns that his net needs to be ready before going out on the water and realizes he has some net mending to do.

- What is God preparing you to do? Is your net ready?
- What resources and people has God put in your path to help you be successful?
- How do you keep track of the events and lessons you've experienced that have helped you along your way?

Chapter 4

Dan learns that when the storms of life roll in, true friends will ride out the storm with you.

- How much of your day is spent building or nurturing relationships and being a true friend to others?
- How are you impacted when you know someone is praying for you?
- What's the difference between telling someone you're praying for them and praying aloud with them in person, on the spot?

Chapter 5

In this chapter everyone is praying for the best but also preparing for the worst. But what about faith?

- When trouble comes, how do you typically respond?
- Do you think there is wisdom in preparing for the worst, or is this demonstrating a lack of faith?

- How do you respond when others act like they're expecting the worst to happen?

Chapter 6

In this chapter, Dan starts heavy chemo treatments nicknamed the "Big Guns," and the battle to survive gets ugly.

- At what point in your life have you been the closest to God?
- How would you describe what it feels like to be close to God?
- How does God communicate with you?

Chapter 7

Dan doesn't want to come to the end of his battle with cancer and regret not trying something that God brought him. Since the medical community says he's dying, he is willing to try just about anything.

- How do you discern whether something was brought to you by God or not?
- If your caregiver, who is trying to help you heal, suggests something you don't believe in or would rather not do, how do you respond?
- What do you do if your caregiver believes you can do something that you think is impossible?

Chapter 8

In this chapter God and Julie lovingly reveal to Dan that he has allowed the boat, the house, the business, and other material things to define him.

- What do you think defines you?

- When your own circumstances are out of control, how do you respond to other people in need?
- What are your thoughts on the pros and cons of joining an accountability group?

Chapter 9

Dan still wrestles daily with the urge to control every outcome. When he finally gets to the end of himself, he realizes he never had control in the first place. People are calling him a great fighter for having survived stage four cancer this long. Dan tells them, "I stopped fighting. I surrendered."

- The next time you come to the end of yourself in a situation, how do you hope to respond?
- If you felt led by God or thought you heard His voice telling you to do something, how would you make sure it was Him?
- Do you think God intentionally uses improbable and impossible circumstances to prove He is working in our lives?

Chapter 10

In this chapter, Dan and Julie sell the boat, foreclose on their home, and go bankrupt. Then Dan discovers his very good friend Marc has a life-threatening brain tumor.

- What area of your life would be the hardest to let go of and turn over to God's control?
- Do you think it's okay to have debt?
- If your good friend or family member were facing a life-threatening and high-risk surgery, what would your last words to him or her be before surgery?

Chapter 11

God allows Dan to experience many firsts in his life, like praying with a customer, ministering to a stranger on an airplane, and going to Haiti on a mission trip. Dan's focus is gradually shifting toward what matters to God.

- In your experience, what are the key factors that keep people from reaching out to others in need?
- What would you do to minimize or eradicate the factors that hold us back from helping others?
- Jesus says in Matthew 25:40, "Truly I tell you, whatever you did for one of the least of these brothers and sisters of mine, you did for me." (NIV) What do you think Jesus would say about the things you are doing for "the least of these?"

Chapter 12

In this chapter God tells Dan to do something that sounds completely ridiculous to his doctor, but Dan does what God says, and God responds with a healing miracle. Then Dan and his friend Marc get baptized in the Gulf of Mexico with thirty of their closest friends.

- If God told you to do something that sounded completely ridiculous, what do you think you would do? If you've experienced this, what did you do?
- For those times where you followed God's instructions in faith, how did He respond?
- Do you think there is value in publicly affirming your commitment to staying true to God's purpose for your life, or should this stay between you and God?

Chapter 13

In this chapter, PM2 is going through the worst downturn in company history. After all God has brought them through and the lessons Dan has learned, he's expecting God to bless PM2. But instead, the company is bleeding profusely. Then God shows Dan who the roadblock is.

- Do you think God ever intentionally withholds His blessing from people in order to develop them?
- Do you think God ever withholds blessings from others because of something you have left undone?
- What anchors are you dragging around that God would like to free you of?

Chapter 14

Finally, free of the anchor, God releases His many blessings on Dan and Julie's life. The business takes off. Their home is restored. Dan is completely cured of cancer. Their marriage is stronger than ever. Through the long hard journey, Dan now realizes God has been grooming him all along to become a fisher of men. Dan now sees himself as a fisherman's apprentice.

- Imagine for a moment that you are a fisherman's apprentice. Who in your circle of influence would you seek out to nurture relationships with?
- If you saw yourself as a fisherman's apprentice, would this change your focus each day and drive any different behaviors?
- Do you think it's possible to mix work or play with being a fisher of men?

Acknowledgments

I am so very grateful to my editor, Julie Breihan, who helped me tell this story without losing my voice in the writing. Many thanks also to my photographer, Diane Gainforth, who captured the essence of the story with her cover shot.

About the Author

Dan Floen lives in Apollo Beach, Florida, with his wife, Julie. Their daughter, Laurel, is now a senior at the University of Alabama at Birmingham. Most weekends you'll find Dan on his boat, wetting a line. In the evening, he'll be relaxing in his favorite old sofa, fingerpicking his guitar. Dan's calling is to share the many lessons, tools, and miracles God gave him in the hope that others will come to know God in a closer way, and maybe even avoid some of his mistakes.

Made in the USA
Coppell, TX
22 November 2021

66207299R00175